Evergreen
A Guide to Writing with Readings

COMPACT 9TH EDITION

Workbook: Practice Exercises

Susan Fawcett

WADSWORTH
CENGAGE Learning™

Australia • Brazil • Japan • Korea • Mexico • Singapore • Spain • United Kingdom • United States

WADSWORTH
CENGAGE Learning™

Evergreen: A Guide to Writing with Readings,
Workbook: Practice Exercises
Compact 9th Edition
Susan Fawcett

Senior Publisher: Lyn Uhl

Director of Developmental Studies: Annie Todd

Senior Development Editor: Judith Fifer

Assistant Editor: Beth Rice

Editorial Assistant: Matt Conte

Media Editor: Amy Gibbons

Senior Marketing Manager: Kirsten Stoller

Marketing Coordinator: Brittany Blais

Marketing Communications Manager:
    Courtney Morris

Content Project Manager: Aimee Chevrette Bear

Art Director: Jill Ort

Print Buyer: Betsy Donaghey

Production Service: Lachina Publishing Services

Text Designer: Cia Boynton

Photo Manager: Jennifer Meyer Dare

Cover Designer: Leonard Massiglia

Compositor: Lachina Publishing Services

For product information and technology assistance, contact us at
Cengage Learning Customer & Sales Support, 1-800-354-9706

For permission to use material from this text or product,
submit all requests online at **www.cengage.com/permissions**.
Further permissions questions can be emailed to
permissionrequest@cengage.com.

Student Edition:
ISBN-13: 978-1-111-35747-4
ISBN-10: 1-111-35747-1

Wadsworth
20 Channel Center Street
Boston, MA 02210
USA

Cengage Learning is a leading provider of customized learning solutions with office locations around the globe, including Singapore, the United Kingdom, Australia, Mexico, Brazil and Japan. Locate your local office at **international.cengage.com/region**.

Cengage Learning products are represented in Canada by Nelson Education, Ltd.

For your course and learning solutions, visit **www.cengage.com**.

Purchase any of our products at your local college store or at our preferred online store **www.cengagebrain.com**.

Printed in Canada
3 4 5 6 7 8 15 14 13

Contents

To the Student

Welcome to the Workbook that accompanies *Evergreen: A Guide to Writing with Readings*, Compact Ninth Edition. Here you will find all the practice exercises for the entire text, chapter by chapter, part by part, in a workbook format that is easy to carry and use. These engaging and enjoyable practices, many of them with interesting visual images, are one of the strengths of *Evergreen*, the most widely-used developmental writing text in the United States. *Evergreen* has guided over two million students through the writing process, from prewriting to final draft. The Ninth Edition was designed to meet the changing needs of a new generation of students, with clear, paced lessons, more coverage of writing the essay, and stimulating, contemporary writing samples. Other special features of *Evergreen* include many student-authored paragraphs and essays, as well as professional writing samples, and additional instruction and practice for English Language Learners (ELL/ESL students).

The Practice exercises in this Workbook are arranged by chapter and part headings, so you can easily read or review that section of the main Compact text before you tackle each exercise. In the main text, you will see oval-shaped practice icons in the margins, showing you exactly where each practice fits in the flow of the lesson. Some of the exercises refer to accompanying full-color illustrations, including ads, paintings, and photographs, which will add critical viewing skills to your writing and thinking practice. Directions before each exercise tell you how to complete it, and many of the exercises include an example that shows you exactly what to do. You can write right in the Workbook, and you can tear out or copy pages if your instructor wants you to complete and submit an exercise.

Enjoy the Workbook for *Evergreen*, Compact Ninth Edition, and let both volumes help you learn to write effectively, which can be the path to success in college as well as in your chosen career.

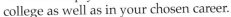

Supplements for Students

The following supplements are available to accompany your text and this Workbook:

- *Evergreen eBook,* a standalone digital version of the text, includes media segments such as author-recorded audio instructions to each chapter as well as live links to websites. The eBook is also available with CourseMate for *Evergreen Compact.*

- CourseMate for *Evergreen Compact*
  Evergreen, Compact Ninth Edition, includes CourseMate for *Evergreen Compact,* a complement to your textbook. CourseMate for *Evergreen Compact* includes:

- An interactive eBook
- Interactive teaching and learning tools:
  - Quizzes
  - Flashcards
  - Videos
  - Test Your Visual IQ
  - ESL Resources
  - and more

To access additional course materials, including CourseMate for *Evergreen Compact,* please visit www.cengagebrain.com. At the CengageBrain.com home page, search for the ISBN of your title (from the back cover of your book) using the search box at the top of the page. This will take you to the product page where these resources can be found.

Preface

This Workbook accompanies *Evergreen: A Guide to Writing with Readings*, Compact Ninth Edition. Here, students will find all the practice exercises, write-on lines, and practice-related visual images that are included within the large-format version of *Evergreen*. These engaging and enjoyable practices are one of the strengths of *Evergreen*, the most widely-used developmental writing text in the United States. To date, *Evergreen* has guided over two million students through the writing process, from prewriting to final draft. This Ninth Edition, like each new edition, was designed to meet the changing needs of a new generation of students, with clear, paced lessons, more coverage of writing the essay, and contemporary writing samples that will motivate your students to read.

The practices in this Workbook are organized consecutively under the chapter and part headings found in the main Compact *Evergreen* text, so students will be able to read or review relevant portions of the text before they work on a practice. In the margins of the Compact text, oval-shaped practice icons indicate precisely where each practice fits in the flow of the lesson, making use of both volumes easy and clear. Some of the practice exercises refer to accompanying full-color illustrations—like ads, paintings, and photographs—which add critical viewing challenges to the grammatical, writing, and thinking tasks your students will undertake in this book. Students can record their answers on the write-on lines and spaces in the Workbook; they can also tear out specific exercises to turn in as homework assignments or quizzes.

The instructor's version of the Workbook is an Annotated Instructor's Edition, with the answers to each practice printed in blue for easy checking. In this AIE you will also find Susan Fawcett's suggested Teaching Tips, ESL Tips, and (new to this edition) Learning Styles Tips, with suggestions for reaching students with certain learning styles, such as visual learners. Many of the student and professional writings found in practice paragraphs and essays are new to this edition, and are intended to interest and motivate students.

As with the large-format version of *Evergreen*, the text was written for diverse student populations, whatever their ethnicity, age, language background, or dominant learning style. Practice exercises for ESL/ELL (English Language Learner) students are included in the Appendix. The Ninth Edition also includes more coverage of essay writing, with two chapters on essay writing in Unit 4 (Chapters 16 and 17), to meet the need of instructors to get students up to speed quickly, and packing more writing instruction into fewer class hours. The new, fresh design of the Ninth Edition has been adapted to this more compact format.

Extensive New Online Teaching Program

Supplements for instructors using the Ninth Edition include the following:

- *Alplia for Evergreen* is an optional student supplement that instructors can order for their classes. *Aplia* provides writing instruction and practice to help you with basic writing and grammar skills. It features ongoing individualized practice with immediate feedback. To learn more, visit http://www.aplia .com/developmentalenglish.

- **Completely revised Test Bank,** authored by Professor Judy Pearce of Montgomery Community College and Dean Ann Marie Radaskiewicz of Western Piedmont Community College, provides current and updated diagnostic, mastery, unit, and chapter tests for every chapter in the book; the Test Bank is available either online or in ExamView® format.

- The *Evergreen PowerLecture*™ is an easy-to-use tool that helps the instructor assemble, edit, and present tailored multimedia lectures. The PowerLecture™ is organized around the topics in the text and allows you to create a lecture from scratch, customize the provided templates, or use the readymade Microsoft PowerPoint slides as they are. The CD-ROM also includes the following resources:

  - Instructor's Manual and Test Bank
  - ExamView® Test Bank, which allows instructors to create, deliver, and customize tests (both print and online)
  - ESL Guide and ESL Resources
  - Videos corresponding to the Reading Selections in the main text
  - Web Links to all websites referenced in the main text
  - and more!

- **Revised Instructor's Manual,** with the author's teaching suggestions for every chapter and reading, sample syllabi, and more. Included in the Instructor's Manual is the *Evergreen Instructor's Guide to Teaching ESL Students,* written by Dr. Donald L. Weasenforth and updated by Catherine Mazur-Jefferies, which provides extensive assistance in teaching classes that include ELL or Generation 1.5 students, including a Language Transfer Chart that shows common errors for each main language group.

- **Instructor Companion Site,** a password-protected website, provides a downloadable version of the Test Bank and Instructor's Manual; **Creative Classroom Links** to teaching strategies and tested classroom activities; resources for preventing plagiarism; customizable rubrics for every paragraph and essay type; and chapter-specific **PowerPoint** slides for classroom use.

Acknowledgments

Thanks to the many instructors and students who provided feedback for this edition of *Evergreen:*

Zoe Albright, Metropolitan Community College–Longview

Mahasveta Barua, University of Delaware

James Beasley, Irvine Valley College

Elisabeth Beccue, Erie Community College

Stephen Black, Southwest Tennessee Community College

Jennifer Bubb, Illinois Valley Community College

Todd Bunnell, Mississippi University for Women

Tamy Chapman, Saddleback College

Susan Chenard, Gateway Community College

Karen Cox, City College of San Francisco

Cynthia A. Crable, Allegany College of Maryland

Kennette Crockett, Harold Washington College (City College of Chicago)

Barbara Danley, Sandhills Community College

Hannah Dentinger, Lake Superior College

Karen Dimanche Davis, Marygrove College

Richard Donovan, Bronx Community College

Gwen Eldridge, Ivy Tech Community College

Lori Farr, Oklahoma City Community College

Laura Feldman, University of New Mexico–Gallup

Jen Ferguson, Cazenovia College

Curtis Harrell, NorthWest Arkansas Community College

Angela Hathikhanavala, Henry Ford Community College

LeiLani Hinds, Honolulu Community College

Deborah Hunt, College of Charleston

Thomas R. Irish, Sauk Valley Community College

Theresa S. Irvin, Columbus State University

Teresa Kozek, Housatonic Community College

Michael J. Kramer, Alvernia College

Patricia A. Malinowski, Finger Lakes Community College

Elizabeth Marsh, Bergen Community College

Larry D. Martin, Hinds Community College, Rankin

Jeanette Maurice, Illinois Valley Community College

Sara McLaughlin, Texas Tech University

Theresa Mohamed, Onondaga Community College

Victoria Monroe, Ivy Tech State College–Bloomington

Stephen Morrow, Oklahoma City Community College

Ellen Olmstead, Montgomery College

Judy Pearce, Montgomery College

Jay Peterson, Atlantic Cape Community College

Anne Marie Prendergast, Bergen Community College

Josh Pryor, Saddleback College

Ann Marie Radaskiewicz, Western Piedmont Community College

Miki Richardson, Southwest Tennessee
Community College

Linda Robinett, Oklahoma City
Community College

Nicholas Salvatore, Community College
of Philadelphia

Mark Schneberger, Oklahoma City
Community College

Roxanna M. Senyshyn, Pennsylvania State
University, Abington College

Larry Silverman, Seattle Central
Community College

Donna C. Slone, Maysville Community &
Technical College

Jeff Thompson, Tennessee State University

Joseph W. Thweatt, Southwest Tennessee
Community College

Priscilla Underwood, Quinsigamond
Community College

Billie A. Unger, Blue Ridge Community &
Technical College

Michael T. Warren, Maplewood
Community College at Kansas City

Elizabeth Wurz, Columbus State
University

We engaged college students in the *Evergreen* review process for the first time.
Professor Jennifer Ferguson of Cazenovia College generously crafted surveys to
evoke honest and very helpful reactions to this edition as it progressed. We thank
her and her terrific students:

Precious C. Allen
Riley Battoglini
Chaz Bedford
Whitney Belcer
Marquis Bennett
Sherard Brown
Shannon Campbell
Noble Cunningham, Jr.
Berly Estevez

Hannah Friedman
Destiney Gonzalez
Marissa J. Harvey
Skyler R. Ludwig
Francesca Romano
Dana Sprole
LaQuana Talford
Teyanna Tanner

I am indebted to the team at Cengage Learning whose market research and vision
helped make *Evergreen*, Compact Ninth Edition, the best book of its kind in the
country: in particular, Annie Todd, Director of Developmental Studies, my Acquisi-
tions Editior; Judith Fifer, Senior Development Editor; Kirsten Stoller, Senior Marketing Manager; Beth Rice, Assistant Editor; Matt Conte, Editorial Assistant; Amy
Gibbons, Media Editor; and Aimee Bear, Content Project Manager. My huge thanks
to Nikki Petel and Lachina Publishing Services, the most gifted compositors I've
ever worked with, for creating this beautiful edition.

Ann Marie Radaskiewicz, Dean of Developmental Education at Western
Piedmont Community College, contributed high-quality research, writing, and
troubleshooting throughout the revision process. With her can-do professionalism and good cheer, Ann has become a treasured colleague and friend. I owe a
special great debt of gratitude to Karen Cox, Associate Professor of English at San
Francisco City College, for her creative teaching ideas, writing, and friendship in
the service of our students. Professor Jennifer Ferguson of Cazenovia College was
the first of many professors who urged me to enrich *Evergreen* with more material
on the essay; she went beyond the call of duty in recruiting student reviewers and
discussing revision ideas along the way. ESL expert and PhD candidate Emmy

Ready assisted me with research, writing, proofreading, and exceptional professionalism, offering to work all night when a crazy deadline loomed.

Nationally-recognized ESL expert Don Weasenforth of the Collin County Community College District provided our practical and nuanced guide to more effectively teaching ESL students in *Evergreen* classes. The guide has been updated with additional help and websites by ESL whiz Catherine Mazur-Jeffries.

Thank you to my English colleagues around the country who helped me find inspiring student essays for the new edition. The process was great fun. My inspiration always has been our students, whose aspirations, hard work, and fortitude in the face of sometimes unthinkable obstacles drive my life's goal of helping them learn and thrive. This year, I had the privilege of speaking with students all over the country as I sought permission to reprint many new examples of good student writing. These conversations with community college students and recent graduates filled me with pride; I spoke with entrepreneurs, nurses, military veterans, engineers, even a former rodeo rider whose essays and paragraphs will surely motivate the students who read this book.

For the great gifts of love and kindness during this difficult year, thank you to my friends, Maggie Smith, Colleen Huff, Trisha Nelson, Bryan Hoffman, Elaine Unkeless, Ginger Chaich, and Laraine Flemming. More every year, family so enriches the journey: my dear husband, the English professor and fiction writer Richard Donovan; therapist, blogger, and brother extraordinaire, David Fawcett; and his partner, my beloved other brother, Edward Brown. I dedicate this edition to our Mom, the watercolor artist Harriet Fawcett, who died in July, 2010 and taught us all that a radiant last chapter is possible. Wishing you all a wonderful term of learning, writing, and realizing your potential.

Evergreen

Compact 9th Edition

Workbook: Practice Exercises

Unit 1

Getting Started

CHAPTER 1

Exploring the Writing Process

A: The Writing Process

B: Subject, Audience, and Purpose

A. The Writing Process

PRACTICE 1

Think of something that you wrote recently—and of which you felt proud—for college, work, or your personal life. Now on paper or with classmates, discuss the *process* you followed in writing it. Did you do any *planning* or *prewriting*—or did you just sit down and start writing? How much time did you spend rewriting and *revising* your work? What one change in your writing process do you think would most improve your writing? Taking more time to prewrite? Taking more time to revise? Improving your grammar and spelling?

Make some notes below; but you will also need to use pages in a notebook or journal for longer writing assignments.

_____

_____

_____

_____

_____

PRACTICE 2

Bring in several newspaper help-wanted sections. In a group with four or five classmates, study the ads in career fields that interest you. How many fields require writing and communication skills? Which job ad requiring these skills most surprised you or your group? Be prepared to present your findings to the class. If your class has Internet access, visit *Monster.com* or other job-search websites and perform the same exercise.

EXPLORING ONLINE

http://www.google.com

Search "Writing: A Ticket to Work… or a Ticket Out" and read the summary. This survey of business leaders finds that good writing is the key to career success. What two facts or comments do you find most striking?

B. Subject, Audience, and Purpose

PRACTICE 3

List five subjects that you might like to write about. Consider your audience and purpose: For whom are you writing? What do you want them to know about your subject? Notice how the audience and purpose will help shape your paper. For ideas, reread the boxed questions in Chapter 1, Part B, of the companion text (*Evergreen*, Compact Ninth Edition).

	Subject	Audience	Purpose
EXAMPLE	my recipe for seafood gumbo	inexperienced cooks	to show how easy it is to make seafood gumbo
1.			
2.			
3.			
4.			
5.			

PRACTICE 4

Jot ideas for the following two assignments, by yourself or in a group with four or five classmates. Notice how your ideas and details differ, depending on the audience and purpose.

1. You have been asked to write a description of your college for local high school students. Your purpose is to explain what advantages the college offers its students. What kinds of information should you include? What will your audience want to know? What information should you leave out?

     _____

     _____

2. You have been asked to write a description of your college for the governor of your state. Your purpose is to persuade him or her to spend more money to improve your college. What information should you include? What will your audience want to know? What information should you leave out?

     _____

     _____

PRACTICE 5

In a group with three or four classmates, read these sentences from real job-application letters and résumés, published in *Fortune* magazine. Each writer's *subject* was his or her job qualifications; the *audience* was an employer, and the *purpose* was to get a job. How did each person undercut his or her own purpose? What writing advice would you give each of these job seekers?

1. I have lurnt Word and computer spreasheet programs.

     _____

2. Please don't misconstrue my 14 jobs as "job-hopping." I have never quit a job.

     _____

3. I procrastinate, especially when the task is unpleasant.

     _____

4. Let's meet, so you can "ooh" and "aah" over my experience.

     _____

5. It is best for employers that I not work with people.

_____

6. Reason for leaving my last job: maturity leave.

_____

7. As indicted, I have over five years of analyzing investments.

_____

8. References: none. I have left a path of destruction behind me.

_____

PRACTICE 6

Study the public service advertisement below and then answer these questions: What *subject* is the ad addressing? Who is the target *audience*? What is the intended *purpose*? In your view, how successful is this ad in achieving its purpose?

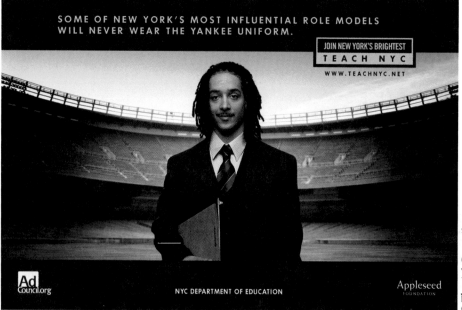

Subject _____

Audience _____

Purpose _____

CHAPTER 2

Prewriting to Generate Ideas

A: Freewriting

B: Brainstorming

C: Clustering

D: Asking Questions

E: Keeping a Journal

A. Freewriting

PRACTICE 1

Do a three-minute focused freewriting on three of these topics:

job	body piercing
friendship	parent (or child)
news	tests

Underline ideas or sentences you like, and that you might like to write more about. Did you surprise yourself by having so much to say about any one topic? Perhaps you would like to write more about that topic.

PRACTICE 2

1. Read over your earlier freewritings and notice your underlinings. Would you like to write more about any underlined words or ideas? Write two or three such words or ideas here:

   Sample answers: Sometimes I feel closer to my children than to my parents.

   I'm often most content on a rainy day.

   _____

   _____

   _____

   _____

2. Now choose one word or idea. Focus your thoughts on it and, on a separate piece of paper or in your notebook, do a ten-minute focused freewriting. Try to stick to the topic as you write but don't worry too much about keeping on track; just keep writing.

B. Brainstorming

PRACTICE 3

Choose one of the following topics that interests you and write it at the top of your paper or computer screen. Then brainstorm. Write anything that comes into your head about the topic. Just let ideas pour out fast!

1. a place I want to go back to
2. my goals in this course
3. my best/worst job
4. qualities that will help me succeed
5. dealing with difficult people
6. an unforgettable person from work, school, or family life

Once you fill a page with your list, read it over, marking the most interesting ideas. Draw arrows or highlight and move text on your screen to connect related ideas. Is there one idea that might be the subject of a paper?

C. Clustering

PRACTICE 4

Choose one of these topics or another topic that interests you. Write it in the center of a piece of paper, or use the diagram below, and then try clustering. Keep writing down associations until you have filled most of the page.

1. heroes
2. holidays
3. food
4. inspiration
5. a dream
6. movies

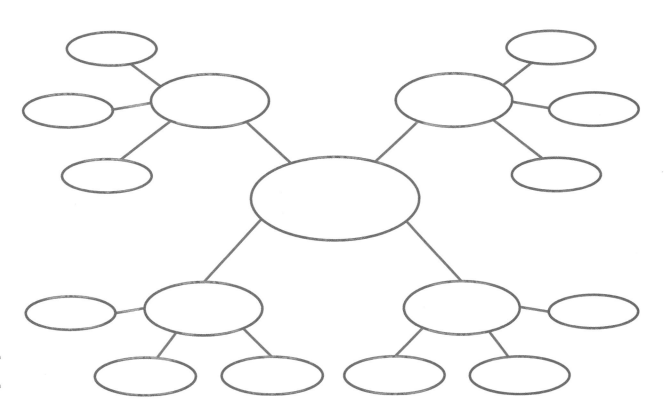

D. Asking Questions

PRACTICE 5

Answer the reporter's six questions on one of the following topics or on a topic of your own choice.

1. career goals
2. sports
3. stress among students

4. music
5. family get-togethers
6. neighbors/neighborhood

Who? _____

What? _____

Where? _____

When? _____

Why? _____

How? _____

PRACTICE 6

Ask and answer at least five questions of your own about one of the topics in Practice 5. Use these questions if you wish: What do I know about this subject? What would I like to know? Where can I find answers to my questions? What would I like to focus on? What is my point of view about this subject? Who is my audience?

E. Keeping a Journal

PRACTICE 7

Get a notebook or set up your computer journal. Write for at least fifteen minutes three times a week.

At the end of each week, reread what you have written or typed. Underline sections or ideas you like and put a check mark next to subjects you might like to write more about.

PRACTICE 8

Choose one passage in your journal that you would like to rewrite and let others read. Mark the parts you like best. Now rewrite and polish the passage so you would be proud to show it to someone else.

Unit 2

Discovering the Paragraph

CHAPTER 3

The Process of Writing Paragraphs

A: Defining and Looking at the Paragraph

B: Narrowing the Topic and Writing the Topic Sentence

C: Generating Ideas for the Body

D: Selecting and Dropping Ideas

E: Arranging Ideas in a Plan or an Outline

F: Writing and Revising the Paragraph

A. Defining and Looking at the Paragraph

PRACTICE 1

Find and underline the **topic sentence** in each of the following paragraphs. Look for the sentence that states the **main idea** of the entire paragraph. Be careful: The topic sentence is not always the first sentence.

Paragraph 1

In the mid-1980s, 340,000 people in the United States owned cell phones. Today, that number is well over 250 million. Worldwide, more than a billion people have gone wireless, and most of them have no idea that inside the sleek, plastic exterior of every cell phone sits a package of electronics laden with hazardous substances called persistent,

© Richard Barnes

Cell phones can be recycled safely at plants like this one in Hilliard, Ohio, but Americans still throw 3 million tons of electronics into the trash each year.

bioaccumulative and toxic chemicals (PBTs). When cell users toss their phones into the trash, PBTs like lead, arsenic, and cadmium leak into the land, air, and water, eventually entering the tissues of animals and humans. Every year, 150 million cell phones—complete with batteries and chargers—are pitched into the garbage instead of being recycled or safely disposed of. As the popularity of cellular phones soars, growing numbers of cell users are creating growing piles of toxic trash.

—Adapted from Rene Ebersole,
"Recycle Cell Phones, Reduce Toxic Trash," *National Wildlife*

Paragraph 2

The summer picnic gave ladies a chance to show off their baking hands. On the barbecue pit, chickens and spareribs sputtered in their own fat and in a sauce whose recipe was guarded in the family like a scandalous affair. However, every true baking artist could reveal her prize to the delight and criticism of the town. Orange sponge cakes and dark brown mounds dripping Hershey's chocolate stood layer to layer with ice-white coconuts and light brown caramels. Pound cakes sagged with their buttery weight and small children could no more resist licking the icings than their mothers could avoid slapping the sticky fingers.

—Maya Angelou, *I Know Why the Caged Bird Sings*

Paragraph 3

Eating sugar can be worse than eating nothing. Refined sugar provides only empty calories. It contributes none of the protein, fat, vitamins, or minerals needed for its own metabolism in the body, so these nutrients must be obtained elsewhere. Sugar tends to replace nourishing food in the diet. It is a thief that robs us of nutrients. A dietary emphasis on sugar can deplete the body of nutrients. If adequate nutrients are not supplied by the diet—and they tend not to be in a sugar-rich diet—they must be leached from other body tissues before sugar can be metabolized. For this reason, a U.S. Senate committee labeled sugar as an "antinutrient."

—Janice Fillip, "The Sweet Thief," *Medical Self-Care*

PRACTICE 2

Each group of sentences below could be unscrambled and written as a paragraph. Circle the letter of the **topic sentence** in each group of sentences. Remember: The topic sentence should state the main idea of the entire paragraph and should be general enough to include all the ideas in the body.

EXAMPLE

a. Next, a social phobia is an intense fear of a social or performance situation, like standing in a checkout line.

b. Agoraphobia, the third type, is a morbid terror of public places.

c. Phobias, the most common anxiety disorder, can be divided into three types.

d. A specific phobia, the first type, is an irrational fear of a specific thing, like spiders, dogs, elevators, or needles.

(Sentence c includes the ideas in all the other sentences.)

1. a. Some physicians use iPhones to show patients videos about their medical conditions and even procedures to be performed.

    b. At New York's Museum of Modern Art, visitors can use their iPhones to get audio information about the art as they stroll the galleries.

    c. Musicians can use the iPhone as a recorder or wind instrument, by blowing into the microphone while touching "holes" on the screen to produce notes.

    d. The iPhone, a hand-held device that functions as a phone, camera, Internet browser, and digital music player, is being used in many creative and innovative ways.

2. a. Invited to join the space program, she trained as an astronaut and flew on the space shuttle *Endeavor* in 1992.

    b. The young Dr. Jemison headed to West Africa, where she worked in the Peace Corps for two years.

    c. Though a childhood teacher urged her to be a nurse, Mae Jemison knew she wanted to be a scientist and doctor.

    d. After eight years at NASA, she became a professor at Dartmouth College and started a company to help poor countries use solar energy.

    e. The life of Dr. Mae Jemison, the first African American female astronaut, is characterized by daring achievements and a strong desire to give back.

    f. A fine student, Jemison entered Stanford University at sixteen and later earned her M.D. degree from Cornell in 1981.

3.   a. The left side of the human brain controls spoken and written language.

    b. The right side, on the other hand, seems to control artistic, musical, and spatial skills.

    c. Emotion is also thought to be controlled by the right hemisphere.

    d. The human brain has two distinct halves, or hemispheres, and in most people, each one controls different functions.

    e. Logical reasoning and mathematics are left-brain skills.

    f. Interestingly, the left brain controls the right hand, and vice versa.

4.   a. As a Bronx Community College student, Oscar Hijuelos showed his gift for writing.

    b. He researched the Cuban music scene of New York in the '50s for his second novel, *The Mambo Kings Play Songs of Love.*

    c. After one year at Bronx Community, he transferred to City College, earning his B.A. in creative writing.

    d. Step by step, Oscar Hijuelos, the son of Cuban immigrants, has become a very successful writer.

    e. While crafting his first two books, Hijuelos earned money selling shoes and writing ad copy for subway cars.

    f. After *Mambo Kings* won the Pulitzer Prize and was made into a film, Hijuelos wrote three more novels and inspired many young writers.

5.   a. Male and female insects are attracted to each other by visual, auditory, and chemical means.

    b. Through its chirping call, the male cricket attracts a mate and drives other males out of its territory.

    c. Butterflies attract by sight, and their brightly colored wings play an important role in courtship.

    d. Some female insects, flies among them, release chemicals called *pheromones* that attract males of the species.

6. a. People who don't know basic algebra can be more easily fooled by dishonest manipulation of numbers.

    b. Because studying algebra has so many benefits, every college student should be required to pass an algebra course.

    c. Learning algebra helps build problem-solving skills and reasoning skills.

    d. According to the U.S. Secretary of Education, Americans must know algebra in order to compete with well-educated citizens from other nations in this global economy.

    e. An understanding of algebra is required in a surprising range of professions, from architect to banker to photographer.

7. a. Albert Einstein, whose scientific genius awed the world, did not speak until he was four and could not read until he was nine.

    b. Inventor Thomas Edison had such severe problems reading, writing, and spelling that he was called "defective from birth," taken out of school, and taught at home.

    c. Many famous people have suffered from learning disabilities.

    d. Swimmer Michael Phelps has Attention Deficit Hyperactivity Disorder (ADHD), yet he developed great discipline and won more gold medals than any Olympian in history.

8. a. Believe it or not, the first contact lens was drawn by Leonardo da Vinci in 1508.

    b. However, not until 1877 was the first thick glass contact actually made by a Swiss doctor.

    c. The journey of contact lenses from an idea to a comfortable, safe reality took nearly five hundred years.

    d. In 1948, smaller, more comfortable plastic lenses were introduced to enthusiastic American eyeglass wearers.

    e. These early glass lenses were enormous, covering the whites of the eyes.

    f. Today, contact lens wearers can choose ultra-thin, colored, or even disposable lenses.

B. Narrowing the Topic and Writing the Topic Sentence

PRACTICE 3

Read each topic sentence below. Circle the topic and underline the controlling idea.

1. A low-fat diet provides many health benefits.

2. *Animal Planet* is both entertaining and educational.

3. Our football coach works to build players' self-esteem.

4. This campus offers many peaceful places where students can relax.

5. My cousin's truck looks like something out of *Star Wars*.

PRACTICE 4

Put a check beside each topic sentence that is focused enough to allow you to write a good paragraph. If a topic sentence is too broad, narrow the topic according to your own interests and write a new topic sentence with a clear controlling idea.

> **EXAMPLES** ____✓____ Keeping a journal can improve a student's writing.
>
> Rewrite: _____
>
> _____ This paper will be about my family.
>
> Rewrite: *My brother Mark has a unique sense of humor.* _____

1. _____ Eugene's hot temper causes problems at work.

   Rewrite: _____

   _____

2. _____ This paragraph will discuss my two closest friends.

   Rewrite: _____

   _____

3. _____ Learning a foreign language has several benefits.

Rewrite: _____

_____

4. _____ Child abuse is something to think about.

Rewrite: _____

_____

5. _____ Company officials should not read employees' e-mail.

Rewrite: _____

_____

PRACTICE 5

Here is a list of broad topics. Choose three that interest you from this list or from your own list in Chapter 1, Practice 3. Narrow each topic, choose your controlling idea, and write a topic sentence focused enough to write a good paragraph about. Make sure that each topic sentence has a clear controlling idea and is a complete sentence.

Overcoming fears	Insider's tour of your community
Popular music	Balancing work and play
Credit cards	A person you like or dislike
An act of cowardice or courage	A time when you were (or were not) in control

1. Narrowed topic: _____

Controlling idea: _____

Topic sentence: _____

_____

2. Narrowed topic: _____

Controlling idea: _____

Topic sentence: _____

_____

3. Narrowed topic: _____

   Controlling idea: _____

   Topic sentence: _____

_____

PRACTICE 6

Many writers adjust the topic sentence after they have finished drafting the paragraph. In a group of three or four classmates, study the body of each of these paragraphs to find the main, or controlling, idea. Then, working together, write the most exact and interesting topic sentence you can for each paragraph.

Paragraph 1

_____

_____

A pet parrot recently saved his owner's life. Harry Becker was watching TV in his living room when he suddenly slumped over with a heart attack. The parrot screamed loudly until Mr. Becker's wife awoke and called 911. In another reported case of animal rescue, a family cat saved six-week-old Stacey Rogers. When the cat heard the baby gasping for breath in her crib, it ran howling to alert the baby's mother, who called paramedics. Even more surprising was an event reported in newspapers around the world. In 1996 in a Chicago zoo, a female gorilla rushed to save a three-year-old boy who fell accidentally into the gorilla enclosure. Still carrying her own baby on her back, the 150-pound gorilla gently picked up the unconscious child and carried him to the cage door to be rescued. Such stories reveal a mysterious and sometimes profound bond between animals and humans.

Paragraph 2

_____

_____

The first advantage of digital photography is easier picture-taking. Gone are the days of toting film to the store to be processed and waiting to see how the pictures turn out. The digital photographer can see instantly whether a shot is good and then snap more pictures if necessary. Another advantage of digital photography is quick and easy processing. At home on a computer, the digital photographer can size or retouch his or her images, print the good ones, or e-mail them to family and friends. Third, with no film or developing costs, digital photography saves money. The photographer can take hundreds of shots and print only the best. A final advantage is the tiny size and weight of digital cameras. Therefore, when an irresistible photo opportunity arises, the digital photographer is more likely to have a camera handy, tucked in a pocket or handbag. Most people treasure their photographs, so any tools that can help capture memories with more ease and less frustration are sure to catch on.

C. Generating Ideas for the Body

PRACTICE 7

Now choose the topic from Practice 5 that most interests you. Write your narrowed topic, controlling idea, and topic sentence here.

Narrowed topic: _____

Controlling idea: _____

Topic sentence: _____

_____

Next, brainstorm. On paper or on the computer, write anything that comes to you about your topic sentence. Just let your ideas pour out. Try to fill at least one page.

D. Selecting and Dropping Ideas

PRACTICE 8

Read through your own brainstorm list from Practice 7. Select the ideas that relate to your topic sentence and drop those that do not. In addition, drop any ideas that just repeat your topic sentence. Be prepared to explain why you drop or keep each idea.

E. Arranging Ideas in a Plan or an Outline

PRACTICE 9

On paper or on the computer, arrange the ideas from your brainstorm list according to some plan or outline. First, group together related ideas; then decide which ideas will come first, which second, and so on.

Keep in mind that there is more than one way to group ideas. Think about what you want to say; then group ideas according to what your point is.

F. Writing and Revising the Paragraph

PRACTICE 10

In your notebook or journal, write a first draft of the paragraph you have been working on.

PRACTICE 11

Check the following paragraphs for adequate support. As you read each one, decide which places need more or better support—specific facts, details, and examples. Then rewrite the paragraphs in your notebook, inventing facts and details whenever necessary and dropping repetitious words and sentences.

Paragraph 1

(1) My uncle can always be counted on when the family faces hardship. (2) Last year, when my mother was very ill, he was there, ready to help in every way. (3) He never has to be called twice. (4) When my father became seriously depressed, my uncle's caring made a difference. (5) Everyone respects him for his willingness to be a real "family man." (6) He is always there for us.

Paragraph 2

(1) Lending money to a friend can have negative consequences. (2) For example, Ashley, a student at Tornado Community College, agreed to lend $200 to her best friend, Jan. (3) This was a bad decision even though Ashley meant well. (4) The results of this loan

were surprising and negative for Ashley, for Jan, and for the friendship. (5) Both women felt bad about it but in different ways. (6) Yes, lending money to a friend can have very negative consequences, like anger and hurt.

Paragraph 3

(1) Many television talk shows don't really present a discussion of ideas. (2) Some people who appear on these shows don't know what they are talking about; they just like to sound off about something. (3) I don't like these shows at all. (4) Guests shout their opinions out loud but never give any proof for what they say. (5) Guests sometimes expose their most intimate personal and family problems before millions of viewers—I feel embarrassed. (6) I have even heard hosts insult their guests and guests insult them back. (7) Why do people watch this junk? (8) You never learn anything from these dumb shows.

PRACTICE 12

Check the following paragraphs for unity. If a paragraph has unity, write U in the blank. If not, write the number of the sentence that does not belong in the paragraph.

Paragraph 1

_____ (1) The first batch of one of the world's most popular soft drinks was mixed in a backyard kettle over a hundred years ago. (2) On May 6, 1886, Dr. John Styth Pemberton heated a mixture of melted sugar, water, coca leaves, kola nuts, and other ingredients. (3) He planned to make one of the home-brewed medical syrups so popular at that time. (4) However, this one tasted so good that Dr. Pemberton decided to sell it as a soda fountain drink for five cents a glass. (5) The first glass of this new drink was sold at Jacob's Pharmacy in Atlanta, Georgia. (6) Atlanta was and still is a wonderful place to live. (7) Pemberton's tasty invention, Coca-Cola, caught on. (8) Today, Coca-Cola is consumed by 140,000 people every minute.

Paragraph 2

_____ (1) Technology enables people like the famous physicist Dr. Stephen Hawking to continue working despite serious physical disabilities. (2) For more than 45 years, Dr. Hawking has lived with Lou Gehrig's disease, which attacks the muscles, but his brilliant mind works perfectly. (3) He can no longer walk, speak, or feed himself. (4) Nevertheless, a high-tech wheelchair with computer attachments allows him to continue his research and stay in touch with friends and colleagues around the world. (5) His computer is hooked up full-time to the Internet. (6) To speak, he chooses words displayed on the computer screen, and then an electronic voice machine pronounces each word. (7) A pressure-sensitive joystick even lets Dr. Hawking make his way through traffic. (8) In his home, infrared remote controls operate doors, lights, and his personal entertainment center. (9) He has three children with his first wife, Jane, and one grandchild. (10) Dr. Hawking continues to search for new ways to overcome his problems through technology.

Paragraph 3

_____ (1) Across the country, thousands of college students and others are attending or performing poetry at "poetry slams." (2) A poetry slam is a competitive event in which participants perform one original poem before an audience. (3) With words, rhymes, and dramatic skill as their only tools, these fast-talking bards have just three minutes to win over the audience. (4) After each performance, judges selected from the audience give a numerical score, usually from 1 to 10. (5) Gymnastics competitions are judged using a similar ten-point scoring system. (6) Although most slammers would love to win first prize, they say that poetry slams also allow them to express their deepest thoughts, boost self-esteem, hone their English skills, and connect with a community of people who "speak from the heart." (7) Poetry slams are gaining popularity as schools, arts organizations, and groups of young writers start poetry clubs or sponsor contests. (8) Now, as online videos of the winning performances reveal the power of poetry slams, the excitement has spread worldwide.

EXPLORING ONLINE

To listen to winning poets, go to **http://www.youtube.com** and search "national poetry slam winners." Would you like to attend or perform at a poetry slam? Why or why not? What do you think is the reason so many people attend slams?

PRACTICE 13

Now read the first draft of your paragraph from Practice 10 with a critical eye. Revise and rewrite it in your notebook or on the computer, checking especially for a clear topic sentence, strong support, and unity.

PRACTICE 14

Exchange *revised* paragraphs with a classmate. Ask specific questions or use the Peer Feedback Sheet from Chapter 3 of the companion text.

When you *give* feedback, try to be as honest and specific as possible; saying a paper is "good," "nice," or "bad" doesn't really help the writer. When you *receive* feedback, think over your classmate's responses; do they ring true?

Now *revise* a second time, with the aim of writing a fine paragraph. Proofread carefully for grammar errors, spelling errors, and omitted words.

CHAPTER 4

Achieving Coherence

A: Coherence Through Order

B: Coherence Through Related Sentences

A. Coherence Through Order

PRACTICE 1

Arrange each set of sentences in logical time order, numbering the sentences 1, 2, 3, and so on, as if you were preparing to write a paragraph. Underline any words and phrases, like *first, next,* and *in 1692,* that give time clues.

1. ___ First, lie on your back with your knees comfortably bent.

   ___ Next, put your hands at your sides or fold them over your chest.

   ___ Finally, focus on your abs and do your crunches slowly, three sets of 10 each.

   ___ Lift your torso until the shoulder blades leave the floor, and then slowly roll back down.

   ___ The perfect crunch should be done slowly and deliberately, working the whole abdominal wall.

2. ___ In 1957, *The Cat in the Hat* made famous both its hat-wearing tomcat with terrible manners and its author.

   ___ Before he died in 1991, Dr. Seuss inspired millions to love language with such creations as the Grinch, Nerds, Wockets, Bar-ba-loots, bunches of Hunches, and fox in sox.

___ *Green Eggs and Ham* came out in 1960 and told a memorable story, using only 55 different words.

___ In his long career, Theodor Geisel, better known as Dr. Seuss, wrote 46 wildly imaginative children's books, now read all over the world.

___ His first book was rejected by 28 publishers, who found it "too strange for children."

___ In 1937, when it finally was published, readers loved the rhythmic march of tongue-twisting, invented words and the wacky characters.

3. ___ One of the judges later deeply regretted his part, but this murderous chapter in American history has never been forgotten.

___ When famous Puritan ministers Increase Mather and his son Cotton Mather published writings in the 1680s "proving" that witches existed, they set the stage for the Salem witchcraft trials.

___ The suspects were promptly jailed based on the girls' testimony, and in June, five judges launched a series of courtroom witch trials.

___ By September, nineteen so-called "witches and wizards" had been found guilty, hanged, or pressed to death with stones.

___ In 1692, two girls had seizures in a Massachusetts village and falsely accused neighbors of putting a curse on them, stirring a witch-hunting hysteria.

PRACTICE 2

Below are topic sentences followed by supporting details. Arrange each group of details according to space order, numbering them 1, 2, 3, and so on, as if you were preparing to write a descriptive paragraph. On the line after each topic sentence, tell what kind of space order you used: *left to right, back to front,* and so forth.

1. Describe a firefighter's uniform. _____

___ fire-retardant pants, called "turnouts"

___ black, hard plastic helmet with flashlight attached

___ steel-reinforced black rubber bunker boots

___ bright yellow, fireproof Kevlar jacket

___ compressed-air face mask

2. Describe the security measures protecting the original Declaration of Independence.

_____

____ room's perimeter ringed with security cameras and motion sensors

____ two armed guards standing next to the bronze and marble shrine

___ the National Archives building in Washington, D.C.

___ parchment of document touched only by decay-preventing helium gas

____ bulletproof glass case

3. Describe a city scene. _____

___ dented trash cans in the alley

___ a bird riding the wind in blue sky

___ rusty metal fire escape zigzagging up from the ground

___ laundry flapping on a line near the eighth floor

___ glimpse of an old rooftop water tower

PRACTICE 3

Arrange the ideas that develop each topic sentence in their **order of importance**, numbering them 1, 2, 3, and so on. *Begin with the most important* (or largest, most severe, most surprising) and continue to the *least* important. Or reverse the order if you think that the paragraph would be more dramatic by beginning with the *least* important ideas and building toward a climax, with the most important last.

1. Cynthia Lopez's first year of college brought many unexpected expenses.

____ Her English professor wanted her to own a college dictionary.

____ All those term papers to write required a computer.

____ She had to spend $90 for textbooks.

____ Her solid geometry class required various colored pencils and felt-tip pens.

2. Alcoholic beverages should not be sold at sporting events.

____ Injuries and even deaths caused by alcohol-induced crowd violence would be eliminated.

____ Fans could save money by buying soft drinks instead of beer.

____ Games and matches would be much more pleasant without the yelling, swearing, and rudeness often caused by alcohol.

3. The apartment needed work before the new tenants could move in.

____ The handles on the kitchen cabinets were loose.

____ Every room needed plastering and painting.

____ Grime marred the appearance of the bathroom sink.

____ Two closet doors hung off the hinges.

B. Coherence Through Related Sentences

PRACTICE 4

What important words are repeated in the following paragraph? Underline them. Circle any pronouns that replace them. Notice the varied pattern of repetitions and pronoun replacements.

I have always considered my father a very intelligent person. His intelligence is not the type usually tested in schools; perhaps he would have done well on such tests, but the fact is that he never finished high school. Rather, my father's intelligence is his ability to solve problems creatively as they arise. Once when I was very young, we were driving through the desert at night when the oil line broke. My father improvised a light, squeezed under the car, found the break, and managed to whittle a connection to join the two severed pieces of tubing; then he added more oil and drove us over a hundred miles to the nearest town. Such intelligent solutions to unforeseen problems were typical of him. In fact, my father's brand of brains—accurate insight, followed by creative action—is the kind of intelligence that I admire and most aspire to.

PRACTICE 5

Read each paragraph carefully. Then write on the lines any synonyms and substitutions that the writer has used to replace the word(s) in italics.

Paragraph 1

According to sports writer Ian Stafford, the British hold the record for winning the world's *oddest competitions.* In one of these bizarre events, contestants contort their faces and are judged on their ugliness. One competitor removed half his dentures and reversed the other half, rolled his eyes, and tucked his nose into his mustache and upper lip to achieve prize-winning ugliness. Another of these eccentric contests is snail racing. Opponents in this case are, of course, snails, which are placed in the center of a thirteen-inch cloth circle. The first to reach the edge of the circle wins. The race often takes four to five minutes, although the all-time champion (owned and trained by an English seven-year-old) finished the course in two minutes. Toe wrestling, bog snorkeling, worm charming—the British have emerged as unconquered rivals in all of these so-called sports. Perhaps you think that sports writer Ian Stafford should win first prize in the Biggest Liar in the World Competition. No, every one of these outlandish games exists. You can check them all out on the Internet.

Oddest competitions are also referred to as _____, _____,

_____, and _____.

Paragraph 2

Lori Arviso Alvord, M.D., spent her childhood playing on the red mesas of a New Mexico Indian reservation. Later, while training to become the first Navajo woman surgeon, she encountered a very different world, the sterilized steel-and-chrome environment of the modern hospital. There, as she broke her culture's taboos against touching the dead and removing parts of the body, she felt disconnected from her Native American heritage. Yet even as the skilled doctor used the latest medical technology to repair injuries and remove tumors, she felt that something important was missing. Returning to her roots to search for answers, she realized that scientific medicine alone cannot restore the harmony among body, mind, and spirit the Navajos call "walking in beauty." This pioneering healer resolved to integrate her culture's ancient healing traditions with high-tech procedures. Her skill with a scalpel begins a patient's healing process, but her blend of healing ceremonies and the involvement of families and neighbors restores the balance of good health.

Lori Arviso Alvord, M.D., is also referred to as _____,

_____, and _____.

Dr. Lori Alvord, surgeon, associate dean, and author, is featured in this ad for the American Indian College Fund. Why does the ad ask, "Have you ever seen a real Indian?"

HAVE YOU EVER SEEN A REAL INDIAN?

AMERICAN INDIAN COLLEGE FUND
EDUCATION IS STRENGTH

PRACTICE 6

Give coherence to the following paragraphs by thinking of appropriate synonyms or substitutions for the words in italics. Then write them in the blanks.

Paragraph 1

J.K. Rowling was not always a multi-millionaire. In fact, before the success of her first book, *Harry Potter and the Philosopher's Stone*, the *best-selling author* endured many hardships. She began writing when her mother was in the final stages of multiple sclerosis. Discovering a gift for writing, the _____ used her grief to deepen her narrative about a boy wizard. After the birth of her daughter, Rowling quit her teaching job to write full time, living on public assistance. When the manuscript was finished, she sent it to twelve different publishers. Unable to foresee the global appeal of Harry Potter, all twelve rejected it. Finally, after a glowing review from the eight-year-old daughter of a publishing company executive, the _____ could at last share her imaginative tales with readers. By the time her last book was released in 2007, the franchise had made over fifteen billion dollars. In just over a decade, J.K. Rowling went from being a struggling mother to a _____.

Paragraph 2

Although *sodas* are hugely popular, experts say that drinking them can have harmful health effects. These _____ are full of high-fructose corn syrup, which contributes to diabetes and high blood pressure. Because they contain sugar but no vitamins, minerals, fiber, or nutrients of any kind, they also contribute to obesity. Surprisingly, diet _____ are not the answer; for reasons that experts don't entirely understand, they actually seem to make many people gain weight. Other research shows that the phosphorus in _____ promotes bone loss, and the acid hastens tooth decay.

For all these reasons, many schools have banned or restricted the sale of _____

to children, who too often reach for a pop-top can instead of a healthier choice like milk,

juice, or water. As more schools put limits on what children can drink, the soda companies

are busy marketing "vitamin water" and fruit juice to keep up with the trend.

PRACTICE 7

Carefully determine the exact relationship between the sentences in each pair below. Then choose a transitional expression that clearly expresses this relationship and write it in the blank. Use the list of transitional expressions in Chapter 4, Part B, of the companion text. Pay attention to punctuation and capitalize the first word of every sentence.*

1. No one inquired about the money found in the lobby. _____, it was given

    to charity.

2. First, cut off the outer, fibrous husk of the coconut. _____ poke a hole

    through one of the dark "eyes" and sip the milk through a straw.

3. The English Department office is on the fifth floor. _____ to it is a small

    reading room.

4. Some mountains under the sea soar almost as high as those on land. One underwater

    mountain in the Pacific, _____, is only 500 feet shorter than Mount Everest.

5. All citizens should vote. Many do not, _____.

6. Mrs. Dalworth enjoys shopping in out-of-the-way thrift shops. _____, she

    loves bargaining with the vendors at outdoor flea markets.

_____

* For practice using conjunctions to join ideas, see Chapter 26, "Coordination and Subordination," in both the companion text and this workbook.

7. In 1887, Native Americans owned nearly 138 million acres of land. By 1932, _____, 90 million of those acres were owned by whites.

8. Kansas corn towered over the fence. _____ the fence, a red tractor stood baking in the sun.

9. Most street crime occurs between 2:00 and 5:00 A.M. _____, do not go out alone during those hours.

10. Dr. Leff took great pride in his work at the clinic. _____, his long hours often left him exhausted.

11. George Washington Carver developed hundreds of uses for a single agricultural product, the peanut. _____, he created peanut butter, peanut cooking oil, and printing ink from this legume.

12. We waited in our seats for over an hour. _____ the lights dimmed, and the Fabulous String Band bounded on stage.

PRACTICE 8

Add **transitional expressions** to this essay to guide the reader smoothly from sentence to sentence. To do so, consider the relationship between sentences (shown in parentheses). Then write the transitional word or phrase that best expresses this relationship.

Oldest Child, Youngest Child—Does It Matter?

A number of studies show that birth order—whether a person is the first-born, middle, or last-born child in the family—can affect both personality and career choice. _____, first-borns carry the weight of their parents' expectations
            (illustration)
and _____ are urged to be responsible and set a good example for their
        (time)
younger siblings. _____, they may develop leadership skills and a strong
            (result)

motivation to achieve. Many eldest children _____ become leaders. High
                                                    (time)

percentages of U.S. presidents and CEOs, _____ , are first-borns.
                                                    (illustration)

Middle children, _____ , get less attention and applause in childhood.
                        (contrast)

_____ , they tend to become flexible and good at resolving conflicts.
    (result)

_____ , some middle children become rebellious or creative as they make
    (addition)

their place in the world. _____ , many choose careers as entrepreneurs,
                                  (time)

negotiators, or businesspeople. _____ , later-born or last-born children,
                                        (addition)

in order to compete with their older siblings, may become rule-breakers or family

clowns. Professionally, babies of the family tend to become musicians, adventurers,

and comedians. _____ , there are countless exceptions to these general
                      (conceding a point)

trends; _____ it is interesting to ponder the evidence that our birth order
              (contrast)

_____ helps shape who we are.
    (emphasis)

PRACTICE 9   **THINKING AND WRITING TOGETHER**

In small groups, discuss what you learned about birth order and personality in
Practice 8. What is your place in the family? Do the typical traits apply to you?
Take notes for later writing while you describe the classic first-born, middle-born,
or youngest child; then apply these traits to yourself or someone you know well
who fills that birth spot. Is the portrait accurate? To learn more, visit **http://www
.birthorderandpersonality.com/.**

PRACTICE 10   **REVIEW**

Most paragraphs achieve coherence through a variety of linking devices: repetition, pronouns,
substitutions, and transitional expressions. Read the following paragraphs with care, noting
the kinds of linking devices used by each writer. Answer the questions after each paragraph.

Paragraph 1

(1) *Slumdog Millionaire* tells the tale of Jamal, a young man from the slums of Mumbai who is one question away from winning India's version of *Who Wants to Be a Millionaire*. (2) As the fast-moving film unfolds, we follow Jamal and Latika, the girl he loved and lost in childhood, from the gritty poverty and child exploitation of India's ghettos into the present. (3) Awarded eight Academy Awards, this celebration of love and hope scores top marks on viewer surveys. (4) *Slumdog Millionaire* is one to see.

—Miguel Bode, *crazy4film.com*

1. What important words appear in both the first and last sentences? _____

   _____

2. In sentences 2 and 3, *Slumdog Millionaire* is referred to as _____

   _____

Paragraph 2

(1) In the annals of great escapes, the flight by seventeen-year-old Lester Moreno Perez from Cuba to the United States surely must rank as one of the most imaginative. (2) At 8:30 on the night of Thursday, March 1, Lester crept along the beach in Varadero, a resort town on the north coast of Cuba. (3) Working quickly, he launched his sailboard—a

Cuban rafters attempting to reach the United States. What would you risk to live in freedom?

surfboard equipped with a movable sail—into the shark-haunted waters off the Straits of Florida. (4) At first guided by the stars and later by the hazy glow from electric lights in towns beyond the horizon, Lester sailed with 20-knot winds toward the Florida Keys, 90 miles away. (5) All night he balanced on the small board, steering through black waters. (6) Just past daybreak on Friday, Lester was sighted 30 miles south of Key West by the Korean crew of the freighter *Tina D.* (7) The boom on his tiny craft was broken. (8) The astonished sailors pulled him aboard, fed him chicken and rice, and finally radioed the U.S. Coast Guard.

—Adapted from Sam Moses, "A New Dawn," *Sports Illustrated*

1. Underline the transitional expressions in this paragraph.

2. What *order* of ideas does the paragraph employ? _____

Paragraph 3

(1) *Phishing* is the term for tricking computer users into revealing sensitive information such as passwords or credit-card numbers. (2) A person who goes phishing first sets up a seemingly official website and e-mail address to pose as a legitimate individual or business. (3) Next, the phisher casts the bait. (4) He or she e-mails unsuspecting individuals to request information, usually threatening account suspension or cancellation if the request is ignored. (5) When an unfortunate recipient takes the bait and sends back the information, the criminal can then reel it in and use it to commit fraud. (6) In one recent phishing case, for example, a young male disguised as an America Online employee sent out messages claiming that members' accounts had problems. (7) The e-mail looked official, with AOL logos and a link to the AOL Billing Center. (8) However, when the victims clicked on that link, they were taken to dummy web page. (9) Anyone who typed in a credit-card number, social security number, bank-account number, or password gave that vital information to the con artist.

1. What important words are repeated in this paragraph? _____

2. What synonyms and pronouns are used for "a person who goes phishing"? _____

_____

3. What transitional expressions are used in sentences 6 and 8? _____

Unit 3

Developing the Paragraph

Illustration

PRACTICE 1

Read each of the following paragraphs of illustration. Underline each topic sentence. Note in the margin how many examples are provided to illustrate each general statement.

Paragraph 1

Random acts of kindness are those little sweet or grand lovely things we do for no reason except that, momentarily, the best of our humanity has sprung…into full bloom. When you spontaneously give an old woman the bouquet of red carnations you had meant to take home to your own dinner table, when you give your lunch to the guitar-playing beggar who makes music at the corner between your two subway stops, when you anonymously put coins in someone else's parking meter because you see the red "Expired" medallion signaling to a meter maid—you are doing not what life requires of you, but what the best of your human soul invites you to do.

—Daphne Rose Kingma, *Random Acts of Kindness*

Paragraph 2

There are many quirky variations to lightning. A "bolt from the blue" occurs when a long horizontal flash suddenly turns toward the earth, many miles from the storm. "St. Elmo's Fire," often seen by sailors and mountain climbers, is a pale blue or green light caused by weak electrical discharges that cling to trees, airplanes, and ships' masts. "Pearl lightning" occurs when flashes are broken into segments. "Ball lightning" can be from an inch to several feet in diameter. Pearls and balls are often mistaken for flying saucers or UFOs, and many scientists believe they are only optical illusions.

—Reed McManus, *Sierra Magazine*

PRACTICE 2

Each example in a paragraph of illustration must clearly relate to and support the general statement. Each general statement in this practice is followed by several examples. Circle the letter of any example that does *not* clearly illustrate the generalization. Be prepared to explain your choices.

EXAMPLE The museum contains many fascinating examples of African art.

a. It houses a fine collection of Ashanti fertility dolls.

b. Drums and shamans' costumes are displayed on the second floor.

c. The museum building was once the home of Frederick Douglass.
   (The fact that the building was once the home of Frederick Douglass is *not an example* of African art.)

1. The International Space Station is designed for efficient use of limited space.

   a. Food has been dehydrated so it can be stored in tiny packages.

   b. Special science laboratories onboard are the size of clothes closets.

   c. Daily life in the space station can be observed by 90 percent of the world's population.

   d. Each little "bedroom" can be folded and stored in a single sleeping bag.

2. Today's global companies sometimes find that their product names and slogans can translate into embarrassing bloopers.

   a. Pepsi's slogan "Come alive with the Pepsi Generation" didn't work in Taiwan, where it meant "Pepsi will bring your ancestors back from the dead."

   b. When General Motors introduced its Chevy Nova in South America, company officials didn't realize that *no va* in Spanish means "it won't go."

   c. In Chinese, the Kentucky Fried Chicken slogan "finger-lickin' good" means "eat your fingers off."

   d. Nike runs the same ad campaign in several countries, changing the ad slightly to fit each culture.

3. Many life-enhancing products that we take for granted were invented by women.

   a. Josephine Cochran invented the dishwasher in 1893, declaring that if no one else would build a machine to perform this boring task, she would do it herself.

b. In 1966, chemist Stephanie Louise Kwoleck patented Kevlar, a fabric five times stronger than steel, now used in bulletproof vests and other important products.

c. Lonnie Johnson got the idea for the famous Supersoaker squirtgun after the homemade nozzle on his sink sprayed water across the room.

4. Since a series of tragic accidents in 2000 and 2001 killed several drivers, the National Association of Stock Car Racing (NASCAR) has taken steps to make the sport safe.

a. All new race car seats wrap around the driver's rib cage and shoulders, providing better support during a crash.

b. The fastest NASCAR track is the one in Talladega, Alabama, where the average race speed is 188 miles per hour.

c. All drivers are now required to wear the head and neck support (HANS) device, a collar that prevents the head from snapping forward or sideways during a wreck.

d. NASCAR tracks now have softer walls and barriers that better absorb the impact of cars at high speeds.

NASCAR driver Dale Earnhardt, Jr., dons his helmet and HANS safety device before the Daytona 500.

© AP Images / Chris O'Meara

5. Single parents must cope with a variety of stresses that couples do not.

   a. With just one paycheck instead of two, even single parents who receive child support can find themselves struggling to pay the monthly bills.

   b. Because single parents have no partner to share errands and household chores, they may have little time for stress-relieving recreation.

   c. Assigning household chores is a way to help children learn good habits.

   d. Stressful emotions like guilt can plague single parents, who wonder how their children will be affected by growing up without a full-time mom or dad.

6. Nature has provided us with many powerful medicines.

   a. Aspirin comes from willow bark, penicillin from fungus, and the cancer drug Taxol from the Pacific yew tree.

   b. Drugs that lower cholesterol and blood pressure are helping people with heart disease lead longer, healthier lives.

   c. A newly discovered compound from a New Zealand deep-sea sponge, called Halichondrin B, has been eliminating tumors in laboratory tests.

   d. Prialt, a drug that blocks pain signals in the human spinal cord, comes from the venom of the deadly cone snail of the Indian and Pacific Oceans.

7. In the Arizona desert, one sees many colorful plants and flowers.

   a. Here and there are patches of pink clover.

   b. Gray-green saguaro cacti rise up like giant candelabra.

   c. Colorful birds dart through the landscape.

   d. Bright yellow poppies bloom by the road.

8. Many meaningful gifts can be created for little cost or even for free.

   a. A hand-drawn book of coupons redeemable for services like "one home-cooked meal," "one car wash," or "an evening of babysitting" costs only time, not money.

   b. For the low price of supplies, handmade gifts like a crocheted scarf, a collection of favorite photos or recipes, or a quilt often become treasured heirlooms.

   c. Go shopping in your own house and gather unopened, unused items—such as soaps, lotions, or candles—to "regift" in gift baskets.

   d. A laptop computer makes a great gift for a student or an adult on the go.

PRACTICE 3

The secret of good illustration lies in well-chosen, well-written examples. Think of one example that illustrates each of the following general statements. Write out the example in sentence form (one to three sentences) as clearly and exactly as possible.

1. A few contemporary singers work hard to send a positive message.

   Example _____

   _____

   _____

2. In a number of ways, this college makes it easy for working students to attend.

   Example _____

   _____

   _____

3. Believing in yourself is 90 percent of success.

   Example _____

   _____

   _____

4. Many teenagers believe they must have expensive designer clothing.

   Example _____

   _____

   _____

5. Growing up in a large family can teach the value of compromise.

   Example _____

   _____

   _____

6. A number of shiny classic cars cruised up and down Ocean Drive.

Example _____

_____

_____

7. Children say surprising things.

Example _____

_____

_____

8. Sadly, rudeness seems more and more common in America.

Example _____

_____

_____

PRACTICE 4   THINKING AND WRITING TOGETHER

Illustrate Acts of Kindness

In the news, we often hear the phrase "random acts of violence"—acts whose unlucky victims are in the wrong place at the wrong time. The phrase "random acts of kindness" reverses this idea in a wonderful way—kind acts whose recipients are often perfect strangers. In a group with four or five classmates, read about random acts of kindness (Practice 1, Paragraph 1, page 39). Now think of one good example of a real-life random act of kindness, performed by you or someone else—either at college or work, or in everyday life. Share and discuss these examples with your group. Which examples are the most striking or moving? Why?

Write up your example in one paragraph. Begin with a clear topic sentence and present the act of kindness as movingly as you can. Refer to the checklist in Chapter 5 of the companion text, and ask your group mates for feedback.

_____

_____

_____

_____

_____

_____

_____

_____

EXPLORING ONLINE

http://www.actsofkindness.org/be-inspired
Read about acts of kindness that people have sent in; click "Contact Us" to submit your group's best writing for possible publication.

CHAPTER 6

Narration

Read the following narrative paragraph carefully and answer the questions:

> The Cherokee people tell the story of a young boy who has been badly wronged by someone he considered a friend. The boy, hurt and furious, tells his grandfather about the incident. His grandfather nods and replies, "At times, I too have felt hatred for those who do great harm and seem to feel no sorrow about it. But hate wears a person down and does not hurt the enemy. It is like taking poison and wishing the enemy would die. I have struggled with these feelings many times. It is as if two wolves live inside me; they live inside you, too. One wolf is good. He is peaceful, generous, compassionate, and wise. He lives in harmony with all those around him and does not easily take offense. He fights only when it is right to do so. But the other wolf lives in me as well—and in you. He is full of anger, envy, self pity, and pain. The smallest thing infuriates him. He cannot think clearly because his anger is so great, yet that anger changes nothing. Sometimes, it is hard to live with two wolves inside me, for both of them struggle to dominate my spirit.
>
> The boy looked intently into his grandfather's eyes and asked, "Which wolf wins, Grandfather?" The grandfather smiled and said quietly, "The one I feed."

1. What is the point of the narrative? _____

_____

2. What events make up this narrative? _____

    _____

    _____

    _____

3. Do you relate to this story? In what way?_____

    _____

    _____

PRACTICE 2

Here are three plans for narrative paragraphs. The events in the plans are not in correct chronological order. The plans also contain events that do not belong in each story. Number the events in the proper time sequence and cross out any irrelevant ones.

1. A combination of talent and hard work has propelled Alicia Keys to musical stardom.

    _____ In 1988, seven-year-old Alicia dazzled her first piano teacher by mastering both classical and jazz pieces.

    _____ By 2005, her distinctive voice and blending of soul, jazz, hip hop, and classical styles had won a huge fan base and four more Grammies.

Alicia Keys in concert

© Stefan M. Prager/Redferns/Getty Images

_____ As a teenager in the "Hell's Kitchen" section of New York City, she wrote her first songs and blossomed as a pianist.

_____ Every year since 1959, the Grammy, the Academy Award of music, has been given to musicians of outstanding achievement.

_____ At age twenty, she released *Songs in A Minor*, the debut album that scored five Grammy awards in 2002, including Best New Artist and Song of the Year for her hit single "Fallin'."

2. In a treasured letter home from the Civil War, my great great-grandfather William, then sixteen, describes an evening of surprising calm.

_____ Suddenly, one of William's buddies spotted Confederate soldiers watching from the opposite bank.

_____ The Civil War lasted from 1861 to 1865.

_____ Yanks and Rebs swam, whooped, and even shared cigarettes together before returning to their camps.

_____ William did not know what signal was given, but instead of shooting, both armies suddenly stripped to their underwear and splashed into the water.

_____ The next morning, these young men continued the slaughter.

_____ After a day of bloody fighting in July 1863, William and his Union company were settling down on a wooded hill above a pond.

3. Some say that the Greek myth of Icarus teaches the importance of moderation and self-control.

_____ Just as his father feared, the blazing sun melted the wax, the wings fell apart, and Icarus plummeted to his death.

_____ To escape from a prison tower in the Mediterranean Sea, the inventor Daedalus made wings for himself and his son Icarus out of feathers, thread, and wax.

_____ Soaring higher and delighting in his ability to fly toward the sun, Icarus ignored his father's advice.

_____ Daedalus and Icarus leapt from the tower and began flying over the sea.

_____ The study of Greek myths can be rewarding and relevant to modern life.

_____ As he strapped on their wings, Daedalus warned his boy not to fly too near the sun, or the heat would melt the wax.

PRACTICE 3   **THINKING AND WRITING TOGETHER**

Carefully examine this picture after you read about Icarus in item 3 above. How does this modern image connect to the story of Icarus? Is the young man also escaping a prison? If so, what might be his prison? Do you think the myth of Icarus is or is not relevant to the modern world? Be prepared to share your thoughts.

Flight of Icarus, Glen Wexler

© Glen Wexler

PRACTICE 4

Here are topic sentences for three narrative paragraphs. Make a plan for each paragraph, placing the events of the narrative in the proper time sequence.

1. When I had trouble with _____ , help came from an unexpected source.

   _____

   _____

   _____

   _____

   _____

   _____

2. The accident (or performance) lasted only a few moments, but I will never forget it.

   _____

   _____

   _____

   _____

   _____

   _____

3. _____ was the craziest day I've ever experienced on the job.
   (day and date)

_____

_____

_____

_____

_____

_____

PRACTICE 5   **THINKING AND WRITING TOGETHER**

Narrate an Experience of Stereotyping

Good narratives have a *point*; they bring to life a moral, lesson, or idea. In a group with four of five classmates, read this narrative passage about "The Latina Stereotype" by Judith Ortiz Cofer and then discuss and answer the questions.

> My first public poetry reading took place at a restaurant where a luncheon was being held before the event. I was nervous and excited as I walked in with a notebook in hand. An older woman motioned me to her table, and thinking (foolish me) that she wanted me to autograph a copy of my newly published slender volume of verse, I went over. She ordered a cup of coffee from me, assuming that I was the waitress. (Easy enough to mistake my poems for menus, I suppose.) I know it wasn't an intentional act of cruelty. Yet of all the good things that happened later, I remember that scene most clearly, because it reminded me of what I had to overcome before anyone would take me seriously.

● What is the point of this story? Exactly what *stereotype* did the writer encounter? What did the woman assume about her and why?

_____

_____

_____

_____

- Have you ever been stereotyped? That is, has anyone ever treated you a certain way based only on your age, clothing, race, gender, major, accent, piercings or other decoration, or even things you are carrying, like books or a beeper? Share a story with the group. What stereotype was imposed on you, and how did you react? Now narrate vividly in writing your experience of stereotyping. You might wish to place your topic sentence, stating the meaning or point, last. Ask your group mates for feedback.

_____

_____

_____

_____

_____

_____

_____

_____

_____

_____

_____

EXPLORING ONLINE

http://www.tolerance.org/

Explore this interesting site about increasing tolerance. Take notes on any ideas for further writing.

CHAPTER 7

Description

Read the following paragraph carefully and answer the questions.

The woman who met us had an imposing beauty. She was tall and large-boned. Her face was strongly molded, with high cheekbones and skin the color of mahogany. She greeted us politely but did not smile and seemed to hold her head very high, an effect exaggerated by the abundant black hair slicked up and rolled on the top of her head. Her clothing was simple, a black sweater and skirt, and I remember thinking that dressed in showier garments, this woman would have seemed overwhelming.

1. What overall impression does the writer give of the woman? _____

_____

_____

2. What specific details support this general impression? _____

_____

_____

_____

_____

3. What kind of order does the writer use? _____

PRACTICE 2

It is important that the details in a descriptive paragraph support the overall impression given in the topic sentence. In each of the following plans, one detail has nothing to do with the topic sentence; it is merely a bit of irrelevant information. Find the irrelevant detail and circle its letter.

1. Magda's sewing shop is crammed with the items of her trade.
   a. racks of clothing awaiting alterations
   b. thread, thimbles, and tailor's chalk scattered on the work table
   c. dress forms for all shapes and sizes in one corner
   d. large mug half full of coffee on the window sill
   e. sewing machine in front of the window

2. The Calle Ocho Festival, named after S.W. 8th Street in Little Havana, is a giant Latino street party.
   a. as far as the eye can see on S.W. 8th Street, thousands of people stroll, eat, and dance
   b. on the left, vendors sell hot pork sandwiches, *pasteles* (spiced meat pies), and fried sweets dusted with powdered sugar
   c. up close, the press of bare-limbed people, blaring music, and rich smells
   d. during the 1980s, Dominican merengue music hit the dance clubs of New York
   e. on the right, two of many bands play mambo or merengue music

3. In the photograph from 1877, Chief Joseph looks sad and dignified.
   a. long hair pulled back, touched with gray
   b. dark eyes gaze off to one side, as if seeing a bleak future
   c. strong mouth frowns at the corners
   d. ceremonial shell necklaces cover his chest
   e. Nez Percé tribe once occupied much of the Pacific Northwest

4. In the video of last night's overtime victory, basketball star Yao Ming looks tired.

 a. his eyes nearly closed, lids heavy

 b. chest heaving, almost panting as he runs down the court

 c. seven feet, six inches tall, towering over his opponents

 d. shoulders slumped a bit

 e. arms hanging limp at his sides

5. Many people are taking personal steps to curb global warming.

 a. hybrid cars in high demand

 b. increasing popularity of public transportation and carpools

 c. recycling a priority in many households

 d. use of special bulbs for energy-saving light

 e. glaciers melting at fast rates

PRACTICE 3

Here are three topic sentences for descriptive paragraphs. Give five specific details that would support the overall impression given in each topic sentence. Appeal to as many of the senses as possible. Be careful not to list irrelevant bits of information.

EXAMPLE   Stopped in time by the photographer, my mother appears confident.

Details:

 a. *her hair swept up in a sophisticated pompadour*

 b. *a determined look in her young eyes*

 c. *wide, self-assured smile*

 d. *her chin held high*

 e. *well-padded shoulders*

(These five details support *confident* in the topic sentence.)

1. This was clearly a music (sports, or computer) lover's room.

    a. _____

    b. _____

    c. _____

    d. _____

    e. _____

2. The buildings on that street look sadly run-down.

    a. _____

    b. _____

    c. _____

    d. _____

    e. _____

3. The beach on a hot summer day presented a constant show.

    a. _____

    b. _____

    c. _____

    d. _____

    e. _____

PRACTICE 4

Pick the description you like best from Practice 3. Prewrite for more details if you wish. Choose a logical order in which to present the best details, make a plan or an outline, and then write an excellent descriptive paragraph. Make notes in the space on the next page, and write the full paragraph in your notebook or journal.

_____

_____

_____

_____

_____

_____

PRACTICE 5 **THINKING AND WRITING TOGETHER**

Describe a Painting

In a group with four or five classmates, study the painting below. Your task is to write one paragraph describing this painting so that someone who has never seen it can visualize it. As a group, craft a good topic sentence that gives an overall impression of the scene. Your topic sentence might take this form:

"George Tooker's 1950 painting, _Subway_, shows (or captures) _the subway as a frightening_

place, prison-like environment. "

Have one person take notes as you brainstorm important details, using rich language to capture the scene. Now decide the best order in which to present your details—right

Subway by George Tooker, 1950
Egg tempera on composition board. 18 ⅛ c 36 ⅛ in. Whitney Museum of Art, New York; Purchase, with funds from the Juliana Force Purchase Award 50.23.

© Estate of George Tooker

to left, center to sides, or some other. Use transitional expressions to guide the reader's eye from detail to detail. Revise the writing to make it as exact and fresh as possible. Be prepared to read your work to the full class.

_____

_____

_____

_____

_____

_____

_____

_____

_____

EXPLORING ONLINE

http://www.artic.edu/aic/

Art Institute of Chicago: Find a work of art that intrigues you and describe it.

http://www.moma.org/

Museum of Modern Art: Find a work of art that intrigues you and write about it.

Process

Read the following how-to paragraph carefully and answer the questions.

If your dog barks too much, the Humane Society recommends an easy way to solve the problem. All you need is a plant mister—a small spray bottle—filled with water and kept handy. First and most important, respond immediately every time your dog barks unnecessarily. Instantly say, "Quiet, Pluto," or whatever the dog's name is, giving one or two squirts of water in the dog's face. Be sure to do this while the dog is barking. Waiting until the dog stops barking may confuse it. If the dog moves away, say, "Quiet" again as you move toward the dog and give it one more squirt of water. Second, repeat this procedure every time the dog barks without a good reason. The dog will soon learn that your saying "Quiet" comes with a squirt of water. Usually two days—about five to ten water treatments—are enough. Third, as time goes by, use the spray bottle only if the dog forgets—that is, rarely. Throughout the training process, remember to be consistent, using the spray technique every single time, and don't forget to reassure your dog that you two are still friends by petting it when it is quiet.

—Eleanor Steiger, Student

1. What should you be able to do after reading this paragraph? _____

_____

_____

2. Are any "materials" necessary for this process? _____

_____

3. How many steps are there in this paragraph? List them.

_____

_____

_____

4. What order does the writer employ? _____

PRACTICE 2

Here are five plans for process paragraphs. The steps for the plans are not in the correct chronological order. The plans also contain irrelevant details that are not part of the process. Number the steps in the proper time sequence and cross out any irrelevant details.

1. The process of taking digital fingerprints, which requires specialized scanning equipment, consists of several simple steps.

_____ The computer converts these finger scans into digital data patterns, mapping points on the patterns.

_____ One by one, the subject places his or her fingers on the optical or silicon scanner surface for a few seconds while the computer scans.

_____ The technician begins by cleaning the subject's fingers with alcohol to remove any dirt or sweat.

_____ For years, the only fingerprints were made by rolling the fingers in wet ink and pressing the fingers onto a card.

_____ At the technician's command, the computer can compare this subject's fingerprint patterns to millions of patterns in the national database and identify possible matches.

2. Stress, which is your body's response to physical or mental pressures, occurs in three stages.

_____ In the resistance stage, your body works hard to resist or handle the threat, but you may become more vulnerable to other stressors, like flu or colds.

_____ If the stress continues for too long, your body uses up its defenses and enters the exhaustion stage.

_____   Trying to balance college courses, parenthood, and work is sure to cause stress.

_____   During the alarm stage (also called *fight or flight*), your body first reacts to a threat by releasing hormones that increase your heart rate and blood pressure, create muscle tension, and supply quick energy.

3. Chewing gum is made entirely by machine.

_____   Then the warm mass is pressed into thin ribbons by pairs of rollers.

_____   First, the gum base is melted and pumped through a high-speed spinner that throws out all impurities.

_____   The gum base makes the gum chewy.

_____   Huge machines mix the purified gum with sugar, corn syrup, and flavoring, such as spearmint, peppermint, or cinnamon.

_____   Finally, machines wrap the sticks individually and then package them.

_____   Knives attached to the last rollers cut the ribbons into sticks.

4. Many psychologists claim that marriage is a dynamic process consisting of several phases.

_____   Sooner or later, romance gives way to disappointment as both partners really see each other's faults.

_____   Idealization is the first phase, when two people fall romantically in love, each thinking the other is perfect.

_____   The last phase occurs as the couple face their late years as a twosome once again.

_____   The third phase is sometimes called the productivity period, when two people work at parenting and career development.

_____   Men and women may have different expectations in a marriage.

_____   As the children leave home and careers mature, couples may enter a stage when they rethink their lives and goals.

5. Helping to save rare stranded sea turtles, our service learning project, was a rewarding series of steps.

——— Inside, we rubbed Vaseline on each turtle's shell and put saline in its eyes; the sickest turtles needed IV fluids.

——— We gently loaded each tired giant in the front seat of a pickup truck and hurried back to the sanctuary.

——— In the fall, when temperatures dropped, we volunteers at the Wellfleet Wildlife Sanctuary raced to the beaches to find any giant sea turtles that had not swum south.

——— Two volunteers so loved working with endangered turtles that they are now pursuing careers in marine biology.

——— Within 12 hours, we drove our patients to the aquarium in Boston, to spend the winter and get well before their release in warm Florida seas.

PRACTICE 3

Here are topic sentences for three process paragraphs. Make a plan for each paragraph, listing in proper time sequence all the steps that would be necessary to complete the process. Now choose one plan and write an excellent process paragraph. Answers will vary.

1. Although I'm still not the life of the party, I took these steps to overcome my shyness at parties.

_____

_____

_____

_____

_____

_____

2. Good kids turning bad: it is a process occurring all over the country.

_____

_____

_____

_____

_____

_____

3. _____ is/was a very complicated (or simple) process.

_____

_____

_____

_____

_____

_____

PRACTICE 4   THINKING AND WRITING TOGETHER

Explain the Process of Intoxication

In a group with four or five classmates, study and discuss these percentages that show rising blood alcohol content (BAC), a measure of intoxication. Now plan and write a paragraph that describes what happens as BAC rises. Your purpose is to inform the public about this process. Write a topic sentence that gives an overview; in the body, include three or four percentages if you wish. In your concluding sentence or sentences, you might wish to emphasize the dangerous human meaning of these numbers. Be prepared to read your paragraph to the full class.

BAC	Effect
0.03%	relaxation, mood change
0.05%	decrease in motor skills; legal driving limit in New York
0.07%	legal driving limit in sixteen states
0.09%	delayed reaction time, decreased muscle control, slurred speech
0.15%	blurred vision, unsteadiness, impaired coordination
0.18%	difficulty staying awake
0.30%	semi-stupor
0.50%	coma and risk of death

Now assume your purpose is to write another paragraph convincing young people not to binge drink. Would BAC percentages help persuade your audience, or would you take another approach? What might that approach be?

_____

_____

_____

_____

_____

_____

_____

_____

EXPLORING ONLINE

http://www.safeyouth.org/

Search for "alcohol abuse" for facts on alcohol's link to violence, depression, and other harmful behaviors.

CHAPTER 9

Definition

A: Single-Sentence Definitions

B: The Definition Paragraph

A. Single-Sentence Definitions

PRACTICE 1

Write a one-sentence definition by **synonym** for each of the following terms. Remember, the synonym should be more familiar than the term being defined.

1. *irate:* _____

2. *to elude:* _____

3. *pragmatic:* _____

4. *fiasco:* _____

5. *elated:* _____

PRACTICE 2

Here are five **class definitions**. Circle the category and underline the distinguishing characteristics in each. You may find it helpful to make a chart.

1. A *haiku* is a Japanese poem that has seventeen syllables.
2. *Plagiarism* is stealing writing or ideas that are not one's own.
3. A *homer* is a referee who unconsciously favors the home team.
4. An *ophthalmologist* is a doctor who specializes in diseases of the eye.
5. The *tango* is a ballroom dance that originated in Latin America and is in 2/4 or 4/4 time.

PRACTICE 3

Define the following words by **class definition**. You may find it helpful to use this form:

"A _____ is a _____
          (noun)   (class or category)

that _____."
                (distinguishing characteristic)

1. *hamburger*: _____

   _____

   _____

2. *bikini*: _____

   _____

   _____

3. *snob*: _____

   _____

   _____

4. *mentor*: _____

_____

_____

5. *adolescence*: _____

_____

_____

PRACTICE 4

Write a one-sentence definition by **negation** for each of the following terms. First say what each term is not; then say what it is.

1. *hero*: _____

_____

_____

2. *final exam*: _____

_____

_____

3. *self-esteem*: _____

_____

_____

4. *intelligence*: _____

_____

_____

5. *freedom of speech*: _____

_____

_____

B. The Definition Paragraph

Read the following paragraph carefully and then answer the questions.

A feminist is *not* a man-hater, a masculine woman, a demanding shrew, or someone who dislikes housewives. A feminist is simply a woman or man who believes that women should enjoy the same rights, privileges, opportunities, and pay as men. Because society has deprived women of many equal rights, feminists have fought for equality. For instance, Susan B. Anthony, a famous nineteenth-century feminist, worked to get women the right to vote. Today, feminists want women to receive equal pay for equal work. They support a woman's right to pursue her goals and dreams, whether she wants to be an astronaut, athlete, banker, or full-time homemaker. On the home front, feminists believe that two partners who work should equally share the housework and child care. Because the term is often misunderstood, some people don't call themselves feminists even though they share feminist values. But courageous feminists of both sexes continue to speak out for equality.

1. The definition here spans two sentences. What kind of definition does the writer use

   in sentence 1? _____

2. What kind of definition appears in sentence 2? _____

3. The paragraph is developed by describing some key beliefs of feminists. What are

   these? _____

   _____

   _____

4. Which point is supported by an example? _____

_____

5. Make a plan or an outline of the paragraph.

_____

_____

_____

_____

_____

_____

_____

_____

PRACTICE 6

Read the following paragraphs and answer the questions.

Induction is reasoning from particular cases to general principles; that is, the scientific method: you look at a number of examples, then come to a general conclusion based on the evidence. For instance, having known twenty-five people named Glenn, all of whom were men, you might naturally conclude, through induction, that all people named Glenn are men. The problem with inductive reasoning here, however, is Glenn Close, the movie actress.

Deduction is reasoning from the general to the particular. One starts from a statement known or merely assumed to be true and uses it to come to a conclusion about the matter at hand. Once you know that all people have to die sometime and that you are a person, you can logically deduce that you, too, will have to die sometime.

—Judy Jones and William Wilson, "100 Things Every
College Graduate Should Know," *Esquire*

1. What two terms are defined? _____

2. What kind of definition is used in both topic sentences? _____

3. In what larger category do the writers place both induction and deduction? _____

_____

4. What example of induction do the writers give? _____

5. What example shows the *problem* with induction? _____

6. What example of deduction do the writers give? _____

_____

PRACTICE 7

Here are some topic sentences for definition paragraphs. Choose one that interests you and make a plan for a paragraph, using whatever method of development seems appropriate. Write your notes below, or in your notebook or journal.

1. An optimist is someone who usually expects the best from life and from people.

2. Prejudice means prejudging people on the basis of race, creed, age, or sex—not on their merits as individuals.

3. A wealthy person does not necessarily have money and possessions, but he or she might possess inner wealth—a loving heart and a creative mind.

4. Registration is a ritual torture that students must go through before they can attend their classes.

5. Bravery and bravado are very different character traits.

_____

_____

_____

_____

_____

_____

_____

| PRACTICE 8 | **THINKING AND WRITING TOGETHER** |

Define a Team Player

Whether or not we play sports, most of us know what it means to be a *team player* on a basketball or soccer team. But these days, many employers also want to hire "team players." What, exactly, are they looking for? What qualities does a team player bring to the job?

In a group with four or five classmates, discuss the meaning of *team player*, listing all the qualities that you think a team player has. List at least eight qualities:

_____   _____

_____   _____

_____   _____

_____   _____

Now craft a topic sentence of definition; have a group member write it down, using the form:

A team player is a(n) _____ who _____.

Choose the three or four most important qualities and write a paragraph defining *team player*. Use examples or details to bring your paragraph to life. Be prepared to share your paragraph with the full class.

_____

_____

_____

_____

_____

_____

_____

_____

_____

_____

_____

_____

_____

_____

_____

_____

_____

EXPLORING ONLINE

http://content.monster.ie/tools/quizzes/teamplayer/

Take the team player quiz, and write about your results.

CHAPTER **10**

Comparison and Contrast

A: The Contrast Paragraph and the Comparison Paragraph

B: The Comparison and Contrast Paragraph

A. The Contrast Paragraph and the Comparison Paragraph

Read the following paragraph carefully and answer the questions.

Certain personality traits, like whether a person is more reactive or proactive, can predict success or its opposite. In his book *The Seven Habits of Highly Effective People*, Steven Covey writes that reactive people tend to sit back and wait for life or circumstances to bring them opportunities. They react instead of act. When good things happen, they are happy, but when bad things happen, they feel like victims. Reactive people often say things like, "There's nothing I can do," "I can't because ... ," and "If only." In the short term, reactive people might feel comfortable playing it safe, holding back, and avoiding challenges; in the long term, though, they are often left dreaming. On the other hand, proactive people know that they have the power to choose their responses to whatever life brings. They act instead of react: If things aren't going their way, they take action to help create the outcome they desire. Proactive people can be recognized by their tendency to say things like "Let's consider the alternatives," "I prefer," "We can," and "I will." In the short term, proactive people might face the discomfort of failing because they take on challenges, set goals, and work toward them. But in the long term, Covey says, proactive people are the ones who achieve their dreams.

1. Can you tell from the topic sentence whether a contrast or comparison will follow? _____

   _____

2. What two personality types are being contrasted? _____

3. What information does the writer provide about reactive people? _____

   _____

4. What parallel information does the writer provide about proactive people? _____

   _____

   _____

5. What pattern does the writer of this paragraph use to present the contrasts? _____

   _____

6. What transitional expression does the writer use to stress the shift from A to B? _____

   _____

PRACTICE 2

This paragraph is hard to follow because it lacks transitional words and expressions that emphasize contrast. Revise the paragraph, adding transitional words of contrast. Strive for variety.

American restaurant portions have increased dramatically between 1985 and the

present, a trend that worries many nutritionists. The small food servings of twenty years

ago were healthy, according to the U.S. Food and Drug Administration (FDA). Modern portions have dangerously ballooned. For example, in 1985, a blueberry muffin weighed just 1.5 ounces. Today's typical muffin is a whopping 5 ounces. Compared with portions in 1985, today's supersized foods pack excess calories. For instance, a turkey sandwich once provided 320 calories. Now it delivers 820 calories, nearly half the fuel a male should consume in one day. The smaller food portions of years past contained reasonable amounts of dietary fat. Today's portions often ooze with fat. In 1985, a typical fast-food hamburger delivered 15 fat grams. Today's burger contains 34 artery-clogging grams—even before the consumer adds extra sauce. Huge portions do give us more for our money: more calories, more fat, more obesity, more heart disease. Don't be a victim of portion distortion.

A picture is worth a thousand words at the U.S. government's "Portion Distortion" website, which contrasts typical food portions 20 years ago and now.

Spaghetti and Meatballs

20 Years Ago   **Today**

500 calories   **??? calories**

How many calories do you think are in today's portion of spaghetti and meatballs?

○ **1,025** ○ **600** ○ **800**

Department of Health and Human Services, National Institutes of Health

EXPLORING ONLINE

http://hp2010.nhlbihin.net/portion/

Learn more about "portion distortion" and maintaining a healthy weight;
take notes on facts or ideas for further writing.

PRACTICE 3

Below are three plans for contrast paragraphs. The points of contrast in the second
column do not follow the same order as the points in the first column. In addition, one
detail is missing. First, number the points in the second column to match those in the first.
Then fill in the missing detail.

1. Shopping at a Supermarket   **Shopping at a Local Grocery**

1. carries all brands   _____ personal service

2. lower prices   _____ closed on Sundays

3. open seven days a week   _____ prices often higher

4. little personal service   _____ _____

5. no credit   _____ credit available for steady customers

2. My Son   **My Daughter**

1. fifteen years old   _____ good at making minor household repairs

2. likes to be alone   _____ likes to be with friends

3. reads a lot   _____ doesn't like to read

4. is an excellent cook   _____ expects to attend a technical college

5. wants to go to chef school   _____ _____

3. Job A   **Job B**

1. good salary   _____ three-week vacation

2. office within walking distance   _____ work on a team with others

3. two-week vacation   _____ one-hour bus ride to office

4. work alone   _____ health insurance

5. lots of overtime   _____ no overtime

6. no health insurance   _____ _____

PRACTICE 4

Here are three topics for either contrast or comparison paragraphs. Compose two topic sentences for each topic, one for a possible contrast paragraph and one for a possible comparison paragraph.

	Topic	**Topic Sentences**
EXAMPLE	Two members of my family	A. *My brother and sister have different attitudes toward exercise.*
		B. *My parents are alike in that they're easygoing.*
1.	Two friends or coworkers	A. _____
		B. _____

2. You as a child and you as
   an adult

   A. _____

   _____

   _____

   B. _____

   _____

   _____

3. Two vacations

   A. _____

   _____

   _____

   B. _____

   _____

   _____

PRACTICE 5

Here are four topic sentences for comparison or contrast paragraphs. For each topic sentence, think of one supporting point of comparison or contrast and explain that point in one or two sentences.

1. When it comes to movies (TV shows, books, entertainment), Demetrios and Arlene have totally different tastes.

   _____

   _____

2. My mother and I have few personality traits in common.

   _____

   _____

3. Although there are obvious differences, the two neighborhoods (blocks, houses) have much in common.

_____

_____

4. Paying taxes is like having a tooth pulled.*

_____

_____

PRACTICE 6

THINKING AND WRITING TOGETHER

Contrast Toys for Boys and Toys for Girls

Retail stores and websites frequently recommend toys for children, often dividing their gift ideas into two groups: "toys for boys" and "toys for girls." These were the top-selling toys in 2008, according to the National Retail Federation.

Top Toys for Boys	**Top Toys for Girls**
1. Video Games	1. Barbie
2. Nintendo Wii	2. Disney Hannah Montana
3. LEGO	3. Dolls (generic)
4. Cars (generic)	4. Bratz
5. Transformers	5. Nintendo Wii
6. Elmo	6. Video Games
7. Star Wars	7. Elmo
8. Hot Wheels	8. Disney High School Musical
9. Remote-Controlled Vehicles	9. Disney Princess
10. Xbox 360	10. American Girl

Make sure every group member knows what these toys are. Then, based on the lists, discuss what contrasting messages are being sent about what boys and girls supposedly

_____

* For more work on this kind of comparison, see Chapter 23, "Revising for Language Awareness," Part D, in the companion text.

like to do. Do these lists put unfair limits on children of either sex? Now plan and write a comparison or contrast paragraph together based on your discussion.

EXPLORING ONLINE

http://www.google.com

Or visit your favorite search engine; search "toys, gender roles" and see what information you find.

B. The Comparison and Contrast Paragraph

PRACTICE 7

Here is a somewhat longer comparison and contrast (two paragraphs). Read it carefully and answer the questions.

Most people don't connect Dr. Gregory House, the brilliant medical detective on the television show *House,* with Sherlock Holmes, the legendary crime-solver invented by writer Sir Arthur Conan Doyle in 1887. The differences are obvious. House is a medical doctor confronting people's illnesses while Holmes is a detective who tracks murderers and jewel thieves. House stars in a TV drama created by David Shore, but Holmes stars in Doyle's four novels and fifty-six short stories. House is a 21st century American man, whereas Holmes is a British character of the last century, with his quaint pipe and old-fashioned plaid cap.

Yet despite these differences, the two sleuths share startling similarities. Both solve mysteries by their brilliant powers of deduction. Both are extremely arrogant, alienating people around them, and both are lazy until a good case rivets their attention. House is notoriously addicted to pain-killers, supposedly to help him cope with a wounded leg; similarly, the fictional Holmes is addicted to cocaine. Dr. Greg House's only true friend is his colleague Dr. Wilson, just as Sherlock Holmes' only friend is his assistant, Dr. Watson. Each of these troubled loners turns to music. House plays the guitar, and Holmes, a violin. "House" is another word for "home," which sounds like Holmes. One TV episode showed House's address as 221B, with the street name covered. Sherlock Holmes fictional address is 221B Baker Street. For those doubters who still say all this is just coincidence, *House* creator David Shore admitted in a 2005 interview that the brilliant and complex Sherlock Holmes inspired him to create Dr. Gregory House.

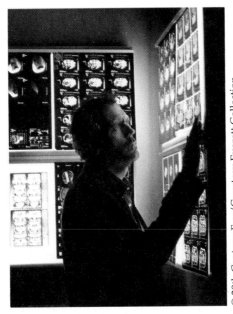

© 20th Century Fox/Courtesy Everett Collection

© The Granger Collection, New York

TV's Dr. House and Sherlock Holmes have more in common than inquiring minds.

1. What two persons or things does this writer compare and contrast? _____

_____

2. What words indicate that both contrast and comparison will follow? _____

_____

3. How are Dr. House and Sherlock Holmes different? _____

_____

4. How are Dr. House and Sherlock Holmes similar? _____

_____

5. On a sheet of paper or in your notebook, make a plan or outline for these paragraphs.

Classification

Read the following paragraph carefully and answer the questions.

In his classic discussion of friendship, the Greek philosopher Aristotle divided friends into three categories, based on the reason for the friendship. *Friendships of utility* are those in which two people are drawn together for mutual benefit. For example, two nurse's aides may develop a friendship through helping each other on the job, or two classmates may become friends because they study together. In this type of friendship, the connection frequently is broken when the situation changes, when one person takes another job or the class ends. In the second type, *friendships of pleasure*, two people find it pleasurable to spend time together. Two passionate lovers fall into this category. Other examples are young people who hang out for fun, golf buddies, or hiking pals. When the pleasure fades, these friends may part ways. Either of these two types, however, can evolve into the more lasting third type, *friendships of the good*, or true friendships. These relationships are based on mutual admiration for the other's values and overall goodness, which creates a desire to interact and offer assistance. Lifelong friendships formed in childhood and friendships that endure despite separations, hardship, or changes in personal circumstances are true friendships. Aristotle's categories might explain why some people consider themselves lucky if they count just one true friend in a lifetime.

1. How many categories are there, and what are they? _____

   _____

2. On what basis does the writer classify friendships? _____

   _____

3. Make a plan of the paragraph on a separate sheet of paper.

PRACTICE 2

Each group of things or persons on the following page has been divided according to a single basis of classification. However, one item in each group does not belong—it does not fit that single basis of classification.

Read each group of items carefully; then circle the letter of the one item that does *not* belong. Next write the single basis of classification that includes the rest of the group.

EXAMPLE   Shirts

    a. cotton

    b. suede

    (c.) short-sleeved

    d. polyester

      material they are made of

1. Shoes
   a. flat heels
   b. 2-inch heels
   c. patent leather heels
   d. 3-inch heels

   _____

2. Dates
   a. very good-looking
   b. sometimes pay
   c. always pay
   d. expect me to pay

   _____

3. Students
   a. moderately hard-working
   b. very hard-working
   c. goof-offs
   d. talkative in class

   _____

4. Contact lenses
   a. soft
   b. green
   c. brown
   d. lavender

   _____

5. Milk

   a. 2 percent fat

   b. whole

   c. chocolate

   d. 1 percent fat

   _____

6. Drivers

   a. obey the speed limit

   b. teenage drivers

   c. speeders

   d. creepers

   _____

PRACTICE 3

Any group of persons, things, or ideas can be classified in more than one way, depending on the basis of classification. For instance, students in your class can be classified on the basis of height (short, average, tall) or on the basis of class participation (often participate, sometimes participate, never participate). Both of these groupings are valid classifications of the same group of people.

Think of two ways in which each of the following groups could be classified.

Group	Basis of Classification
EXAMPLE Bosses	(A) _how demanding they are_
	(B) _how generous they are_
1. Members of my family	(A) _____
	(B) _____
2. Hurricanes	(A) _____
	(B) _____
3. Fans of a certain sport	(A) _____
	(B) _____

4. Vacations   (A) _____

                            (B) _____

5. Fitness magazines   (A) _____

                            (B) _____

PRACTICE 4

Listed below are three groups of people or things. Decide on a single basis of classification for each group and the categories that would develop from your basis of classification. Finally, write a topic sentence for each of your classifications.

	Group	**Basis of Classification**	**Categories**
EXAMPLE	Professors at Pell College	*methods of* _____ *instruction* _____	*lectures* _____ *class discussions* _____ *both* _____ _____

TOPIC SENTENCE: *Professors at Pell College can be classified according to their methods of instruction: those who lecture, those who encourage class discussions, and those who do both.*

_____

Group	**Basis of Classification**	**Categories**
1. Car owners	_____ _____	_____ _____ _____ _____

TOPIC SENTENCE: _____

_____

_____

2. Credit-card users   _____   _____

                                          _____   _____

                                                                         _____

                                                                         _____

TOPIC SENTENCE: _____

_____

_____

3. Ways of reacting   _____   _____

    to a crisis   _____   _____

                                                                         _____

                                                                         _____

TOPIC SENTENCE: _____

_____

_____

PRACTICE 5

Now choose the classification in Practice 4 that most interests you and make a plan or outline for a paragraph on a separate sheet of paper. As you work, make sure that you have listed all possible categories for your basis of classification. Remember, every car owner or credit-card user should fit into one of your categories. Finally, write your paragraph, describing each category briefly and perhaps giving an example of each.

PRACTICE 6

THINKING AND WRITING TOGETHER

Classify Students on Campus

In a group with four or five classmates, discuss some interesting ways in which you might classify the students at your college. List at least five possible ways. You might focus on students in just one place—like the computer lab, swimming pool, coffee stand, library, or an exam room during finals week.

_____

_____

_____

_____

_____

Then come up with one basis of classification, either serious or humorous. For example, you could classify swimmers according to their level of expertise or splashing, students during finals week according to their fashion statements, or students standing in line for coffee according to their degree of impatience.

_____

Now choose the most interesting basis of classification. Name three or four categories that cover the group, and write a paragraph classifying your fellow students. You might wish to enrich your categories with details and examples. Be prepared to read your paragraph to the full class.

_____

_____

_____

_____

_____

_____

CHAPTER 12

Cause and Effect

Read this paragraph and answer the questions.

Sadly, this college is part of a national trend: Date rape is on the rise. To stop date rape, college administrators and students must understand and deal with its possible causes. First, some fraternities and male peer groups on campus promote an attitude of disrespect toward women. This mentality sets the stage for date rape. Second, alcohol and drugs erode good judgment and self-control. The kegs, barrels, and bags consumed at many parties here put students at risk, including the risk of date rape. A third cause of date rape is miscommunication between men and women. Men and women often have different ideas of what date rape is or even if it exists. We need campus workshops in which we can discuss this issue openly and come to some understanding between the sexes. Date rape is a serious problem that can ruin lives. We can make a difference by addressing the causes of date rape: the male mentality of disrespect, heavy campus use of alcohol and drugs, and the differing views of men and women.

—Michael White Moon, Student

1. Underline the topic sentence. Does this paragraph discuss the causes or effects of

   date rape? _____

2. Do you agree with this student's analysis of the problem? Would you name other

   causes, and if so, which? _____

   _____

3. On a separate sheet of paper, make a plan of this paragraph.

4. Does Mr. White Moon discuss the three causes in a logical order? Why or why not?

_____

_____

PRACTICE 2

To practice separating cause from effect, write the cause and the effect contained in each item below.

EXAMPLE   Fewer people are attending concerts at the Boxcar Theater because ticket prices have nearly doubled.

Cause: _ticket prices nearly doubled_____

Effect: _fewer people attending concerts_____

1. A thunderstorm was approaching, so we moved our picnic into the van.

   Cause: _____

   Effect: _____

2. Seeing my father suffer because he could not read motivated me to excel in school.

   Cause: _____

   Effect: _____

3. One study showed that laughter extended the lives of cancer patients.

   Cause: _____

   Effect: _____

4. Americans are having fewer children and doing so later in life. Some experts believe this is why they are spending more money every year on their pets.

   Cause: _____

   Effect: _____

5. Many doctors urged that trampolines be banned because of an "epidemic" of injuries to children playing on them.

   Cause: _____

   Effect: _____

6. I bought this glow-in-the-dark fish lamp for one reason only: it was on sale.

   Cause: _____

   Effect: _____

7. As more people spend time surfing the Internet, television viewing is declining for the first time in fifty years.

   Cause: _____

   Effect: _____

8. For years, Charboro cigarettes outsold all competitors as a result of added ammonia. This ammonia gave smokers' brains an extra "kick."

   Cause: _____

   First Effect: _____

   Second Effect: _____

PRACTICE 3

List three causes *or* three effects to support each topic sentence below. First, read the topic sentence to see whether causes or effects are called for. Then think, jot, and list your three best ideas.

1. The huge success of Barbie (or some other toy, game, or product) has a number of causes.

   _____

   _____

   _____

2. There are several reasons why AIDS continues to spread among teenagers, despite widespread knowledge about the deadly nature of the disease.

_____

_____

_____

3. Reading books by authors of many nationalities, instead of just American and English authors, has many positive (or negative) effects on American students.

_____

_____

_____

PRACTICE 4

Now choose one topic from Practice 3 that interests you and write a paragraph of cause or effect on notebook paper. Before you write a draft, think and make a plan. Have you chosen the three most important causes or effects and decided on an effective order in which to present them? As you write, use transitional expressions to help the reader follow your ideas.

PRACTICE 5   **THINKING AND WRITING TOGETHER**

Analyze Possible Reasons for the "Happy Holidays Heart Attack"

In a group of four or five classmates, read this passage aloud. Then follow the directions.

For years, researchers have known that deadly heart attacks increase during the winter holiday season. Many "year-round" risk factors for heart disease are known: smoking, high blood pressure, high cholesterol, diabetes, lack of exercise, and age, but these alone do not explain what hospital workers call the "Merry Christmas coronary" and the "Happy New Year heart attack." Studies show that the number of cardiac deaths is higher on December 25 than any other day of the year, second highest on December 26, and third highest on January 1. Adding to the mystery, these numbers hold true across the country, even in places with warm climates, like Los Angeles and Miami.

—Brad Orlean, healthstyles.com, 12/20/08

What do you think are the causes or reasons why so many people suffer heart attacks on Christmas and New Year's? Choose a group member to jot your ideas; then discuss and brainstorm possible causes for this phenomenon. List your strongest three causes in the order of importance. Advise your friends and family members about one important step they should take to stay healthy during the holidays.

Ideas _____

_____

_____

_____

_____

Causes

(1) _____

_____

(2) _____

_____

(3) _____

_____

Persuasion

PRACTICE 1

Read the following persuasive paragraph carefully and answer the questions.

   American women should stop buying so-called women's magazines because these publications lower their self-esteem. First of all, publications like *Glamour* and *Cosmo* appeal to women's insecurities and make millions doing it. Topics like "Ten Days to Sexier Cleavage" and "How to Attract Mr. Right" lure women to buy 7 million copies a month, reports Claire Ito in *The Tulsa Chronicle*, May 4, 2009. The message: women need to be improved. Second, although many people—especially magazine publishers—claim these periodicals build self-esteem, they really do the opposite. One expert in readers' reactions, Deborah Then, says that almost all women, regardless of age or education, feel worse about themselves after reading one of these magazines. Alice, one of the women I spoke with, is a good example: "I flip through pictures of world-class beauties and six-foot-tall skinny women, comparing myself to them. In more ways than one, I come up short." Finally, if women spent the money and time these magazines take on more self-loving activities—studying new subjects, developing mental or physical fitness, setting goals and daring to achieve them—they would really build self-worth. Sisters, seek wisdom, create what you envision, and above all, know that you can.

—Rochelle Revard, Student

1. What is this paragraph arguing for or against? _____

   _____

2. What audience is the writer addressing? _____

3. Which reason is supported by facts? _____

What are the facts, and where did the writer get them? _____

_____

_____

4. Which reason answers the opposition? _____

5. Which reason is supported by an example? _____

What is the example? _____

_____

6. Which reason appeals to an authority? _____

Who is the authority? _____

_____

PRACTICE 2

Read the following paragraph carefully and answer the questions.

This state should offer free parenting classes, taught by experts, to anyone who wishes to become a parent. First and most important, such parenting classes could save children's lives. Every year, over 2 million American children are hurt, maimed, or killed by their own parents, according to the National Physicians Association. Some of these tragedies could be prevented by showing parents how to recognize and deal with their frustration and anger. Next, good parenting skills do not come naturally, but must be learned. Dr. Phillip Graham, chairman of England's National Children's Bureau, says that most parents have "no good role models" and simply parent the way they were parented. The courses would not only improve parenting skills but might also identify people at high risk of abusing their children. Third, critics might argue that the state has no business getting involved in parenting, which is a private responsibility. However, the state already makes decisions about who is a fit parent—in the courts, child-protection services, and adoption agencies—but often this is too late for the well-being of the child. Finally, if we do nothing, the hidden epidemic of child abuse and neglect will continue. We train our children's teachers, doctors, day-care workers, and bus drivers. We must also educate parents.

1. What is this paragraph arguing for or against? _____

   _____

   _____

2. Which reason appeals to an authority for support? _____

   Who is the authority? _____

3. Which reason answers the opposition? _____

4. Which reason includes facts? What is the source of these facts? _____

   _____

   _____

5. What consequence does the writer predict if parenting classes are not offered? _____

   _____

6. Does this writer convince you that parenting classes might make a difference? If you
   were writing a persuasion paragraph to oppose or support this writer, what would your
   topic sentence be?

   _____

   _____

   _____

PRACTICE 3

In the companion text, you learned five basic methods of persuasion: **facts, referring to
an authority, examples, predicting the consequence**, and **answering the opposition.** Ten
topic sentences for persuasive paragraphs follow. Write one reason in support of each topic
sentence, using the method of persuasion indicated.

Facts

1. A stop sign should be placed at the busy intersection of Hoover and Palm streets.

   Reason: _____

   _____

   _____

2. People should not get married until they are at least twenty-five years old.

   Reason: _____

   _____

   _____

Referring to an Authority

(If you cannot think of an authority offhand, name the kind of person who would be an authority on the subject.)

3. These new Sluggo bats will definitely raise your batting average.

   Reason: _____

   _____

   _____

4. Most people should get at least one hour of vigorous exercise three times a week.

   Reason: _____

   _____

   _____

Examples

5. Pets should be allowed in children's hospital rooms because they speed healing.

   Reason: _____

   _____

   _____

6. Mace and pepper spray should be legalized because they can prevent crime without causing permanent injury.

Reason: _____

_____

_____

_____

Predicting the Consequence

7. Companies should (should not) be allowed to conduct random drug testing on employees.

Reason: _____

_____

_____

_____

8. The federal government should (should not) prohibit the sale of handguns through the mail.

Reason: _____

_____

_____

_____

Answering the Opposition

(State the opposition's point of view and then refute it.)

9. This college should (should not) drop its required-attendance policy.

Reason: _____

_____

_____

_____

10. Teenagers should (should not) be required to get their parents' permission before being allowed to have an abortion.

Reason: _____

_____

_____

_____

PRACTICE 4

Each of the following sentences tells what you are trying to persuade someone to do. Beneath each sentence are four reasons that attempt to convince the reader that he or she should take this particular course of action. Circle the letter of the reason that *seems irrelevant, illogical,* or *untrue.*

1. If you wanted to persuade someone to do holiday shopping earlier, you might say that

   a. shopping earlier saves time.

   b. more gifts will be in stock.

   c. stores will not be overly crowded.

   d. Usher shops early.

2. If you wanted to persuade someone to buy a particular brand of cereal, you might say that it

   a. is inexpensive.

   b. contains vitamins and minerals.

   c. comes in an attractive box.

   d. makes a hearty breakfast.

3. If you wanted to persuade someone to move to your town, you might say that

   a. two new companies have made jobs available.

   b. by moving to this town, he or she will become the happiest person in the world.

   c. there is a wide selection of housing.

   d. the area is lovely and still unpolluted.

4. If you wanted to persuade someone to vote for a particular candidate, you might say that she

a. has always kept her promises to the voters.

b. has lived in the district for thirty years.

c. has substantial knowledge of the issues.

d. dresses very fashionably.

5. If you wanted to persuade someone to learn to read and speak a foreign language, you might say that

a. knowledge of a foreign language can be helpful in the business world.

b. he or she may want to travel in the country where the language is spoken.

c. Enrique Iglesias sings in two languages.

d. being able to read great literature in the original is a rewarding experience.

6. If you wanted to persuade someone to quit smoking, you might say that

a. smoking is a major cause of lung cancer.

b. smoking stains teeth and softens gums.

c. ashtrays are often hard to find.

d. this bad habit has become increasingly expensive.

PRACTICE 5

As you write persuasive paragraphs, make sure that your reasons can withstand close examination. Here are some examples of *invalid* arguments. Read them carefully. Decide which method of persuasion is being used and explain why you think the argument is invalid. Refer to the list of methods of persuasion in Chapter 13 of the companion text.

1. Men make terrible drivers. That one just cut right in front of me without looking.

Method of persuasion: _____

Invalid because _____

_____

2. Many people have become vegetarians during the past ten or fifteen years, but such people have lettuce for brains.

   Method of persuasion: _____

   Invalid because _____

   _____

3. Candy does not really harm children's teeth. Tests made by scientists at the Gooey Candy Company have proved that candy does not cause tooth decay.

   Method of persuasion: _____

   Invalid because _____

   _____

4. Stealing pens and pads from the office is perfectly all right. Everyone does it.

   Method of persuasion: _____

   Invalid because _____

   _____

5. We don't want _____ in our neighborhood. We had a

   _____ family once, and they made a lot of noise.

   Method of persuasion: _____

   Invalid because _____

   _____

6. If our city doesn't build more playgrounds, a crime wave will destroy our homes and businesses.

   Method of persuasion: _____

   Invalid because _____

   _____

CHAPTER 13 Persuasion **101**

7. Studying has nothing to do with grades. My brother never studies and still gets As all the time.

   Method of persuasion: _____

   Invalid because _____

   _____

8. Women bosses work their employees too hard. I had one once, and she never let me rest for a moment.

   Method of persuasion: _____

   Invalid because _____

   _____

9. The Big Deal Supermarket has the lowest prices in town. This must be true because the manager said on the radio last week, "We have the lowest prices in town."

   Method of persuasion: _____

   Invalid because _____

   _____

10. If little girls are allowed to play with cars and trucks, they will grow up wanting to be men.

    Method of persuasion: _____

    Invalid because _____

    _____

PRACTICE 6 **THINKING AND WRITING TOGETHER**

Persuade Through Humor

Advertisements bombard us every day—through TV, newspapers, magazines, billboards, store windows, and the labels on people's clothing and possessions. The billions of dollars that Americans spend on brand-name products tell us that ads are very persuasive, usually making their argument with a strong visual image and a few catchy words. To expose the great power of advertising, a group called Adbusters creates stylish spoof ads for real

Copyright © Cengage Learning. All rights reserved.

products. The goal is to expose the truth that real-life ads often hide. In a group of four or five classmates, study the ad below and then answer the questions.

What hugely popular product is being "busted" by the Adbusters spoof below? What is the persuasive message of this ad? Working together, write down the ad's "topic sentence" and argument. How effective is Adbuster's ad? Does it successfully answer the "opposition"—that is, McDonald's worldwide campaign to convince us to buy more Big Macs?

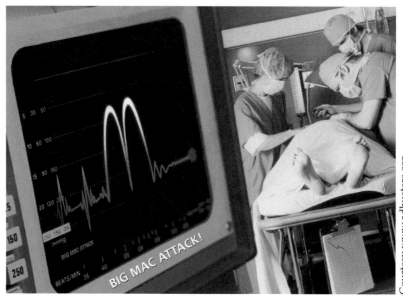

Courtesy www.adbusters.org

_____

_____

_____

_____

_____

_____

_____

_____

_____

_____

_____

_____

_____

_____

EXPLORING ONLINE

http://www.adbusters.org/spoofads

Study other Adbuster spoof ads, especially those for fashion, alcohol, and tobacco. Pick the funniest and write about its persuasive message. For help creating your own print ad, go to **https://www.adbusters.org/spoofads/printad.** In your group, create a persuasive ad, perhaps using the slogan, "Got _____?"

Unit 4 Writing the Essay

CHAPTER 14

The Process of Writing an Essay

A. Looking at the Essay

PRACTICE 1

Read this student essay carefully and then answer the questions.

BOTTLE WATCHING

(1) Every time I see a beer bottle, I feel grateful. This reaction has nothing to do with beer. The sight reminds me of the year I spent inspecting bottles at a brewery. That was the most boring and painful job I've ever had, but it motivated me to change my life.

(2) My job consisted of sitting on a stool and watching empty bottles pass by. A glaring light behind the conveyor belt helped me to spot cracked bottles or bottles with something extra—a dead grasshopper, for example, or a mouse foot. I was supposed to grab such bottles with my hooked cane and break them before they went into the washer. For eight or nine hours a day that was all I did. I got dizzy and sore in the eyes. I longed to fall asleep. I prayed that the conveyor would break down so the bottles would stop.

(3) After a while, to put some excitement into the job, I began inventing little games. I would count the number of minutes that passed before a broken bottle would come by, and I would compete against my own past record. Or I would see how many broken bottles I could spot in one minute. Once, I organized a contest for all the bottle watchers with a prize for the best dead insect or animal found in a bottle—anything to break the monotony of the job.

(4) After six months at the brewery, I began to think hard about my goals for the future. Did I want to spend the rest of my life looking in beer bottles? I realized that I wanted a job I could believe in. I wanted to use my mind for better things than planning contests for bleary-eyed bottle watchers. I knew I had to hand in my hook and go back to school.

(5) Today I feel grateful to that terrible job because it motivated me to attend college.

—Pat Barnum, Student

1. Which sentence in the introductory paragraph is the thesis statement? _____

   _____

2. Did Mr. Barnum's introduction catch and hold your interest? Why or why not? _____

   _____

3. Underline the topic sentences in paragraphs 2, 3, and 4.

4. What is the controlling idea of paragraph 2? _____

5. What is the controlling idea of paragraph 3? What examples support this idea? _____

   _____

   _____

6. What do you like best about this essay? What, if anything, would you change?

   _____

   _____

   _____

B. Writing the Thesis Statement

Revise each vague thesis statement, making it more specific. Remember, a good thesis statement should have a clear controlling idea and indicate what the rest of the essay will be about.

EXAMPLE   Watching TV news programs has its good points.

Watching news programs on TV can make one a more

informed and responsible citizen.

1. A visit to the emergency room can be interesting.

    _____

2. I will write about my job, which is very cool.

    _____

    _____

3. Professors should teach better.

    _____

    _____

4. There are many unusual people in my family.

    _____

    _____

5. School uniforms are a good idea.

    _____

    _____

PRACTICE 3

Eight possible essay topics follow. Pick three that interest you. For each one, **narrow** the topic, choose your **controlling idea**, and then compose a specific **thesis statement**.

a volunteer experience   handling anger (or other emotion)

when parents work   a story or issue in the news now

an addictive habit   a problem on campus or at work

the value of pets   advantages or disadvantages of Internet research

EXAMPLE   Subject: *handling anger*

Narrowed subject: *my angry adolescence*

Controlling idea: *channeling adolescent anger into art*

Thesis statement: *In a photography workshop for "at-risk" teenagers, I learned that anger can be channeled positively into art.*

1. Subject:_____

    Narrowed subject: _____

    Controlling idea: _____

    Thesis statement : _____

2. Subject: _____

    Narrowed subject: _____

    Controlling idea: _____

    Thesis statement: _____

3. Subject: _____

    Narrowed subject: _____

    Controlling idea: _____

    Thesis statement: _____

C. Generating Ideas for the Body

PRACTICE 4

Choose one of the thesis statements you wrote in Practice 3 and generate ideas to develop an essay. Using your favorite prewriting method, try to fill at least a page. If you get stuck, reread the thesis statement to focus your thoughts or switch to another prewriting method.

D. Organizing Ideas into an Outline

PRACTICE 5

Complete this outline as if you were planning the essay. First, state in sentence form each problem that will develop the topic sentence: unappetizing food, slow service, and high prices. Then develop each with details and examples.

1. **INTRODUCTION and thesis statement:**	Because the student cafeteria has many problems, the college should hire a new administrator to see that it is properly managed in the future.
2. **Topic sentence:**	Foremost among the cafeteria's problems are unappetizing food, slow service, and high prices.

Problem 1: _____

_____

_____

_____

Problem 2: _____

_____

_____

_____

Problem 3: _____

_____

_____

_____

3. Topic sentence:

A new administrator could do much to improve these terrible conditions.

Step 1. Set minimum quality standards

—personally oversee purchase of healthful food

—set and enforce rules about how long food can be left out

—set cooking times for hot meals

Step 2. Reorganize service lines

—study which lines are busiest at different times of the day

—shift cooks and cashiers to those lines

—create a separate beverage line

Step 3. Lower prices

—better food and faster service would attract more student customers

—cafeteria could then lower prices

4. CONCLUSION

PRACTICE 6

Write from two to four topic sentences to support each of the thesis statements that follow. (First you may wish to brainstorm or freewrite on paper or on the computer screen.) Make sure that every topic sentence really supports the thesis statement and that every one could be developed into a good paragraph. Then arrange your topic sentences in a rough outline in the space provided.

EXAMPLE Before you buy a computer, do these three things.

Topic sentence: *Decide how much you can spend, and determine*

your price range.

Topic sentence: *Examine the models that are within your price*

range.

Topic sentence: *Shop around; all computer dealers are not*

created equal.

1. I vividly recall the sights, smells, and tastes of _____

_____

Topic sentence: _____

_____

Topic sentence: _____

_____

Topic sentence: _____

_____

Topic sentence: _____

_____

2. Living alone has both advantages and disadvantages.

Topic sentence: _____

_____

Topic sentence: _____

_____

Topic sentence: _____

_____

Topic sentence: _____

_____

3. Doing well at a job interview requires careful planning.

Topic sentence: _____

_____

Topic sentence: _____

_____

Topic sentence: _____

_____

Topic sentence: _____

_____

PRACTICE 7

Now choose *one* thesis statement you have written, or write one now. Generate ideas for the body and organize them in an outline for an essay of your own. (For ideas, reread the thesis statements you wrote for Practice 3, page 108.) Your outline should include your thesis statement; two to three topic sentences; and supporting details, facts, and examples. Prewrite every time you need ideas; revise the thesis statement and the topic sentences until they are sharp and clear.

E. Ordering and Linking Paragraphs in the Essay

PRACTICE 8

Plans for three essays follow, each containing a thesis statement and several topic sentences in scrambled order. Number the topic sentences in each group according to *an order that makes sense*. Be prepared to explain your choices.

1. **Thesis statement**: An immigrant who wishes to become a U.S. citizen must complete a three-stage naturalization process.

   Topic sentences:

   _____ After submitting an application, the would-be citizen interviews with an immigration officer and takes tests on the English language and American civics.

   _____ An immigrant who meets general requirements for minimum length of residency and good moral character begins by filling out Form N-400, the Application for Naturalization.

   _____ Applicants who perform well in the interview and on the tests take the Oath of Allegiance to the United States in a moving group ceremony, thus becoming American citizens.

2. **Thesis statement:** To meet the demands of a growing computer industry and aging population, the fastest growing job markets through 2016 will be in the computer and medical fields.

   Topic sentences:

   _____ A second group of medical jobs will exist in private homes, where health-care aides will be needed to tend the elderly.

   _____ Skilled computer software engineers, systems designers, and database administrators will find many job opportunities from which to choose.

   _____ In hospitals and doctors' offices, the need for medical assistants, pharmacy technicians, and dental hygienists will grow rapidly.

3. Thesis statement: The practice of tai chi can improve one's concentration, health, and peace of mind.

Topic sentences: _____ In several ways, tai chi boosts physical health.

_____ Peace of mind increases gradually as one becomes less reactive.

_____ Concentrating on the movements of tai chi in practice promotes better concentration in other areas of life.

PRACTICE 9

Now, go over the essay outline that you developed in Practice 7 and reconsider which paragraphs should come first, which second, and so forth. Does time order, space order, or order of importance seem appropriate to your subject? Number your paragraphs accordingly.

PRACTICE 10

Read the essay that follows, noting the paragraph-to-paragraph *links*. Then answer the questions.

SKIN DEEP

(1) What do Johnny Depp, Lady Randolph Churchill, Whoopi Goldberg, and Charles Manson all have in common? Perhaps you guessed tattoos: body decorations made by piercing the skin and inserting colored pigments. In fact, tattoos have a long and nearly worldwide history, ranging from full-body art to a single heart, from tribal custom to pop-culture fad.

(2) The earliest known tattoo was found on the mummy of an Egyptian priestess dating back to 2200 B.C. Tattoos were also used in the ancient world to decorate Japanese noblemen, mark Greek spies, and hide expressions of fear on Maori tribesmen in New Zealand. Full-body tattooing was practiced for centuries in the South Seas; in fact, the word *tattoo* comes from the Tahitian word *tattaw*. In medieval times, small tattoos were common in Europe. For instance, in 1066, after the famous Battle of Hastings, the only way that the body of the Anglo Saxon King Harold could be identified was by the word *Edith* tattooed over his heart.

(3) For the next 600 years, however, Europeans lost interest in tattoos. Then, in the 1700s, explorers and sailors rekindled public excitement. Captain Cook, returning from a trip to Tahiti in 1761, described the wonders of tattoos. Cook enthusiastically paraded

a heavily tattooed Tahitian prince named Omai through England's finest drawing rooms. People were intrigued by the colorful flowers, snakes, and geographical maps covering Omai's body. Although large tattoos were too much for the British, the idea of a pretty little bee or royal crest on the shoulder was very appealing. Tattooing remained popular with Europe's royalty and upper classes through the nineteenth century. The Prince of Wales, the Duke of York, Tsar Nicholas of Russia, and Winston Churchill's mother all had tattoos.

(4) When tattooing first reached America, on the other hand, its image was definitely not refined. American soldiers and sailors, feeling lonely and patriotic during World War II, visited tattoo parlors in South Pacific ports and came home with *Mother* or *Death Before Dishonor* inked into their arms. Soon motorcyclists started getting tattoos as part of their rebellious, macho image. The process was painful, with a high risk of infection, so the more elaborate a cyclist's bloody dagger or skull and crossbones, the better.

(5) Tattooing did not remain an outlaw rite of passage for long. Safer and less painful methods developed in the 1970s and 1980s brought tattooing into the American mainstream, especially among the young. Designs ranged from one butterfly to black-and-white patterns like Native American textiles to flowing, multicolored, stained-glass designs. With the media documenting the tattoos of the rich and famous, tattooing became a full-blown fad by the 1990s. Now the one-time symbols of daring have become so common that many rebels are having their tattoos removed. About one-third of all the work performed by tattoo artists in the United States is "erasing" unwanted tattoos.

Tattoo artist at work

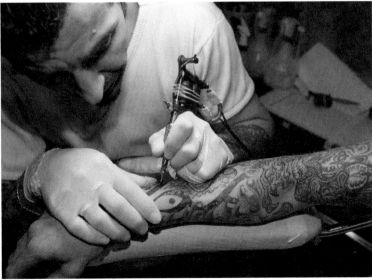

© Atlantide Phototravel/Corbis

1. What transitional expressions does this writer use to link paragraphs? (Find at least two.)

   _____

   _____

2. How does the writer link paragraphs 1 and 2? _____

   _____

3. How does the writer link paragraphs 4 and 5? _____

   _____

F. Writing and Revising Essays

PRACTICE 11

On notebook paper, write a first draft of the essay you have been working on in Practices 7 and 9.

PRACTICE 12

Now, carefully read over the first draft of your essay from Practice 11 and **revise** it, referring to the checklist of questions in Chapter 14, Part F, of the companion text. You might wish to ask a peer reviewer for feedback before you revise. Ask specific questions or use the Peer Feedback Sheet in Chapter 3 of the companion text. Take your time and write the best essay you can. Once you are satisfied, **proofread** your essay for grammar and spelling errors. Neatly write the final draft or print a final copy.

CHAPTER 15

The Introduction, the Conclusion, and the Title

A: The Introduction

B: The Conclusion

C: The Title

A. The Introduction

Read each of the following essay introductions. Then circle the letter of the method the writer used to begin the essay.

1.   "I was up at bat, and I struck out. Right away, I got so angry that I wanted to throw my bat, but then I remembered mindfulness, and I didn't do it." With these words, ten-year-old Ricky Toledo told his classmates how he had refrained from one of the furious outbursts that had repeatedly gotten him in trouble at school. In a five-week program at their school in New Mexico, Ricky and his classmates had been receiving mindfulness training, learning such stress-reduction techniques as sitting quietly and practicing gentle breathing.

This essay begins with a

    a. direct quotation.

    b. single-sentence thesis statement.

    c. general idea that is narrowed to a specific thesis statement.

2.   According to the American Diabetes Association, 26 million Americans now have diabetes, and that total is expected to double or even triple by 2050. These shocking numbers mirror the rise in obesity. Type 2 diabetes, by far the most common type, results directly from poor eating and lifestyle habits even though certain groups are genetically at more risk. Learning the facts about diabetes and making necessary changes can save millions of lives.

This essay begins with a(n)

    a. illustration or anecdote (a brief narrative).

    b. surprising fact or idea.

    c. contradiction.

B. The Conclusion

PRACTICE 2

Read each of the following essay conclusions. Circle the letter of the method the writer used to conclude the essay.

1.   The facts are beyond question. Texting while driving kills, just as do other forms of distracted driving, like chatting on a cell phone or driving drunk. Human lives are at stake. Florida legislators must pass this law that makes texting while driving illegal.

This essay concludes with a

    a. call to action.

    b. final point.

    c. question.

2.   Nearly all the students who agreed to give up their Blackberries and smartphones for five days thought the experiment was worthwhile although they had felt lost without their phones. Some experienced near-panic during the first day or two. A number

admitted that, by day five, they felt liberated and began to notice things on campus that they had not seen before: trees, signs, architectural details, and the huge number of other students talking on phones or texting even when they were with other friends at the time. Asked whether they would use their phones less in the future, however, students in the experiment all said no way, absolutely not.

This essay concludes with a

    a. call to action.

    b. question.

    c. final point.

C. The Title

PRACTICE 3

Read these titles carefully. Then write a sentence or two describing what you expect each essay to be about, based only on its title.

1. What is ADD (Attention Deficit Disorder)? A Personal Story

    _____

    _____

2. Serious Gamer: Video Games in the Medical Sciences

    _____

    _____

3. Three Reasons to Become a Vegetarian

    _____

    _____

CHAPTER 16

Types of Essays, Part 1

A: The Illustration Essay

B: The Narrative Essay

C: The Descriptive Essay

D: The Process Essay

E: The Definition Essay

A. The Illustration Essay

Read this student's illustration essay and answer the questions.

OTC: ONLY TAKE CARE!

(1) Many people take over-the-counter (OTC) medications for headaches, colds, and such. Over 100,000 OTC medications are for sale in stores, a number that surprised me even though I am pursuing my Pharmacy Technician certification. Most consumers think that OTC drugs are harmless because no prescription is needed, but, in fact, they can be hazardous to your health.

(2) Aspirin, for instance, is so common that people think it cannot hurt them. Every day, 43 million people take aspirin for pain, swelling or fever; some take it on their doctors' orders to prevent a heart attack or stroke. An excellent drug if used correctly, aspirin can cause bleeding in the organs or even a brain bleed. Coated aspirin helps protect from stomach bleeding, but only your doctor can say whether the dangers are worth the risks. Many people don't know that those on blood thinners like warfarin

should never take aspirin or that aspirin can cause serious brain, liver, and other damage in children and teens who have fevers; this condition is called Reyes Syndrome. A widespread myth among teenagers that mixing Coca Cola with aspirin "gets you high" is not true; however, it can cause bleeding.

(3) A second illustration is cold medications. The decongestants in many of these can dangerously raise blood pressure in people who take blood pressure medications and in those on certain antidepressants. People with irregular heartbeats can be "set off" by the stimulants in these drugs. A serious new problem with cold medications is addiction to a chemical found in over 100 of them, called Dextromethorphan (DXM). More and more young people are abusing cold medications for the DXM high. Overdoses and deaths have been reported.

(4) Sleep aids are yet another example of problematic OTCs. Not being able to fall or stay asleep is a nerve-wracking problem for many people, but instead of studying their own habits to try and solve the problem naturally, often they just pop a pill. Most sleep aids contain antihistamines, which can cause not only drowsiness but also side effects during the day like sleepiness or headaches. Sleeping pills can become addictive, and people who use them should never drink alcohol. Studies differ as to whether these medications even work.

(5) These are just three examples of OTC medications and their possible side effects. Easy access to these drugs means that mistakes and abuse are common. As a consumer, it's up to you to protect your body and your health. Always read the Drug Facts label on everything you take. Ask your doctor or pharmacist about both your OTC and prescription medications to make sure there are no interactions among them.

—Bradley K. Knight, Student

1. Underline or highlight the **thesis statement**. What main examples does this student use to support the thesis and develop the essay?

   _____

2. Now, underline or highlight the **topic sentences**. Label the parts of this essay by writing these labels in the left margin opposite the correct part:

   IN Introduction   E1 Example 1 and details
   C   Conclusion   E2 Example 2 and details
                             E3 Example 3 and details

3. What transitional expressions of illustration help introduce each example?

   _____

4. The writer mentions in the introduction that he is pursuing a certain certification. Is this sentence relevant to the paper, or should it be dropped?

   _____

5. Mr. Knight drew on his curriculum to find a topic for his illustration essay. Have you learned material in your own courses that might interest your classmates? Can this material be presented through examples?

_____

PRACTICE 2

Often a writer will notice specific examples first, see a pattern, and then come up with a generalization—a thesis statement or topic sentence. In a group with four or five classmates, examine the photographs below of houses designed by the great American architect, Frank Lloyd Wright (1867–1959). Can your group make any *general statements* about Wright's houses, based just on these *examples*? Write down your generalizations.

Frank Lloyd Wright's Fallingwater, Mill Run, PA

Art Resource, NY. © Frank Lloyd Wright Foundation, Scottsdale, AZ/Artists Right Society (ARS), NY

The Robie House, Chicago, IL
© Rick Geharter/Lonely Planet Images

The Massaro House, Mahopac, NY
© David Allee

PRACTICE 3

1. Choose a topic from the list below or one your instructor has assigned. Make sure you can develop it well with examples. Then brainstorm, cluster, or freewrite to get as many examples as possible. Choose the best ones. You're on your way.

   1. Role models (positive or negative)
   2. Failure as an effective teacher
   3. Qualities (or skills) that many employers look for
   4. TV shows that send a violent (hopeful, or other) message

5. Everyday action steps to protect the environment

6. Three people in the news who exemplify honesty or commitment to principles

7. The skills, values, or traits that would make your friend a good store manager (police officer, cartoonist, and so forth)

8. Musicians or artists of a particular type (R&B, tropical Latin, surrealist, French impressionist, and so on) or three works by the same artist

9. Experiences that shaped your attitudes toward education (or family or work)

10. Unusual places to go on dates (or to study, de-stress, get married, and so on)

11. Writer's choice: _____

2. Many students find using a graphic organizer helpful as they plan an essay. In your notebook, draw a blank 8 by 11-inch organizer like the one on pages 167–168 of the companion text or use the illustration essay organizer on the CourseMate for *Evergreen Compact*. In it, create an outline for your essay. The information you write in each box will become a paragraph.

PRACTICE 4

Now, referring to your plan, write the best first draft you can. Aim for clarity as you help the reader develop an understanding of each category in your illustration. Check your paragraphing, and use *transitional expressions** to guide the reader from example to example.

Let your draft cool for an hour or a day; then reread it as if you were a helpful, eagle-eyed stranger. Now revise and rewrite, emphasizing clarity, completeness, and keeping your reader in mind. Is each paragraph developed fully? Do transitions make the flow of ideas clear? Proofread for spelling, grammar, and sentence errors.

B. The Narrative Essay

PRACTICE 5

In a group with four or five classmates, discuss the picture of the Vietnam Memorial on the next page. Why do you think this man is here? What is he holding? What do you guess is the expression on his face? What *story* does this picture tell?

---

* For a list of transitional expressions of illustration, see Chapter 5 in the companion text.

A visitor at the Vietnam Memorial

PRACTICE 6

Read this student's narrative essay and answer the questions.

MY BLACK DOG

(1) I arrived at this college excited about changing my life. I was no longer the immature young man who thought education was boring. Through a neighbor in the field, I had become interested in studying to be a nuclear medicine technologist. My neighbor works in a cardiologist's office, interacts with patients, and does all the stress testing. He helped me pick a program, and I enrolled. But soon after starting school, I began to feel overwhelmed, upset, and irritated much of the time; I had no idea that this was the Black Dog.

(2) The fact is I could barely keep up with all the assignments, tests, and papers in five challenging classes. Further, this was an unfamiliar environment where math skills and brains ruled, not smart (make that stupid) remarks. I worried about failing but was embarrassed to talk to anyone—not my neighbor, not even my wife. One day she told me I was turning into a mean guy.

(3) In the student lounge, I happened to see a pamphlet published by the health service. It was mostly a list of questions, such as "Are you irritable, anxious, withdrawn?" "Do you often feel fatigued or low in energy?" "Do you experience extreme sadness or

angry outbursts?" I was surprised to find myself answering "yes" to most of the questions. The pamphlet was on male depression. Like many guys, the last thing I wanted to do was face this and talk about it. In my mind, depression was not manly. Reading that 10 percent of college students are depressed and a third of freshman feel overwhelmed helped a little.

(4) That night, I told my wife what was going on and decided to see a counselor. Amazingly, counseling at the college is free to students. I never loved talking about my insecurities, but it did help, especially problem solving with someone impartial. The counselor, Ron, encouraged me to use other campus resources, get a tutor, and improve the way I manage time. Ron, who knew that I like history, told me that the great leader Winston Churchill fought depression, which he called "the Black Dog". Before long, I felt more like the master of my Black Dog instead of the victim. I am still always rushing, but I don't feel so overwhelmed. My anger is gone, and my grades have climbed from Cs and Ds to As and Bs.

(5) It's impressive that the college has these programs, and I urge anyone who's feeling depressed to reach out, discuss it, and get help. No one should suffer alone because depression grows more vicious in isolation.

—Paul Frey, Student

1. Instead of a thesis statement that tells the point of the story, Mr. Frey writes, "But soon after starting school, I began to feel overwhelmed, upset, and irritated much of the time; I had no idea that this was the Black Dog." Why do you think he does not define "Black Dog" in the first paragraph?

   _____

   _____

2. Underline the topic sentences of paragraphs 2, 3, and 4. What main incidents make up the story?

   _____

   _____

3. What is the point of this narrative? Is it effective that the writer does not reveal the point until paragraphs 3 and 4?

   _____

   _____

4. The introduction, the incidents of the story, and the conclusion together form an outline for the narrative essay. Before sitting down to write, this student made such an outline to guide him as he wrote.

PRACTICE 7

1. Choose a topic from the list below or one your instructor has assigned. Take your time deciding. Think of a story you want to tell—one with a point.

   1. A favorite family story or a story from your ethnic tradition
   2. An immigrant's journey
   3. The story behind a key scientific discovery or invention
   4. How you chose your major or career path
   5. Someone's battle with a serious illness
   6. An important historical event
   7. The plot line of a movie or TV show you would like to produce
   8. The story of someone who inspires you (based on an interview you conduct)
   9. Learning a new language (or other subject or skill)
   10. An unforgettable incident you witnessed
   11. Writer's choice:_____

2. Many students find using a graphic organizer helpful as they plan an essay. In your notebook, draw a blank 8 by 11-inch organizer like the one on pages 171–172 of the companion text or use the illustration essay organizer on the CourseMate for *Evergreen Compact*. In it, create an outline for your essay. The information you write in each box will become a paragraph.

PRACTICE 8

Follow your plan and write the best first draft you can. Make sure to include all the key events, and aim for a smooth flow that will keep the reader interested. Conveying the meaning or point of the story and keeping it moving are the keys to good narration. As you write, inspire yourself by thinking of great storytellers you know or have heard. Use transitional expressions of time to help the reader follow.* Conclude with a final point

_____

* For a list of transitional expressions of time, see Chapter 6 in the companion text.

or idea that follows from the story you have just narrated. Does your title capture the essence of the tale and make people want to read on?

Let your draft cool for an hour or a day; then reread it as if you were a helpful stranger. Now revise and rewrite, avoiding wordiness and keeping your reader in mind. Proofread for spelling, grammar, and sentence errors.

C. The Descriptive Essay

PRACTICE 9

Read this student's descriptive essay and answer the questions.

TORNADO

(1) Tornados are one of the most terrifying natural events that occur, destroying homes and ending lives every year. On April 29th, 1995, a calm, muggy night, I learned this firsthand. Joey, a buddy I grew up with, agreed to travel across state with me so we could visit a friend in Lubbock, Texas. Joey and I were admiring the blue bonnets, which went on for miles like little blue birds flying close to the ground. The warm breeze brushed the tips of the blue bonnets and allowed them to dance under the clear blue sky. In the distance, however, we could see darkness.

(2) As we drove, thunderclouds continued to rumble in, like an ocean tide rolling closer and closer to the beach front, and within minutes the entire landscape was calm and dark. It looked like a total eclipse of the sun, and the blue bonnets were now completely still and somber. The rain began to trickle down out of the sky. The sound of the rain as it hit our car was like that of pins dropping on a metal surface. The intensity of the rain increased as we ventured further into the eye of the storm.

(3) As we approached an overpass, we noticed a parking lot of cars underneath. By now, the rain had created a wall of water, which surrounded our car. We decided to pull over and sprint to the underpass to join the other frightened observers. What Joey and I were unaware of was that a tornado was already on the ground frantically spinning towards our position. The whirling "finger of God" was approaching us.

(4) The sound surrounding us was outrageous, like a steam locomotive roaring, whining, and whistling with an awful high-pitched roar. The rain had almost stopped, but the wind was nearly blowing us off the ground as we huddled together under the overpass. We could hear the screeching of car tires as they started sliding across the rain-soaked pavement. Electrical explosions lit up the darkened sky as the tornado ripped over power lines, snapping them as if they were toothpicks. Screams erupted from the crowd as the tornado crossed directly over us, smashing large objects into the overpass pavement but leaving us untouched.

(5) Shortly thereafter the sky was bright again, revealing only shattered pieces of fence posts and telephone poles. Everyone unraveled from the huddle that had protected them moments earlier. The sun started poking holes in the dark rumbling sky; the wind and rain had ceased, leaving it morbidly calm. The sun burned away every trace of darkness. It was amazing to look back and see a mile long trail of destruction surrounded by homes and fences that were totally untouched. I remember thinking how amazing this moment was, and how grateful I was to be alive.

—Wesley Duke, Student

1. This writer's thesis statement is actually two sentences. Underline or highlight them.

2. Every paragraph in this essay describes one scene or aspect of the topic. How many scenes or aspects are described, and what are they?

   _____

   _____

3. This essay combines excellent, specific description with narration. What order does the writer use?

   _____

4. Which of the five senses does Mr. Duke emphasize in paragraph 4? Give some examples.

   _____

   _____

5. The thesis statement, the scenes or phases in the description, and the conclusion together form an **outline** for the descriptive essay. Before sitting down to write, Mr. Duke made a detailed outline to guide his writing process.

PRACTICE 10

In a group with four or five classmates, study the diagram on the next page showing the body position recommended for desk workers and students. This position avoids eyestrain, back and neck injury, and hand or wrist injury. In your group, convert the information shown here into the outline for a memo or short essay. Your audience is office workers and students; your purpose is to *describe* healthy workstation posture.

First, jot details that describe each important part of the diagram. Select the most important points to include and arrange them according to space order in an outline. If you have time, draft a clear essay or memo. Be prepared to share your work with the class.

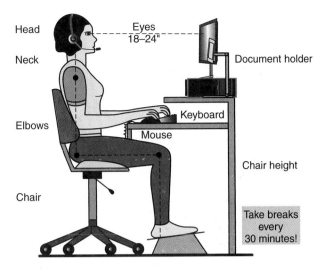

Head

Eyes
18–24"

Neck

Document holder

Elbows

Keyboard

Mouse

Chair height

Chair

Take breaks
every
30 minutes!

PRACTICE 11

1. Choose a topic from the list below or one your instructor has assigned. Take your time deciding. Think of a subject that will make a good description, perhaps an important scene or experience that you can still see in your mind's eye.

    1. The rituals and decorations of a holiday you know well
    2. A place that people don't want to see, such as a public dump, a prison, or a very poor neighborhood
    3. The scene of a historic event or battle as you imagine it
    4. A lively public place, such as a campus hang-out, a fitness center, or a dance club
    5. A tourist attraction or a place of natural beauty
    6. Your present or future workplace, including setting, people, and action
    7. A computer, vehicle, or piece of equipment from your job
    8. Your family portrait
    9. The settings and costumes of a movie you admire
    10. A scene you will never forget
    11. Writer's choice: _____

2. Many students find using a graphic organizer helpful as they plan an essay. In your notebook, draw a blank 8 by 11-inch organizer like the one on pages 175–176 of the companion text or use the illustration essay organizer on the CourseMate for

Evergreen Compact. In it, create an outline for your essay. The information you write in each box will become a paragraph.

PRACTICE 12

Now referring to your plan, write the best first draft you can. Mentally see, hear, and smell the subject. Your *words* are your camera, paints, or graphic design program, so don't settle for the first words that occur to you. Follow the order of space or time, whichever you have selected, and be sure to use transitional expressions of space* or time[†] to guide the reader along. For inspiration, you might reread the conclusion of "Day of the Dead" before you conclude your paper.

Let your draft cool for an hour or a day; then reread it as if you were a helpful stranger. Now revise and rewrite, emphasizing exact language, avoiding wordiness, and keeping your reader in mind. Is each paragraph developed fully? Do transitions make the flow of ideas clear? Proofread for spelling, grammar, and sentence errors.

D. The Process Essay

PRACTICE 13

Read this student's process essay and answer the questions.

THE MIRACLE OF BIRTH

(1) A woman is pregnant for approximately nine months. Within that time are three stages or trimesters, "tri" meaning three. Many women have said they loved being pregnant, but I like to refer to the trimesters as the puking stage, the fat stage, and the always-have-to-pee stage.

(2) In the first trimester, the baby is developing its nervous system and other important little body parts; while all of this is happening inside, the mom-to-be is usually puking her guts up. The fun doesn't stop there, however. Hormone levels skyrocket, and all of a sudden, mom-to-be is crying over the slightest thing, such as a McDonald's commercial that she finds unbearably sweet.

(3) The second trimester is often slightly gentler on one's stomach, perhaps because that stomach has doubled in size, along with mom's butt and thighs. The baby is growing

---

* For a list of transitional expressions of space order, see Chapter 7 of the companion text.

† For a list of transitional expressions of time, see Chapter 6 of the companion text.

fast now, and the vital organs are developing. The baby is beginning to do somersaults, and suddenly there is a new stabbing sensation, almost as if baby is using mom's ribs for gymnastic rings. Comfort is now a thing of the past.

(4) In the third trimester, baby is happily gaining about a pound a week, but for the mother, the last stage of pregnancy never goes by fast enough. As all the intricate fine-tunings of development are happening on baby's major organs, hair, and skin, for some odd reason, sleep for mom is completely out of the question. Perhaps the lack of sleep is due to the up-and-coming gymnast in her stomach or the five hundred trips to the bathroom that mom must make in one night. The many sleepless nights may also be attributed to her anticipation of bladder control or actually having a waist again.

(5) Pregnancy is a wonderful experience as long as puking, gaining forty to sixty pounds, and stumbling in and out of bed do not bother the mom-to-be. To me, pregnancy was a bummer, but like the old saying goes, "no pain, no gain." The end definitely justifies the means, and now that I am almost back to normal functioning with a beautiful, crying baby, the fun really starts.

—Heather Artley, Student

1. Underline or highlight this writer's thesis statement. What process does her essay

   discuss? _____

2. How many stages or steps make up this process? What are they?

   _____

3. Underline or highlight the topic sentences in paragraphs 2, 3, and 4. What order does

   the writer employ? _____

4. Is her tone serious or light? What words or phrases tell you this?

   _____

   _____

PRACTICE 14

In a group with four or five classmates, study the diagram on the next page showing that heart disease is actually a *process*. Read about the four stages.

Do you know anyone who is likely in the process of developing heart disease? How would you go about learning more about this process and how to stop or reverse it? Come up with least two trustworthy sources of information on heart disease. Be prepared to share your thoughts.

Heart disease is a process affecting 16,800,000 Americans.

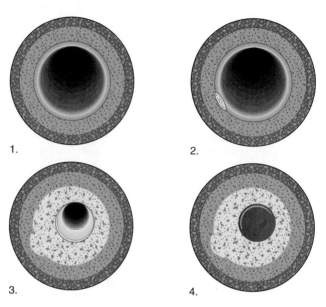

1.

2.

3.

4.

Stage 1. Normal arteries are healthy and open. Stage 2. Cholesterol begins to be deposited in a damaged or inflamed artery wall. Stage 3. Cholesterol continues to build up, narrowing the artery. Stage 4. The artery becomes so clogged that a blood clot can block it, causing heart attack or stroke.

PRACTICE 15

1. Choose a topic from the list below or one your instructor has assigned. Take your time as you pick a process to describe that interests *you*.

   1. A process that will help new students at your college learn how to register (how to drop or add courses, how to meet people on campus, how to apply for financial aid, and so on)

   2. How to get action on a community problem

   3. How to begin tracing your family's genealogy

   4. How to teach a child a skill or value

   5. How to perform a procedure at your workplace (help an elderly person dress, make Hollandaise sauce, handle a crime scene, and so on)

   6. How to set up a program or piece of technology (such as a cell phone, e-mail, a website, or a blog)

   7. The yearly cycle of a crop (corn, wheat, oranges, cocoa, and so on)

8. How to impress the boss (in-laws, professor, person you are dating)

9. An important process you learned in another course (stages of human moral development, how a lake becomes a meadow, and so on)

10. How to get an A in _____

11. Writer's choice: _____

2. Many students find using a graphic organizer helpful as they plan an essay. In your notebook, draw a blank 8 by 11-inch organizer like the one on pages 178–179 of the companion text or use the illustration essay organizer on the CourseMate for *Evergreen Compact*. In it, create an outline for your essay. The information you write in each box will become a paragraph.

PRACTICE 16

Now referring to your plan, write the best first draft you can. Clear language and logical organization are keys to good process writing. Pay special attention to paragraphing; if the process is 3–6 steps, make each step a paragraph; if more, combine several steps per paragraph. Remember to use transitional expressions of time to help the reader follow.*

Let your draft cool for an hour or a day; then reread it as if you were a helpful, eagle-eyed stranger. Now revise and rewrite, avoiding wordiness and keeping your reader in mind. Proofread for spelling, grammar, and sentence errors.

E. The Definition Essay

PRACTICE 17

Read this student's definition essay and answer the questions.

MORE THAN JUST GOOD

(1) I lean against our mango tree, waiting. The taxi is twenty minutes late, something only Americans like me would notice here in Costa Rica. I hear the roar of an engine that needs maintenance. A small gray Toyota speeds past and returns a few moments later, horn blasting. The driver sticks his head out the window and says, "Hello my friend, we go?" While I squeeze into the passenger seat, he says, "I no see you, *lo siento*. But *pura vida* man, where you going?" We seem to hit every pothole, and my body is jostled

---

* For a list of transitional expressions for process, see Chapter 8 of the companion text.

like a child playing with an old doll. Yet despite being late to meet my parents, despite the car having no air conditioning, and despite the driver's choice to blast salsa music loud enough for the entire neighborhood to throw a party, everything is indeed *pura vida*.

(2) The Spanish phrase *pura vida* is not just a Costa Rican slogan printed on t-shirts, and it does not merely mean "pure life." No other Latin American could tell you what it means beyond "something that *Ticos* (Costa Ricans) say." The American culture lacks a similar idea. Often foreigners try to add *pura vida* to their pocket-dictionary vocabularies, but *pura vida* isn't planned. To experience *pura vida*, one must squeeze the best out of every experience—even bad lemons are used to make sweet *limonada*.

(3) *Pura vida* exists in the little things that make Costa Rica precious to the locals who have given so much to their country. *Pura vida* is the flavor of *chilero* sauce that spices up the rice and bean dish of *gallo pinto* that sits on their plates three meals a day. It is the plantain slices fried up to sweeten their palates when the rice and beans are finished. *Pura vida* is children and adults playing soccer together in the abandoned dirt field next door. They yell, "Oooooopaaa!" in unison when their only soccer ball is accidentally kicked into traffic. *Pura vida* is the sweet ocean air that blows in from the Pacific coast, rolls up the western mountains, and seeps throughout the central valley.

(4) While traveling the coast, I stop at a roadside spot that advertises rice, beans, and meat. I am greeted warmly by a waiter who wants to practice his English. "Hey man, you American?" he asks loudly, "You come to Costa Rica?" making sure that everyone can hear him. I nod, and when I tell him that I actually live here, he smiles and replies, "*pura vida.*"

(5) This is the simple life, the pure life where you work hard to feed the family you love. Costa Rica is built on communities, friendship, and a willingness to help each other. When Ticos say *pura vida*, it's not just that life is good now. Life has always been good, and, if it's up to them, always will be.

—Anders Nelson, Student

1. In this essay, paragraph 1 introduces the term to be defined, but the thesis statement occurs in paragraph 2. Underline or highlight it.

2. How does the writer develop the definition of *pura vida* in paragraphs 3 and 4?

    _____

    _____

3. Mr. Nelson uses careful description to help readers see and experience his subject. What descriptive details did you find especially powerful and effective?

    _____

    _____

4. Let this student's work inspire you. Can you think of a term from your home town, neighborhood, or native country that might lend itself to an essay of definition? Write ideas here. Ask some classmates if they would like to read more about the term.

_____

PRACTICE 18

In a group with several classmates, look closely at the poster below, which is called *The Illiterate*. The picture seems to compare someone who cannot read and write with a blindfolded man walking off a cliff. What does the picture say about being illiterate? Does it accurately *define* illiteracy? Do you know anyone who is illiterate? If you were writing an essay called *The Illiterate*, how would you explain the term?

The Illiterate by Aleksei Radakov

Hoover Institution Archives, Stanford University

PRACTICE 19

1. Choose a topic from the list below or one your instructor has assigned. You might wish to define a term from an important college course, your job, or your culture. Decide what type of definition you will use.

    1. A special term from sports, technology, business, art, or psychology

    2. An environmental term (*global warming, endangered species, recycling, deforestation*, and so on)

    3. A friend

    4. Poverty

    5. Immigrant

    6. Maturity

    7. A disease or medical condition, such as diabetes, autism, depression, or alcoholism

    8. A slang term in current use

    9. A term from another language or culture (*salsa, joie de vivre, manga, machismo*, and so on)

    10. Hate (for ideas, see *What is Hate?* **http://www.media-awareness.ca/english/ issues/online_hate/index.cfm**)

    11. Writer's choice: _____

2. Many students find using a graphic organizer helpful as they plan an essay. In your notebook, draw a blank 8 by 11-inch organizer like the one on pages 181–182 of the companion text or use the illustration essay organizer on the CourseMate for *Evergreen Compact*. In it, create an outline for your essay. The information you write in each box will become a paragraph.

PRACTICE 20

Now referring to your plan, write the best first draft you can. Aim for clarity as you help the reader develop an understanding of this word or term. Check your paragraphing, and use *transitional expressions** to guide the reader from point to point.

Let your draft cool for an hour or a day; then reread it as if you were a helpful, eagle-eyed stranger. Now revise and rewrite, emphasizing exact language, avoiding wordiness, and keeping your reader in mind. Is each paragraph developed fully? Do transitions make the flow of ideas clear? Proofread for spelling, grammar, and sentence errors.

---

* For a list of transitional expressions, see Chapter 4 of the companion text.

CHAPTER 17

Types of Essays, Part 2

A: The Comparison and the Contrast Essay

B: The Classification Essay

C: The Cause and Effect Essay

D: The Persuasive Essay

A. The Comparison and the Contrast Essay

Read this student's essay and answer the questions.

BAREBACK BRONC RIDING VERSUS BULL RIDING

(1) There are many different events in the sport of rodeo. Two of the best-known, bareback bronc riding and bull riding, might seem quite similar to the casual onlooker. Although they are both rough stock (bucking) events, they differ in the equipment required, riding technique, animal size, and bucking style.

(2) Bareback bronc riding requires a lot of equipment for a safe and successful ride. The bareback rigging is probably most important. It is a combination of wood and leather, molded into a suitcase-type handle for the rider to wedge his hand in while wearing a thick leather glove. Another important piece of equipment is the neck roll, a thick pad attached to the back of the neck with long straps to prevent whiplash or fractures during

the ride and dismount. Bareback riders are also required to wear straight-shanked, free-spinning spurs with rounded rowels (or wheels) to keep from cutting the horse. A vest and chaps are optional safety features for the legs and torso.

(3) Bareback bronc riding also entails a very unnatural technique. In this event, the rider positions himself almost completely reclined on the horse, with his head near the flanks and his feet at the shoulders. Once the gate is opened, the rider is required to "mark out" the horse. This means that the rider must reach up with his legs and mash his spurs into the horse's neck before the first buck is made. The rider is then judged on his spurring ability, which is done by pulling his feet in an upward motion and into an almost spread-eagle position.

(4) Size and bucking style of a bronc differ as well. An average bucking horse weighs between 1200 and 1500 pounds and is approximately five and one-half feet tall at the top of the shoulder. These horses are extremely quick and generally buck straight down the arena.

(5) In contrast to bareback bronc riding, bull riding does not require a rigging. Instead, a woven grass rope and a thin leather glove are used. The protective vest is a requirement in this event due to the rather aggressive nature of the bulls. No neck roll is needed in this event because there is little strain on the neck. The spurs in bull riding have fixed rowels with sharp ends, and the shanks are angled inward at a forty-five degree angle to make gripping easy. Helmets and face masks are optional safety features for this event.

(6) Unlike bronc riding, bull riding technique is fairly natural. The rider sits in the upright position, straddling the bull just behind the shoulders. There is no mark out requirement in bull riding, and spurring is just a scoring bonus. Usually only the most experienced riders practice spurring.

(7) Bulls differ from horses in both weight and bucking style. Bulls are heavier, with an average weight between 1500 and 2100 pounds, and they stand approximately five feet tall at the top of the shoulders. Although they buck fairly slowly, they are very powerful and very aggressive. Unlike broncs, bulls seldom buck straight down the arena; instead they often fade from side to side, spin, and twist.

(8) In short, there are many differences between bareback bronc riding and bull riding. The primary elements that set these events apart are the variations in equipment, riding technique, size, and bucking style. Both events, however, thrill rodeo fans and riders.

—Matt Bodson, Student

1. Underline or highlight the thesis statement and topic sentences in this essay. Will this writer compare or contrast bronc and bull riding? What words tell you this?

   _____

2. Does this writer follow the *all A; then all B* pattern or the *AB, AB, AB* pattern? If you aren't sure, label each part of the essay in the left margin. Use the terms below listed in scrambled order. A is bronc riding; B is bull riding.

B, point 2	**B, points 3 and 4**	**C = Conclusion**	**A, point 1**
A, point 2	**IN = Introduction**	**A, points 3 and 4**	**B, point 1**

_____

3. Do you think Mr. Bodson picked a subject that he knows a lot about? What aspects of the essay give you this impression?

_____

4. If this writer asked you for peer feedback, what would you say? What do you like most about this essay? Do you have any suggestions for improvement?

_____

PRACTICE 2

Comparing and contrasting two things requires concentration and focus. A few moments of thought usually are _not_ enough to perceive all the similarities or differences. In a group with four or five classmates, practice paying close attention: study the two photographs below until you spot _four differences_ between them. Work quietly and jot your answers; be prepared to share.

_____

_____

_____

_____

_____

© iStock

PRACTICE 3

1. Choose a topic from the list below or one your instructor has assigned. Bear in mind that the most interesting essays usually compare two things that are different or contrast two things that are similar. Otherwise, you run the risk of saying the obvious ("Cats and dogs are two different animals").

   1. Your mother's or father's childhood and your own

   2. Two cultural attitudes about one subject

   3. A neighborhood store and a chain store (bookstore, restaurant, music store, and so on)

   4. Two politicians, entertainers, athletes, public figures, artists, or historical figures

   5. Your expectations about parenthood (a job, or college) versus the realities

   6. Two different social networking websites (like Facebook and MySpace)

   7. A traditional doctor and an alternative healer

   8. Two views on a controversial issue

   9. A book and a movie based on that book

   10. Two job or career options you are considering

   11. Writer's choice: _____

2. Many students find using a graphic organizer helpful as they plan an essay. In your notebook, draw a blank 8 by 11-inch organizer like the one on pages 187–188 of the companion text or use the illustration essay organizer on the CourseMate for *Evergreen Compact*. In it, create an outline for your essay. The information you write in each box will become a paragraph.

PRACTICE 4

Once your plan is finalized, write the best first draft you can. Refer to your plan to make sure you have included every point of comparison or contrast. If any section seems weak, prewrite for more details and revise. Organization is very important in a comparison or contrast essay, so use *transitional expressions** to highlight the order and guide the reader from point to point.

Let your draft cool for an hour or a day; then reread it as if you were a helpful, eagle-eyed stranger. Now revise and rewrite, emphasizing completeness, clear organization,

---

* For a list of transitional expressions of comparison and contrast, see Chapter 10 of the companion text.

and exact language. Is each point developed fully? Do transitions make the flow of ideas clear? Proofread for spelling, grammar, and sentence errors.

B. The Classification Essay

Although the classification essay is usually serious, the pattern can make a good humorous essay, as this student's paper shows. Read it and answer the questions.

THE POTATO SCALE

(1) For years, television has been the great American pastime. Nearly every household has at least one TV, which means that people are spending time watching it, unless, of course, they bought it to serve as a plant stand. Television viewers can be grouped in many ways—by the type of shows they watch (but there is no accounting for taste) or by hours per week of watching (but that seems unfair since a working, twelve-hour-a-week viewer could conceivably become a fifty-hour-a-week viewer if he or she were out of a job). So I have developed the Potato Scale. The four major categories of the Potato Scale rank TV viewers on a combination of leisure time spent watching, intensity of watching, and the desire to watch versus the desire to engage in other activities.

(2) First, we have the True Couch Potatoes. They are diehard viewers who, when home, will be found in front of their televisions. They no longer eat in the dining room, and if you visit them, the television stays on. *TV Guide* is their Bible. They will plan other activities and chores around their viewing time, always hoping to accomplish these tasks in front of the tube. If a presidential address is on every channel but one, and they dislike the president, they will tune into that one channel, be it Bugs Bunny reruns or Polynesian barge cooking. These potatoes would never consider turning off the box.

(3) The second group consists of the Pseudo Couch Potatoes. These are scheduled potatoes. They have outside interests and actually eat at the table, but for a certain period of time (let's say from seven to eleven in the evening), they will take on the characteristics of True Couch Potatoes. Another difference between True and Pseudo Potatoes deserves note. The True Potato must be forced by someone else to shut off the television and do something different; however, if the Pseudo Potato has flipped through all the channels and found only garbage, he or she still has the capacity to think of other things to do.

(4) Third, we have the Selective Potatoes. These more discriminating potatoes enjoy many activities, and TV is just one of them. They might have a few shows they enjoy watching regularly, but missing one episode is not a world-class crisis. After all, the show will be on next week. They don't live by *TV Guide*, but use it to check for interesting

specials. If they find themselves staring at an awful movie or show, they will gladly, and without a second thought, turn it off.

(5) The fourth group consists of Last Resort Potatoes. These people actually prefer reading, going to the theater, playing pickup basketball, walking in the woods, and many other activities to watching television. Only after they have exhausted all other possibilities or are dog tired or shivering with the flu, will they click on the tube. These potatoes are either excessively choosy or almost indifferent to what's on, hoping it will bore them to sleep.

(6) These are the principal categories of the Potato Scale, from the truly vegetable to the usually human. What type of potato are you?

—Helen Petruzzelli, Student

1. Underline or highlight the thesis statement and the topic sentences. Note that they form a clear outline of this well-organized classification essay.

2. The entire essay classifies people on the basis of their television viewing habits. Into how many categories are the TV viewers divided? What are they?

_____

_____

3. Does the writer's order make sense? What is the logic in presenting True Couch Potatoes first, Pseudo Couch Potatoes second, Selective Couch Potatoes third, and Last Resort Couch Potatoes fourth?

_____

4. How successful is Ms. Petruzzelli's essay? Does it inspire you with any ideas for a humorous essay of your own?

_____

PRACTICE 6

In a group with four or five classmates, examine the food pyramid on the next page. It shows what doctors believe to be the healthiest proportion of foods to eat in an ideal daily diet. How is *classification* used in the pyramid? How many food *classes* or *groups* are shown here? Label each food group in the white space; use nouns to keep your labels parallel. How do your group's personal eating habits compare to the ideal? Be prepared to share your findings.

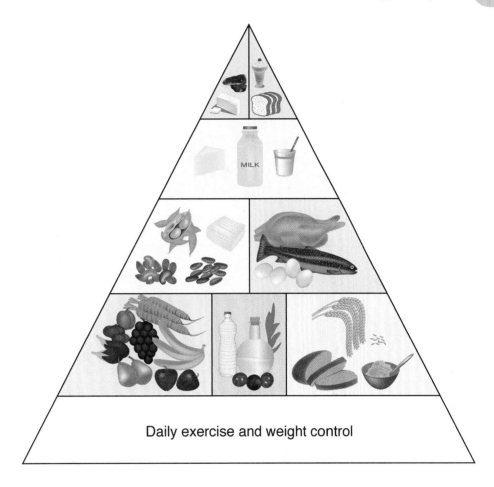

Daily exercise and weight control

PRACTICE 7

1. Choose a topic from the list below or one your instructor has assigned, and then "try on" different bases of classification until you find one that inspires you. (For instance, you could discuss members of your family on the basis of how they spend their leisure time . . . or how good they are at home repairs . . . or how they handle stress.)

   1. Members of your family

   2. People studying in the library

   3. Your monthly expenses

   4. Your coworkers

   5. College students' attitudes toward plagiarism

6. Dog owners

7. Job options in your career field

8. Teenagers whom you interview (about the value of education, hope about the future, or other subject)

9. Items in your desk drawer, handbag, or car trunk

10. Drivers

11. Writer's choice: _____

2. Many students find using a graphic organizer helpful as they plan an essay. In your notebook, draw a blank 8 by 11-inch organizer like the one on pages 190–191 of the companion text or use the illustration essay organizer on the CourseMate for *Evergreen Compact*. In it, create an outline for your essay. The information you write in each box will become a paragraph.

PRACTICE 8

Now, referring to your plan, write the best first draft you can. Aim for clarity as you help the reader develop an understanding of each category in your classification. Check your paragraphing, and use *transitional expressions** to guide the reader from category to category.

Let your draft cool for an hour or a day; then reread it as if you were a helpful, eagle-eyed stranger. Now revise and rewrite, emphasizing clarity, completeness, and keeping your reader in mind. Is each paragraph developed fully? Do transitions make the flow of ideas clear? Proofread for spelling, grammar, and sentence errors.

C. The Cause and Effect Essay

PRACTICE 9

Read this student's cause and effect essay and answer the questions.

TRADING MY BROWN SHIRT FOR A BACKPACK

(1) The words "economic downturn" didn't mean much on the front of a newspaper, but then I got laid off. Suddenly, those weren't just words but the beginning of a long

---

* For a list of transitional expressions of classification, see Chapter 11 of the companion text.

chain of events in my life. I liked my job at the United Parcel Service, and I had received many positive performance reviews, so I didn't think the rising unemployment rate was going to touch me. People still have to ship packages, right? Wrong. Getting my pink slip had powerful effects on my lifestyle and plans, but not all the effects have been bad ones.

(2) After losing my job, I have had to make major financial changes. My unemployment check is about half what I was making at UPS, so I have to budget very carefully. I used to take my fiancé out to a nice dinner almost every week. Now our dates involve pizza and rented movies. We also had to postpone our wedding until I'm back on my feet. The hardest change by far has been moving back in with my dad because I couldn't make the rent on my apartment.

(3) Although I was prepared to have less money, one effect I didn't expect from losing my job was the negative feelings I would have. I was embarrassed to tell my family what had happened, worried that my fiancé would think less of me, and angry that events I couldn't control had ruined my life. It was strange and depressing not having the job to go to every day. Maybe some wouldn't consider delivering packages a career, but I liked my work, it paid well, and I was outside driving a truck all day. So it's not just the money I miss; it's the job.

(4) The one positive effect of getting laid off is that it forced me to reconsider college. When I got a good job shortly after high school, it confirmed my decision to head straight into the "real world." Now that there are so few full-time jobs with benefits out there, getting more education and training seems like the logical move. A counselor at the unemployment office encouraged me to attend a career fair at San Francisco Community College. I ended up taking placement exams and enrolling that same afternoon.

(5) So here I am in a freshman writing class, returning to school the spring I expected to be getting married and hunting for a nice apartment. So far I'm enjoying college more than I thought. I feel proud to be pursuing my Emergency Medical Technician (EMT) certificate. When I'm done, I'll be driving around in an ambulance instead of a delivery truck, and I have a feeling I'm going to like it.

—Alex Silvio, Student

1. Underline or highlight the thesis statement and the topic sentences in paragraphs 2, 3, and 4.

2. Does the writer discuss causes or effects? What are they?

_____

3. Reread Mr. Silvio's concluding paragraph. Is it effective? Why or why not?

_____

PRACTICE 10

In a group with four or five classmates, study the famous painting below by Pablo Picasso, called *Guernica*. The painting depicts the bombing of the town of Guernica, Spain in 1937, but it is widely thought to be a brilliant depiction of the effects of war. What are these effects? Picasso usually used vivid colors. Why do you think he created this painting without color, in black, white and gray?

Art Resource, NY. © 2009 Estate of Pablo Picasso/Artists Rights Society (ARS), NY

PRACTICE 11

1. Choose a topic from the list below or one your instructor has assigned. Make sure your topic lends itself to cause and effect analysis. This list and the one in Chapter 12 will give you ideas. Write a clear thesis statement that identifies your subject and indicates whether causes or effects will be emphasized. Then prewrite a number of possible causes or effects, so you can choose the most important ones to develop your essay. Decide on a logical order in which to present them.

   1. What are the reasons why you are attending college?

   2. What are the reasons for the popularity of a certain product, musical group, or game?

   3. What caused you to do something you are (or are not) proud of?

   4. Analyze the main causes of a problem in society (like child abuse or teen pregnancy).

   5. What causes a hurricane, tornado, or other natural disaster?

   6. Choose an event in history that interests you and analyze its causes.

   7. What are the effects of shyness on someone's life (or pride, rage, curiosity or the lack of it)?

8. Write a letter urging a young person not to make a bad choice with serious negative consequences (such as joining a gang or dropping out of school).

9. What are the effects of a new experience (a trip, military service, living in another country, dorm life)?

10. What are the effects of a divorce, death, or other loss?

11. Writer's choice: _____

2. Many students find using a graphic organizer helpful as they plan an essay. In your notebook, draw a blank 8 by 11-inch organizer like the one on pages 194–195 of the companion text or use the illustration essay organizer on the CourseMate for *Evergreen Compact*. In it, create an outline for your essay. The information you write in each box will become a paragraph.

PRACTICE 12

Now referring to your plan, write the best first draft you can. Make sure that that each cause and/or effect you discuss is clear to you and the reader. Is the order logical? Tie each cause or effect into your thesis statement and main idea. Use *transitional expressions** to help the reader follow what happened.

Let your draft cool for an hour or a day; then reread it as if you were a helpful, eagle-eyed stranger. Now revise and rewrite, emphasizing clarity and a thoughtful explanation of causes or effects. Is each paragraph developed fully? Do transitions make the flow of ideas clear? Proofread for spelling, grammar, and sentence errors.

D. The Persuasive Essay

PRACTICE 13

This student's persuasive essay won a national essay contest sponsored by CCBA (Community College Baccalaureate). Read it and answer the questions.

IMAGINE A FOUR-YEAR COMMUNITY COLLEGE

(1) Imagine four-year institutions that allow for a pace and schedule that meet the needs of nontraditional students with non-academic obligations. Imagine institutions with an affordability that allows students to pay their own tuition as it comes due, in

_____

* For a list of transitional expressions of cause and effect, see Chapter 12 of the companion text.

the absence of family wealth or large scholarships. Imagine colleges that take pride in their program and the philosophy of open admissions, rather than their ability to selectively admit few while turning down many. Imagine institutions like these all over the country, allowing continuity of family, work, and community between students and their hometowns. You have just imagined community colleges with four-year degree programs. Schedule, affordability, and open admissions policies make community colleges ideal to offer four-year degrees.

(2) A key concept of community colleges is to tailor offerings to students with small, sporadic amounts of time available for classes. I work, help run a non-profit honor society on campus, attend full time classes, and am a cadet in the Corona de Tucson Firefighter Academy. Without the flexible schedule that Pima Community College affords me, I would be unable to complete all of these tasks simultaneously. Community colleges generally have very accommodating schedules, with courses available nights and weekends, self-paced on campus, and even online. Students who deserve and desire to complete a bachelor's degree may simply not have the availability to schedule classes between 7 A.M. and 5 P.M. but the community college would meet their needs.

(3) It is no coincidence that many students attending community colleges fall in the category of working poor. During freshman year, I struggled to pay tuition and book expenses; it was a year before I began receiving scholarships. Working in the food service industry, I had limited funds; luckily, I was able to utilize the library's books on reserve when I could not pay for my own. I saved thousands of dollars attending Pima Community College compared to what the University of Arizona would have charged me for the same number of credits. Yet my situation is not unique; millions of students would love to attend lavish universities, but incurring debts or failing to receive competitive scholarships deter worthy students from acquiring higher education. This is not to mention the fact that some full-capacity universities turn down valedictorians simply because they receive more perfect applications than they have seats available.

(4) Sometimes students need more than flexible hours or tuition to attend college; they need something nearby. Community colleges are exactly what the name entails, institutions of the community. Pima Community College has six campuses around town and online courses available. This has given me the ability to live with my sister and help her with mortgage payments while attending school. The community emphasis of these colleges allows students to stay in and help their community, family, and friends while pursuing higher education and personal enrichment. To imagine a solution to a problem and make it a reality is a staple of college education. Many have imagined a four-year community college—it must become a reality.

—John Windham, Student

1. What is this writer arguing *for*? Underline the thesis statement.

_____

_____

2. In the introduction, instead of a thesis statement, the writer asks readers three
   times to "Imagine . . . ." The last sentence of the conclusion says, "You have just
   imagined community colleges with four-year degree programs." How effective is this
   introduction?

   _____

   _____

3. What three features of community colleges does the writer discuss in his
   argument?

   _____

4. This writer uses himself as an example throughout the essay. Is this persuasive? Would
   you say that his experience makes him an authority?

   _____

PRACTICE 14

In a group of four or five classmates, look closely at the public service
advertisement below, which appeared on buses and billboards. Like many
advertisements, this one is trying to *persuade* the viewer to adopt or agree with
a certain view. Working together, write down the ad's "thesis statement" and
argument. How persuasive is this ad?

Courtesy Friends of Animals

YOU LOOK JUST AS STUPID WEARING THEIRS.

www.friendsofanimals.org

PRACTICE 15

1. Choose a topic from the list below or one your instructor has assigned. If possible, choose a subject you feel strongly about. Argue for or against, as you wish.

   1. I deserve a better grade on my _____ assignment (or in this course).

   2. America should control guns with stricter laws.

   3. All animal testing of medicines should be banned, even if such testing would save human lives.

   4. Every college student should be required to give three credit hours' worth of community service a year.

   5. The United States government should provide universal health care to all citizens.

   6. A college education is (not) worth the time and money.

   7. Gay couples should be allowed to adopt children in all states.

   8. I am a good fit for the position of _____.

   9. To better prepare students for the world of work, this college should do three things.

   10. The United States must find and deport all illegal aliens, including students with expired visas.

   11. Writer's choice: _____

2. Many students find using a graphic organizer helpful as they plan an essay. In your notebook, draw a blank 8 by 11-inch organizer like the one on pages 198–199 of the companion text or use the illustration essay organizer on the CourseMate for *Evergreen Compact*. In it, create an outline for your essay. The information you write in each box will become a paragraph.

PRACTICE 16

Now referring to your plan, write the best first draft you can. Aim for clarity and persuasive power as you explain why your stand is the right one. Make sure your reasons follow the most effective order, and carefully choose *transitional expressions** to introduce each reason. Remember, factual support is key to a winning essay.

Let your draft cool for an hour or a day; then reread it as if you were a helpful, eagle-eyed stranger. Now revise and rewrite for clarity and ample support. Is each paragraph and reason developed fully? Do transitions make the flow of ideas clear? Does your conclusion bring the point home? Proofread for spelling, grammar, and sentence errors.

---

* For a list of transitional expressions for persuasion, see Chapter 13 of the companion text.

Summarizing, Quoting, and Avoiding Plagiarism

A: Avoiding Plagiarism

B: Writing a Summary

C: Using Direct and Indirect Quotation

A. Avoiding Plagiarism

PRACTICE 1

What is your college's policy on plagiarism? That is, what consequences or penalties follow if a student is found to have plagiarized a paper or other work? The reference librarian can help you find this information.

B. Writing a Summary

PRACTICE 2

In a group with three or four other classmates, choose an essay from the companion text or this workbook to summarize. Read your chosen essay in the group, aloud if possible. Then each person should write a one-paragraph summary of it, referring to the checklist in Chapter 18, Part B, of the companion text (15–20 minutes).

Now read your finished summaries aloud to your group. How well does each writer briefly capture the meaning of the original? Has he or she kept out personal opinion? What suggestions for improvement can you offer? Your instructor may wish to have the best summary in each group read aloud to the whole class.

PRACTICE 3

Flip through a copy of a current magazine: *Newsweek, People, Essence, Wired,* or another. Pick one article that interests you, read it carefully, and write a one- to three-paragraph summary of the article, depending on the length of the article. The points you include in your summary should reflect the emphasis of the original writer. Try to capture the essence of the article. Remember to give your source at the beginning, to keep out personal opinion, and to check your summary for plagiarism. Refer to the checklist in Chapter 18, Part B, of the companion text.

C. Using Direct and Indirect Quotation

PRACTICE 4

Following are passages from two sources. Read each one, and then, as if you were writing a paper, quote two sentences from each, one directly quoting the author's words and one indirectly quoting the author's ideas. Review the boxed ways to introduce quotations in Chapter 18, Part C, of the companion text and try several methods. Finally, write a brief summary of each passage. Check your work to avoid plagiarism.

Source 1

In most cultures throughout history, music, dance, rhythmic drumming, and chanting have been essential parts of healing rituals. Modern research bears out the connection between music and healing. In one study, the heart rate and blood pressure of patients went down when quiet music was piped into their hospital coronary care units. At

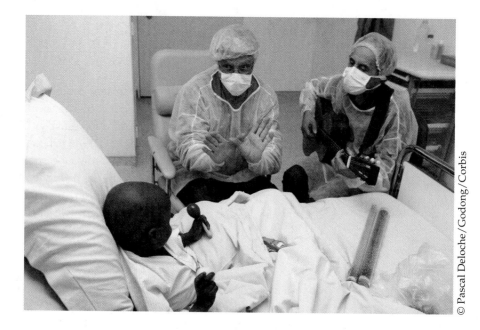

In the children's cancer ward in Villejuif, France, musicians play for a patient during music therapy.

the same time, the patients showed greater tolerance for pain and less anxiety and depression. Similarly, listening to music before, during, or after surgery has been shown to promote various beneficial effects—from alleviating anxiety to reducing the need for sedation by half. When researchers played Brahms' "Lullaby" to premature infants, these babies gained weight faster and went home from the hospital sooner than babies who did not hear the music. Music may also affect immunity by altering the level of stress chemicals in the blood. An experiment at Rainbow Babies and Children's Hospital found that a single thirty-minute music therapy session could increase the level of salivary IgA, an immunoglobulin that protects against respiratory infections.

Institute of Noetic Sciences with William Poole.
The Heart of Healing. Atlanta:
Turner Publishing, 1993: 134. Print.

Direct quotation: _____

_____

Indirect quotation: _____

_____

Summary:

_____

_____

_____

_____

_____

_____

Source 2

Assuming they reach maturity with consciousness intact, the current crop of teenagers will have spent years watching commercials. No one has done the numbers on what happens if you factor in radio, magazine, newspaper advertisements, and billboards, but today's teens probably have spent the equivalent of a decade of their lives being bombarded by bits of advertising information. In 1915, a person could go entire weeks without observing an ad. The average adult today sees three thousand every day.

James B. Twitchell, *Adcult USA*. New York: Columbia University Press, 1996: 2. Print.

Direct quotation: _____

_____

Indirect quotation: _____

_____

Summary:

_____

_____

_____

_____

_____

_____

PRACTICE 5

Following are four sources and four quotations from student papers. If the student has summarized, directly quoted, or indirectly quoted the source correctly, write C. If you believe the source is plagiarized, write P; then revise the student's work as if it were your own to avoid plagiarism.

- Does each student clearly distinguish between his or her ideas and the source's?
- Does each student give enough information so that a reader could locate the original source?

Source 1

"Binge drinking, according to criteria used in periodic surveys by the Harvard researchers, is defined as five or more drinks on one occasion for a man or four or more drinks on one occasion for a woman. Students who reported one or two such episodes in the two weeks preceding the survey were classified as occasional binge drinkers; those reporting three or more were considered frequent binge drinkers."

Okie, Susan. "Survey: 44% of College Students Are Binge Drinkers."
Washington Post 25 Mar. 2002: A6. Print.

Student's Version

_____ Binge drinking is a dangerous problem on campuses, but college administrators are not doing enough to stop it. An amazing 44 percent of college students are binge drinkers. Let us define binge drinking as five or more drinks on one occasion for a man or four or more drinks on one occasion for a woman. College officials need to ask why so many students are drinking dangerously.

Source 2

"The image of the Kitchen God (alternatively known as the Hearth God) usually stood above the family stove, from where he would observe the household. Every New Year he was said to visit heaven to give an account of the behavior of the family in the past year."

Willis, Roy. *Dictionary of World Myth*. London:
Duncan Baird Publishers, 1995: 116. Print.

Student's Version

_____ My Chinese grandmother has a Kitchen God above her stove. It says in the dictionary that this is a special god who observes the household and then visits heaven every New Year to report on the behavior of the family in the past year.

Source 3

"The risk of stroke increases with the number of fast-food restaurants in a neighborhood . . . . Researchers found [that] residents of neighborhoods with the highest number of fast-food restaurants had a 13 percent higher relative risk of suffering ischemic strokes than those living in areas with the lowest numbers of restaurants."

American Heart Association. "Number of Fast-food Restaurants in Neighborhood Associated with Stroke Risk." *ScienceDaily*. Science Daily LLC 20 Feb. 2009. Web. 24 Feb. 2009.

Student's Version

_____ According to a news release by the American Heart Association, people who live near fast-food restaurants like McDonald's or Wendy's are at a higher risk for strokes than those who do not. As the number of restaurants rises, so does the risk.

Source 4

"As alpine glaciers around the world succumb to warming, scientists are reaping grand harvests of frozen organic objects—and with them previously unavailable information on past wildlife, human culture, genetics, climate, and more. Tissues with intact DNA and archaeological objects of wood and bone provide pictures that stone tools only hint at, and because they can all be radio-carbon dated, there is little guessing about chronology."

Krajick, Kevin. "Melting Glaciers Release Ancient Relics." *Science* 19 Apr. 2002: 454–456. Print.

Student's Version

_____ There might be a positive side to global warming after all. Kevin Krajick reports in *Science*, April 19, 2002, that melting glaciers are providing scientists with many objects and tissue samples that will give them "previously unavailable information on past wildlife, human culture, genetics, climate and more."

CHAPTER 19

Strengthening an Essay with Research

A: Improving an Essay with Research

B: Finding and Evaluating Outside Sources: Library and Internet

C: Adding Sources to Your Essay and Documenting Them Correctly

A. Improving an Essay with Research

PRACTICE 1

Choose one of the following: either your favorite paper written this term or a paper on a topic assigned by your instructor. Then read through your paper, marking any spots where an outside source—fact, statistic, expert opinion, or quotation—might strengthen your essay. Write down any questions that you want to answer.

_____

_____

_____

_____

_____

B. Finding and Evaluating Outside Sources: Library and Internet

PRACTICE 2

In your college or local library, find the answers to the following questions; in your notebook or on separate paper, write the answers and the complete source for each piece of information. Your instructor might wish to have you work in competing teams.

1. List the full titles of five novels by Toni Morrison. What major prize did she win and in what year?

2. How many acres of rain forest are destroyed every day in Brazil?

3. What is the average hourly wage of men in the United States? Of women?

4. How many murders were committed in your town or city last year? Is the number up or down from ten years ago?

5. What was the newspaper headline in your hometown or city on the day and year of your birth? What stories dominated page 1?

PRACTICE 3

In your college or local library, find at least two excellent additions from outside sources that will improve your essay: a fact, statistic, example, quotation, or expert opinion. Write the information from each source precisely on 4 × 6 note cards, using quotation marks as you learned in Chapter 18, Part C, of the companion text, or make copies. Write down everything you will need later to cite the source: the book or magazine, article name, author name(s), and so on. Spell everything perfectly; copy exact punctuation of titles, and don't forget page numbers.

PRACTICE 4

Go to **www.fedstats.gov** and learn how to find statistics quickly and easily. Answer these questions:

1. How many people live in the United States? _____

2. What is the leading cause of death in American men? Women? _____

_____

3. What is the leading export from your state? _____

4. How many different ethnic groups live in your state? _____

_____

5. How many new AIDS cases were reported in your state last year? What groups were

   hardest hit? _____

_____

PRACTICE 5

Using one of the suggested search engines, find at least two good pieces of information to strengthen your essay—facts, statistics, expert opinions, and so on. Hone your search words and evaluate what you find. Take careful notes, and cut and paste or print the information you need. Did you find any good material that you were not expecting? (Did you find exciting information on another subject that you might use in another paper? Be sure to take down any information you might use in the future.)

C. Adding Sources to Your Essay and Documenting Them Correctly

PRACTICE 6

Below are five sources a student has compiled for a research essay on the history of the Olympics. Using the MLA models in the companion text to guide you, prepare a Works Cited list for the paper that includes all five sources, properly formatted and in alphabetical order.

- A book by Nigel Spivey called *The Ancient Olympics: A History* that was published in New York, New York by Oxford University Press in 2006

- An article in the August 18, 2008, issue of *Time* magazine called "A Brief History of: Olympic Medals" written by Claire Suddath and appearing on page 19

- A website called *The Ancient Olympic Games Virtual Museum* that was presented by Dartmouth College and last updated on January 11, 2004 (the student viewed it on January 10, 2009 at http://devlab.dartmouth.edu/olympics/)

- A book by David Wallechinsky and Jaime Loucky titled *The Complete Book of the Olympics: 2008 Edition* published by Aurum Press in London in 2008, 1,200 pages long

- An article from the *Wall Street Journal—Eastern Edition* newspaper called "The Real History of the Olympics" that was written by Kyle Smith and appeared on page W11 on Feb. 10, 2006

Works Cited

_____

_____

_____

_____

_____

_____

_____

_____

_____

_____

_____

PRACTICE 7

Now, using two of the three methods—summary, direct quotation, or indirect quotation—add your research findings to your essay. Review Chapters 18 and 19 in the companion text if you need to. Aim to achieve two things: First, try to add the new material gracefully, using introductory phrases so that it relates clearly to your ideas in the essay. Second, be careful to avoid plagiarism by documenting your sources correctly, both inside the essay and in your Works Cited list.

CHAPTER 20

Writing Under Pressure: The Essay Examination

A: Budgeting Your Time

B: Reading and Understanding the Essay Question

C: Choosing the Correct Paragraph or Essay Pattern

D: Writing the Topic Sentence or the Thesis Statement

A. Budgeting Your Time

PRACTICE 1

Imagine that you are about to take the two-hour history test shown below. Read the test carefully, noting the point value of each question, and then answer the questions that follow the examination.

> Part I   Answer both questions. 15 points each.
>
> 1. Do you think that the Versailles Peace Treaty was a "harsh" one? Be specific.

2. List the basic principles of Karl Marx. Analyze them in terms of Marx's claim that they are scientific.

Part II   Answer two of the following questions. 25 points each.

3. Describe the origins of, the philosophies behind, and the chief policies of either Communist Russia or Fascist Italy. Be specific.

4. What were the causes of Nelson Mandela's presidential victory in South Africa in 1994?

5. European history of the nineteenth and twentieth centuries has been increasingly related to that of the rest of the world. Why? How? With what consequences for Europe?

Part III   Briefly identify ten of the following. 2 points each.

a. John Locke

b. Franco-Prussian War

c. Stalingrad

d. Cavour

e. Manchuria, 1931

f. Entente Cordiale

g. Existentialism

h. Jacobins

i. The Opium Wars

j. Social Darwinism

k. The Reform Bill of 1832

l. The most interesting reading you have done this term (from the course list)

1. Which part would you do first and why? _____

_____

How much time would you allot to the questions in this part and why? _____

_____

2. Which part would you do second and why? _____

_____

How much time would you allot to the questions in this part and why? _____

_____

3. Which part would you do last and why? _____

_____

How much time would you allot to the questions in this part and why? _____

_____

_____

B. Reading and Understanding the Essay Question

Read each essay question and underline key words. Then, on the lines beneath the question, describe in your own words exactly what the question requires: (1) What directions does the student have to follow? (2) How many parts will the answer contain?

EXAMPLE   What were the <u>causes</u> of the Cold War? What were its chief <u>episodes</u>? <u>Why</u> has there <u>not</u> been a "hot" war?

Student must *(1) tell what caused the Cold War (two or more causes),*

(2) mention main events of Cold War, (3) give reasons why we haven't

had a full-scale war. The essay will have three parts: causes, main events,

and reasons

1. State Newton's First Law and give examples from your own experience.

Student must _____

_____

_____

2. Choose one of the following terms. Define it, give an example of it, and then show how it affects *your* life: (a) freedom of speech, (b) justice for all, (c) equal opportunity.

Student must _____

_____

_____

3. Shiism and Sunni are the two great branches of Islam. Discuss the religious beliefs and the politics of each branch.

Student must _____

_____

4. Name and explain four types of savings institutions. What are three factors that influence one's choice of a savings institution?

Student must _____

_____

5. Steroids: the athlete's "unfair advantage." Discuss.

Student must _____

_____

_____

6. Discuss the causes and consequences of the Broad Street cholera epidemic in mid-nineteenth-century London. What was the role of Dr. John Snow?

Student must _____

_____

7. Define the Monroe Doctrine of the early nineteenth century and weigh the arguments for and against it.

Student must _____

_____

8. The sixteenth century is known for the Renaissance, the Reformation, and the Commercial Revolution. Discuss each event, showing why it was important to the history of Western civilization.

Student must _____

_____

_____

9. Erik Erikson has theorized that adult actions toward children may produce either (a) trust or mistrust, (b) autonomy or self-doubt, (c) initiative or guilt. Choose one of the pairs above and give examples of the kinds of adult behavior that might create these responses in a child.

Student must _____

_____

_____

_____

10. Simón Bolívar may not have been as great a hero as he was believed to be. Agree or disagree.

Student must _____

_____

_____

_____

C. Choosing the Correct Paragraph or Essay Pattern

PRACTICE 3

You should have no trouble deciding what kind of paragraph or composition to use if the question uses one of the terms just defined—*contrast, trace, classify*, and so on.

However, questions are often worded in such a way that you have to discover what kind of paragraph or essay is required. What kind of paragraph or essay is required by each of the following questions?

EXAMPLE   What is *schizophrenia*?
(*Write a paragraph to. . . .*)   _____*define*_____

1. In one concise paragraph, give the main ideas of Simone de Beauvoir's famous book *The Second Sex*.   _____

2. What is the difference between veins and arteries?   _____

3. Follow the development of Wynton Marsalis's musical style.   _____

4. How do jet- and propeller-driven planes differ?   _____

5. Who or what is each of the following: the Gang of Four, Ho Chi Minh, Tiananmen Square?   _____

6. Explain the causes of the American Civil War.   _____

7. Explain what is meant by "magical realism."   _____

8. Take a stand for or against legalizing marijuana in this country. Give reasons to support your stand.   _____

9. Give two recent instances of military hazing that you consider "out of control."   _____

10. Divide into groups the different kinds of websites giving out medical information.   _____

D. Writing the Topic Sentence or the Thesis Statement

PRACTICE 4

Here are eight examination questions. Write a topic sentence or thesis statement for each question by using the question as part of the answer. Pretend that you know all the material. Even though you may not know anything about the subjects, you should be able to formulate a topic sentence or thesis statement based on the question.

1. Contrast high school requirements in Jamaica with those in the United States.

   Topic sentence or thesis statement: _____

   _____

2. Do you think that the terrorist attacks of September 11, 2001, had any positive effects

   on Americans?

   Topic sentence or thesis statement: _____

   _____

   _____

3. What steps can a busy person take to reduce the destructive impact of stress in his or her life?

   Topic sentence or thesis statement: _____

   _____

   _____

4. Gay couples should be allowed to adopt children. Agree or disagree with this statement.

   Topic sentence or thesis statement: _____

   _____

   _____

5. Assume that you manage a small shop that sells men's apparel. What activities would

    you undertake to promote the sale of sportswear?

    Topic sentence or thesis statement: _____

    _____

    _____

6. The U.S. government should cover the medical costs of AIDS. Agree or disagree with

    this statement.

    Topic sentence or thesis statement: _____

    _____

    _____

7. The state should subsidize students in medical school because the country needs

    more doctors. Agree or disagree with this statement.

    Topic sentence or thesis statement: _____

    _____

    _____

8. Does religion play a more vital role in people's lives today than it did in your parents'

    generation?

    Topic sentence or thesis statement: _____

    _____

    _____

Unit 5 Improving Your Writing

CHAPTER 21

Revising for Consistency and Parallelism

A: Consistent Tense

B: Consistent Number and Person

C: Parallelism

A. Consistent Tense

PRACTICE 1

Read the following sentences carefully for meaning. Then correct any inconsistencies of tense by changing the verbs that do not accurately show the time of events.

EXAMPLE   I took a deep breath and opened the door; there stands a well-dressed man with a large box.

Consistent: I took a deep breath and opened the door; there stands a
stood
well-dressed man with a large box.

or

take   *open*
Consistent: I took a deep breath and opened the door; there stands a
well-dressed man with a large box.

1. Two seconds before the buzzer sounded, Lebron James sank a basket from midcourt, and the crowd goes wild.

2. Nestlé introduced instant coffee in 1938; it takes eight years to develop this product.

3. We expand our sales budget, doubled our research, and soon saw positive results.

4. For twenty years, Dr. Dulfano observed animal behavior and seeks clues to explain the increasing violence among human beings.

5. I knew how the system works.

6. I was driving south on Interstate 90 when a truck approaches with its high beams on.

7. Two brown horses graze quietly in the field as the sun rose and the mist disappeared.

8. Lollie had a big grin on her face as she walks over and kicked the Coke machine.

9. Maynard stormed down the hallway, goes right into the boss's office, and shouts, "I want curtains in my office!"

10. The nurses quietly paced the halls, making sure their patients rest comfortably.

PRACTICE 2

Inconsistencies of tense are most likely to occur within paragraphs and longer pieces of writing. Therefore, it is important to revise your writing for tense consistency. Read this paragraph for meaning. Then revise, correcting inconsistencies of tense by changing incorrect verbs.

It was 1850. A poor German-born peddler named Levi Strauss came to San Francisco, trying to sell canvas cloth to tent makers. By chance he met a miner who complained that sturdy work pants are hard to find. Strauss had an idea, measures the man, and makes him a pair of canvas pants. The miner loved his new breeches, and Levi Strauss goes into business. Although he ordered more canvas, what he gets is a brown French cloth called *serge de Nîmes,* which Americans soon called "denim." Strauss liked the cloth but had the next batch dyed blue. He became successful selling work pants to such rugged men as cowboys and lumberjacks. In the 1870s, hearing about a tailor in Nevada adding copper rivets to a pair of the pants to make them stronger, Strauss patents the idea. When he died in 1902, Levi Strauss was famous in California, but the company keeps growing. In the 1930s, when Levi's jeans became popular in the East, both men and women wear them. By 2000, people all over the world had purchased 2.5 billion pairs of jeans.

PRACTICE 3

The following paragraph is written in the past tense. Rewrite it in consistent present tense. Cross out each past tense verb and write the present tense form above it. Make sure all verbs agree with their subjects.*

The desert heat was vicious under the burlap that camouflaged me. I lay in my "Ranger grave," Army slang for the shallow holes soldiers dug into the sand, just big enough to conceal their bodies. A few thoughts worked their way through the haze of my brain, but mostly I dreamed about water—icy, sparkling water. I almost heard the clink of ice cubes in a Mason jar, dripping with condensation. I barely noticed the fine sand in my eyes. I didn't have enough fluid in my body to make tears. "Water truck!" The call floated down the nearly invisible line of graves that stretched across the sand. I peeked out as the water truck drove away through shimmering waves of heat. It left behind a water buffalo, a huge tank of water for the ground troops in our area. As the new guy in the squad, I had to fill our canteens. With my monkey suit for chemical attack, my machine gun, and extra ammo, I trudged out. The desert coated me with sand. My helmet felt huge on my head. Finally, I reached the tank and mentally pumped myself up. I was a paratrooper, a member of the 82nd Airborne, elite fighting force of the U.S. Army! My sense of duty and my mental ice pushed me onward. I sipped a little hot water, filled the canteens, and dragged them back to the men.

—Ray Christian, Student

———

* For more work on agreement, see Chapter 28, "Present Tense (Agreement)," in the companion text and in this workbook.

Poster for the first
Frankenstein movie, 1931

PRACTICE 4

The following paragraph is written in the present tense. Rewrite it in consistent past tense,* crossing out each present tense verb and writing the past tense form above it.

In the summer of 1816, four friends share a house in Switzerland. Days of rain force them to stay indoors. They begin telling ghost stories to ease the boredom. For awhile, they read aloud from *Tales of the Dead*, a collection of horror stories full of eerie graveyards, swirling fog, and restless spirits. Then one night, they decide to hold a contest to see who can write the most frightening ghost story. All four feel eager to compete. Two of the friends—Percy Bysshe Shelley and Lord Byron—are already famous poets. The other two—Dr. John Polidori and Mary Wollstonecraft Godwin, Shelley's wife-to-be—are also writers. Midnight passes, and they retire to their bedrooms. Mary closes her eyes,

_____

* For more work on the past tense, see Chapter 29, "Past Tense," in the companion text and in this workbook.

and imagination takes over. In her mind's eye, she sees a science student kneeling beside a creature he constructed. It is a hideous corpse of a man, but suddenly, it twitches with life. Horror-stricken, the young man runs away from his creation, hoping that the spark of life will sputter and die. Later, though, he wakes to find the monster standing over his bed. Following this nightmare, Mary writes her novel *Frankenstein* in a two-month rush. Published in 1818, *Frankenstein* becomes a classic, read by people around the world.

PRACTICE 5

Longer pieces of writing often use both the past tense and the present tense. However, switching correctly from one tense to the other requires care. Read the following essay carefully and note when a switch from one tense to another is logically necessary. Then revise verbs as needed.

A QUICK HISTORY OF CHOCOLATE

Most of us now take solid chocolate—especially candy bars—so much for granted that we find it hard to imagine a time when chocolate didn't exist. However, this delicious food becomes an eating favorite only about 150 years ago.

The ancient peoples of Central America began cultivating cacao beans almost 3,000 years ago. A cold drink made from the beans is served to Hernando Cortés, the Spanish conqueror, when he arrives at the Aztec court of Montezuma in 1519. The Spaniards took the beverage home to their king. He likes it so much that he kept the formula a secret. For the next 100 years, hot chocolate was the private drink of the Spanish nobility. Slowly, it makes its way into the fashionable courts of France, England, and Austria. In 1657, a Frenchman living in London opened a shop where devices for making the beverage are sold at a high price. Soon chocolate houses appeared in cities throughout Europe. Wealthy clients met in them, sipped chocolate, conducted business, and gossip.

During the 1800s, chocolate became a chewable food. The breakthrough comes in 1828 when cocoa butter was extracted from the bean. Twenty years later, an English firm mixed the butter with chocolate liquor, which results in the first solid chocolate. Milton Hershey's first candy bar come on the scene in 1894, and Tootsie Rolls hit the market two years later. The popularity of chocolate bars soar during World War I when they are given to soldiers for fast energy. M&Ms gave the industry another boost during World War II; soldiers needed candy that wouldn't melt in their hands.

On the average, Americans today eat ten pounds of hard chocolate a year. Their number-one choice is Snickers, which sold more than a billion bars every year. However, Americans consume far less chocolate than many Western Europeans. The average Dutch person gobbled up more than fifteen pounds a year while a Swiss packed away almost twenty pounds. Chocolate is obviously an international favorite.

B. Consistent Number and Person

PRACTICE 6

Correct any inconsistencies of **number** in the following sentences. Also make necessary changes in verb agreement.

EXAMPLE   1. A singer must protect ~~their~~ *his or her* voice.

1. An individual's self-esteem can affect their performance.
2. Jorge started drinking diet sodas only last November, but already he hates the taste of it.
3. The headlines encouraged us, but we feared that it wasn't accurate.

4. The defendant has decided that he will represent oneself.

5. Dreams fascinate me; it is like another world.

6. If a person doesn't know how to write well, they will face limited job opportunities.

7. Oxford University boasts of the great number of ancient manuscripts they own.

8. Always buy corn and tomatoes when it is in season.

9. The average American takes their freedom for granted.

10. Women have more opportunities than ever before. She is freer to go to school, get a job, and choose the kind of life she wants.

PRACTICE 7

Correct the shifts in **person** in these sentences. If necessary, change the verbs to make them agree with any new subjects.

    EXAMPLE   One should eliminate saturated fats from ~~your~~ *one's* diet.

1. Sooner or later, most addicts realize that you can't just quit when you want to.

2. One problem facing students on this campus is that a person doesn't know when the library will be open and when it will be closed.

3. One should rely on reason, not emotion, when they are forming opinions about such charged issues as abortion.

4. I have reached a time in my life when what others expect is less important than what one really wants to do.

5. Members of the orchestra should meet after the concert and bring your instruments and music.

6. The wise mother knows that she is asking for trouble if you let a small child watch violent television shows.

7. The student who participates in this program will spend six weeks in Spain and Morocco. You will study the art and architecture firsthand, working closely with an instructor.

8. You shouldn't judge a person by the way they dress.

9. If you have been working that hard, one needs a vacation.

10. People who visit the Caribbean for the first time are struck by the lushness of the landscape. The sheer size of the flowers and fruit amazes you.

PRACTICE 8

The following paragraph consistently uses third person singular—*the job applicant, the job seeker, he or she.* For practice in revising for consistency, rewrite the paragraph in **consistent third person plural.** Begin by changing *the job applicant* to *job applicants.* Then change verbs, nouns, and pronouns as necessary.

In a job interview these days, the job applicant should stress his or her personal skills, rather than only technical skills. This strategy could increase his or her chances of getting hired. The job seeker should point out such skills as speaking and writing confidently, working well on a team, solving problems quickly, or managing people. These days, many employers assume that if an applicant has excellent "soft skills" like these, he or she can be trained in the technical fine points of the job.

_____

_____

_____

_____

_____

PRACTICE 9

Revise the following essay for inconsistencies of person and number. Correct any confusing shifts (changing words if necessary) to make the writing clear and *consistent* throughout.

IS OUR IDEA OF RACE CHANGING?

What is race, anyway? Is it skin color, country of origin, cultural traditions, biology? The students in Samuel Richards' sociology class at Pennsylvania State University are pondering these questions. Professor Richards encourages him or her to move beyond the black and white labels most people apply to themself and others.

To make his point that race and ethnicity are complex aspects of identity, Richards began offering a DNA test to any student who wanted to learn more about their racial heritage. Most students, naturally curious about his or her ancestors, rushed to sign up. The DNA tests were performed through a simple mouth swab by a professor of genetics, Mark Shriver. He tested for four DNA groups: Western European, West African, East Asian, and Native American.

The results received national attention. Many students discovered that he or she was mixed race, including some who believed they were 100 percent Caucasian or Asian. One white student, for example, learned that 14 percent of his DNA was African and 6 percent East Asian. "I was like, oh my God, that's me," he recalls. A.J. Dobbins knew he was black and perhaps had a white ancestor, but he was amazed to learn that one's DNA is 28 percent Caucasian, 70 percent sub-Saharan African, and 2 percent Native American.

Many hope that this experiment will chip away at prejudice, shaking people out of his rigid thinking. Critics, however, say the genetic tests are incomplete. They call DNA testing a fad and scoff at some of Richard's students who hoped to test multiracial in order to upset his or her parents. Yet more and more everyday people and celebrities are getting their DNA tested. Columnist Leonard Pitts, Jr., Oprah, and Brazilian soccer star Obina, to name just three, have used DNA results and historic records to trace one's heritage.

C. Parallelism

Rewrite each of the following sentences, using parallel structure to accent parallel ideas.

EXAMPLE The summer in Louisiana is very hot and has high humidity. *The summer*

in Louisiana is very hot and humid.

1. Teresa is a gifted woman—a chemist, does the carpentry, and she can cook.

   _____

   _____

2. The shape of the rock, how big it was, and its color reminded me of a small turtle.

   _____

   _____

3. He is an affectionate husband, a thoughtful son, and kind to his kids.

   _____

   _____

4. Marvin was happy to win the chess tournament and he also felt surprised.

   _____

   _____

5. Dr. Tien is the kindest physician I know; she has the most concern of any physician I know.

   _____

   _____

6. Joe would rather work on a farm than spending time in an office.

_____

_____

7. Every afternoon in the mountains, it either rains or there is hail.

_____

_____

8. *Sesame Street* teaches children nursery rhymes, songs, how to be courteous, and being kind.

_____

_____

9. Alexis would rather give orders than taking them.

_____

_____

10. His writing reveals not only intelligence but also it is humorous.

_____

_____

PRACTICE 11

Write one sentence that is parallel to each sentence that follows, creating pairs of parallel sentences.

EXAMPLE On Friday night, she dressed in silk and sipped champagne.

On Monday morning, she put on her jeans and crammed for a history test.

1. When he was twenty, he worked seven days a week in a fruit store.

   _____

   _____

2. The child in me wants to run away from problems.

   _____

   _____

3. The home team charged enthusiastically onto the field.

   _____

   _____

4. "Work hard and keep your mouth shut" is my mother's formula for success.

   _____

   _____

5. The men thought the movie was amusing.

   _____

   _____

PRACTICE 12

The following paragraph contains both correct and faulty parallel structures. Revise the faulty parallelism.

During World War II, United States Marines who fought in the Pacific possessed a powerful weapon that was also unbeatable: Navajo Code Talkers. Creating a secret code, Code Talkers sent and were translating vital military information. Four hundred twenty

Navajos memorized the code, and it was used by them. It consisted of both common Navajo words and there were also about 400 invented words. For example, Code Talkers used the Navajo words for *owl, chicken hawk,* and *swallow* to describe different kinds of aircraft. Because Navajo is a complex language that is also uncommon, the Japanese military could not break the code. Although Code Talkers helped the Allied Forces win the war, their efforts were not publicly recognized until the code was declassified in 1968. On August 14, 1982, the first Navajo Code Talkers Day honored these heroes, who not only had risked their lives but also been developing one of the few unbroken codes in history.

PRACTICE 13

The following essay contains both correct and faulty parallel structures. Revise the faulty parallelism.

VINCENT VAN GOGH

Vincent Van Gogh sold only one painting in his lifetime, but his oil paintings later influenced modern art and establishing him as one of the greatest artists of all time. Born in Holland in 1853, Van Gogh struggled to find an inspiring career. After failing as a tutor and being a clergyman, he began to paint. Van Gogh's younger brother Theo supported him with money and also sending art supplies. Eventually, Van Gogh went to live with Theo in Paris, where the young artist was introduced to Impressionism, a style of painting that emphasizes light at different times of day. Using vivid colors and also with broad brush strokes, Van Gogh made powerful pictures full of feeling. His favorite subjects were landscapes, still lifes, sunflowers, and drawing everyday people. Perhaps his most famous picture, "Starry Night," shows a wild night sky over a French village, with the moon and stars swirling in fiery circles.

Starry Night, Vincent Van Gogh

When mental illness or feeling depressed clouded Van Gogh's spirit, Theo gentle and firmly urged him to keep painting. Gradually, however, the penniless Van Gogh sank into insanity and feeling despair. *Wheatfield with Crows*, completed shortly before his death, shows a darkening sky spattered black with crows. Van Gogh committed suicide in 1890; his devoted brother died six months later. Theo's widow Johanna took the paintings back to Holland and working hard to get recognition for her brother-in-law's genius. Thanks to Theo's encouragement during Vincent's lifetime and Johanna who made efforts after his death, the dynamic paintings of Van Gogh today are admired, studied, and receive love all over the world.

EXPLORING ONLINE

http://www.vangoghmuseum.nl/vgm/index.jsp

Visit the Van Gogh Museum in the Netherlands and explore. Take notes on your experience.

http://www.vangoghgallery.com/

Find "Wheatfield with Crows." Do you see any details in the painting that would suggest it was made just before the artist committed suicide?

CHAPTER 22

Revising for Sentence Variety

A: Mix Long and Short Sentences

B: Use a Question, a Command, or an Exclamation

C: Vary the Beginnings of Sentences

D: Vary Methods of Joining Ideas

E: Avoid Misplaced and Confusing Modifiers

F: Review and Practice

A. Mix Long and Short Sentences

PRACTICE 1

Revise and rewrite the following paragraph in a variety of sentence lengths. Recombine sentences in any way you wish. You may add connecting words or drop words, but do not alter the meaning of the paragraph. Compare your work with a fellow student's.

    The park is alive with motion today. Joggers pound up and down the boardwalk. Old folks watch them from the benches. Couples row boats across the lake. The boats are green and wooden. Two teenagers hurl a Frisbee back and forth. They yell and leap. A shaggy white dog dashes in from nowhere. He snatches the red disk in his mouth. He bounds away. The teenagers run after him.

_____

_____

_____

_____

_____

_____

B. Use a Question, a Command, or an Exclamation

PRACTICE 1A

Go back through some essays you have already written. Choose an essay, and change the first sentence to a question, a command, or an exclamation. You may want to exchange papers with a classmate, to compare your new introductions.

C. Vary the Beginnings of Sentences

PRACTICE 2

Rewrite the following sentences by shifting the adverbs to the beginning. Punctuate correctly.

EXAMPLE He skillfully prepared the engine for the race.

Skillfully, he prepared the engine for the race. _____

1. Two deer moved silently across the clearing.

_____

2. The chief of the research division occasionally visits the lab.

   _____

3. Proofread your writing always.

   _____

4. Children of alcoholics often marry alcoholics.

   _____

5. Jake foolishly lied to his supervisor.

   _____

PRACTICE 3

Begin each of the following sentences with an appropriate adverb. Punctuate correctly.

1. _____ the detective approached the ticking suitcase.

2. _____ Maria Sharapova powered a forehand past her opponent.

3. _____ she received her check for $25,000 from the state lottery.

4. _____ he left the beach.

5. _____ the submarine sank out of sight.

PRACTICE 4

Write three sentences of your own that begin with adverbs. Use different adverbs from those in Practices 2 and 3; if you wish, use *graciously, furiously, sometimes.* Punctuate correctly.

1. _____

2. _____

3. _____

PRACTICE 5

Underline the prepositional phrases in each sentence. Some sentences contain more than one prepositional phrase. Rewrite each sentence by shifting a prepositional phrase to the beginning. Punctuate correctly.

EXAMPLE A large owl <u>with gray feathers</u> watched us <u>from the oak tree.</u>

From the oak tree, a large owl with gray feathers watched us.

1. The coffee maker turned itself on at seven o'clock sharp.

   _____

   _____

2. A growling Doberman paced behind the chainlink fence.

   _____

   _____

3. A man and a woman held hands under the street lamp.

   _____

   _____

4. They have sold nothing except athletic shoes for years.

   _____

   _____

5. A group of men played checkers and drank iced tea beside the small shop.

   _____

   _____

PRACTICE 6

Begin each of the following sentences with a different prepositional phrase. Refer to the list and be creative. Punctuate correctly.

1. _____ we ordered potato skins, salad, and beer.

2. _____ a woman in horn-rimmed glasses balanced her checkbook.

3. _____ everyone congratulated Jim on his promotion.

4. _____ one can see huge sculptures in wood, metal, and stone.

5. _____ three large helium-filled balloons drifted.

PRACTICE 7

Write three sentences of your own that begin with prepositional phrases. Use these phrases if you wish: *in the dentist's office, under that stack of books, behind his friendly smile.* Punctuate correctly.

1. _____

2. _____

3. _____

D. Vary Methods of Joining Ideas*

PRACTICE 8

Combine each pair of short sentences into one sentence with a compound predicate. Use *and, but, or,* and *yet.* Punctuate correctly.

EXAMPLE   Toby smeared peanut butter on a thick slice of white bread.
He devoured the treat in thirty seconds.

Toby smeared peanut butter on a thick slice of white bread and devoured the

treat in thirty seconds.

---

* For work on joining ideas with coordination and subordination, see Chapter 26, "Coordination and Sub-ordination," in the companion text and this workbook.

1. Americans eat more than 800 million pounds of peanut butter.
   They spend more than $1 billion on the product each year.

   _____

   _____

2. Peanut butter was first concocted in the 1890s.
   It did not become the food we know for thirty years.

   _____

   _____

3. George Washington Carver did not discover peanut butter.
   He published many recipes for pastes much like it.

   _____

   _____

4. The average American becomes a peanut butter lover in childhood.
   He or she loses enthusiasm for it later on.

   _____

   _____

5. Older adults regain their passion for peanut butter.
   They consume great quantities of the delicious stuff.

   _____

   _____

PRACTICE 9

Complete the following compound predicates. Do *not* repeat the subjects.

1. Three Korean writers visited the campus and _____

   _____

2. The singer breathed heavily into the microphone but _____

   _____

3. Take these cans to the recycling center or _____

_____

4. The newspaper printed the story yet _____

_____

5. Three men burst into the back room and _____

_____

PRACTICE 10

Write three sentences with compound predicates. Be careful to punctuate correctly.

1. _____

2. _____

3. _____

PRACTICE 11

Combine the following pairs of sentences by converting the first sentence into an *-ing* modifier. Make sure the subject of the main clause directly follows the *-ing* modifier. Punctuate correctly.

EXAMPLE Jake searched for his needle-nose pliers.
He completely emptied the tool chest.

Searching for his needle-nose pliers, Jake completely emptied the tool chest.

1. She installed the air conditioner.
She saved herself $50 in labor.

_____

_____

2. The surgeons raced against time.
    The surgeons performed a liver transplant on the child.

    _____

    _____

3. They conducted a survey of Jackson Heights residents.
    They found that most opposed construction of the airport.

    _____

    _____

4. Three flares spiraled upward from the little boat.
    They exploded against the night sky.

    _____

    _____

5. Virgil danced in the Pennsylvania Ballet.
    Virgil learned discipline and self-control.

    _____

    _____

6. The hen squawked loudly.
    The hen fluttered out of our path.

    _____

    _____

7. The engineer made a routine check of the blueprints.
    He discovered a flaw in the design.

    _____

    _____

8. Dr. Jackson opened commencement exercises with a humorous story.
    He put everyone at ease.

    _____

    _____

PRACTICE 12

Add either an introductory *-ing* modifier *or* a main clause to each sentence. Make sure that each *-ing* modifier refers clearly to the subject of the main clause.

EXAMPLE *Reading a book a week,* Jeff increased his vocabulary.

Exercising every day, *I lost five pounds* .

1. _____, she felt a sense of accomplishment.

2. Growing up in Hollywood, _____

_____

3. _____, the father and son were reconciled.

4. Interviewing his relatives, _____

_____

5. _____, the wrecking ball swung through the air and smashed into the brick wall.

PRACTICE 13

Write three sentences of your own that begin with *-ing* modifiers. Make sure that the subject of the sentence follows the modifier and be careful of the punctuation.

1. _____

_____

2. _____

_____

3. _____

_____

PRACTICE 14

Combine each pair of sentences into one sentence that begins with a past participial modifier. Convert the sentence containing a form of *to be* plus a past participle into a past participial modifier that introduces the new sentence.

EXAMPLE   Duffy was surprised by the interruption.
He lost his train of thought.

Surprised by the interruption, Duffy lost his train of thought.

1. My mother was married at the age of sixteen.
    My mother never finished high school.

    _____

    _____

2. The 2:30 flight was delayed by an electrical storm.
    It arrived in Lexington three hours late.

    _____

    _____

3. The old car was waxed and polished.
    It shone in the sun.

    _____

    _____

4. The house was built by Frank Lloyd Wright.
    It has become famous.

    _____

    _____

5. The Nineteenth Amendment was ratified in 1920.
    It gave women the right to vote.

    _____

    _____

6. The manuscript seems impossible to decipher.
   It is written in code.

   _____

   _____

7. Dr. Bentley will address the premed students.
   He has been recognized for his contributions in the field of immunology.

   _____

   _____

8. Mrs. Witherspoon was exhausted by night classes.
   She declined the chance to work overtime.

   _____

   _____

PRACTICE 15

Complete each sentence by filling in *either* the past participial modifier *or* the main clause. Remember, the past participial modifier must clearly refer to the subject of the main clause.

> **EXAMPLE** Wrapped in blue paper and tied with string, *the gift arrived* .
>
> *Chosen to represent the team*, Phil proudly accepted the trophy.

1. Made of gold and set with precious stones, _____

2. Overwhelmed by the response to her ad in *The Star*, _____

   _____

3. _____ , Tom left no forwarding

   address.

4. _____ , we found a huge basket

   of fresh fruit on the steps.

5. Astonished by the scene before her, _____

PRACTICE 16

Write three sentences of your own that begin with past participial modifiers. If you wish, use participles from this list:

shocked	dressed	hidden	bent
awakened	lost	stuffed	rewired

Make sure that the subject of the sentence clearly follows the modifier.

1. _____

   _____

2. _____

   _____

3. _____

   _____

PRACTICE 17

Combine the following pairs of sentences by making the *second sentence* an appositive. Punctuate correctly.

These appositives should occur at the *beginning* of the sentences.

EXAMPLE   My uncle taught me to use watercolors.
He is a well-known artist.

A well-known artist, my uncle taught me to use watercolors.

1. Dan has saved many lives.
   He is a dedicated firefighter.

   _____

   _____

2. Acupuncture is becoming popular in the United States.
   It is an ancient Chinese healing system.

   _____

   _____

3. The Cromwell Hotel was built in 1806.
   It is an elegant example of Mexican architecture.

   _____

   _____

These appositives should occur in the *middle* of the sentences. Punctuate correctly.

EXAMPLE His American history course is always popular with students.
   It is an introductory survey.

   His American history course, an introductory survey, is always popular with

   students.

4. The Korean Ping-Pong champion won ten games in a row.
   She is a small and wiry athlete.

   _____

   _____

5. The pituitary is located below the brain.
   It is the body's master gland.

   _____

   _____

6. The elevator shudders violently and begins to rise.
   It is an ancient box of wood and hope.

   _____

   _____

These appositives should occur at the *end* of the sentences. Punctuate correctly.

EXAMPLE   I hate fried asparagus.
It is a vile dish.

I hate fried asparagus, a vile dish.

7. Jennifer flaunted her new camera.
It was a Nikon with a telephoto lens.

_____

_____

8. At the intersection stood a hitchhiker.
He was a young man dressed in a tuxedo.

_____

_____

9. We met for pancakes at the Cosmic Cafe.
It was a greasy diner on the corner of 10th and Vine.

_____

_____

PRACTICE 18

Write three sentences using appositives. In one sentence, place the appositive at the *beginning*; in one sentence, place the appositive in the *middle*; and in one sentence, place it at the *end*.

1. _____

_____

2. _____

_____

3. _____

_____

PRACTICE 19

Combine each pair of sentences by changing the second sentence into a relative clause introduced by *who, which,* or *that.* Remember, *who* refers to persons, *that* refers to persons or things, and *which* refers to things.

These sentences require nonrestrictive relative clauses. Punctuate correctly.

EXAMPLE My cousin will spend the summer hiking in the Rockies.
She lives in Indiana.

My cousin, who lives in Indiana, will spend the summer hiking in the Rockies.

1. Scrabble has greatly increased my vocabulary.
It is my favorite game.

_____

_____

2. Contestants on game shows often make fools of themselves.
They may travel thousands of miles to play.

_____

_____

3. Arabic is a difficult language to learn.
It has a complicated verb system.

_____

_____

The next sentences require restrictive relative clauses. Punctuate correctly.

EXAMPLE He described a state of mind.
I have experienced it.

He described a state of mind that I have experienced.

4. The house is for sale.
    I was born in it.

    _____

    _____

5. My boss likes reports.
    They are clear and to the point.

    _____

    _____

6. People know how intelligent birds are.
    They have owned a bird.

    _____

    _____

PRACTICE 20

Combine each pair of sentences by changing one into a relative clause introduced by *who, which,* or *that*. Remember, *who* refers to persons, *that* refers to persons or things, and *which* refers to things.

Be careful of the punctuation. (Hint: *Which* clauses are usually set off by commas and *that* clauses are usually not.)

1. Her grandfather enjoys scuba diving.
    He is seventy-seven years old.

    _____

    _____

2. You just dropped an antique pitcher.
    It was worth two thousand dollars.

    _____

    _____

3. Parenthood has taught me acceptance, forgiveness, and love.
   It used to terrify me.

   _____

   _____

4. James Fenimore Cooper was expelled from college.
   He later became a famous American novelist.

   _____

   _____

5. The verb *to hector* means "to bully someone."
   It derives from a character in Greek literature.

   _____

   _____

E. Avoid Misplaced and Confusing Modifiers

PRACTICE 21

Correct any confusing, misplaced, or dangling modifiers. Rearrange words or rewrite as necessary.

1. Plump sausages, the dinner guests looked forward to the main course.

   _____

   _____

2. Soaring over the treetops in a hot air balloon, the view was spectacular.

   _____

   _____

3. Powered by hydrogen, the engineers designed a new kind of car.

_____

_____

4. I introduced my boyfriend to my father, who wanted to marry me.

_____

_____

5. Revised to highlight his computer expertise, Marcelo was proud of his new résumé.

_____

_____

6. Jim, who loved to lick car windows, drove his dog to the vet.

_____

_____

7. Banging inside the dryer, Carla heard the lost keys.

_____

_____

8. We complained about the proposed building to the mayor, which we found ugly and too large for the neighborhood.

_____

_____

F. Review and Practice

PRACTICE 22

Revise and then rewrite this essay, aiming for sentence variety. Vary the length and pattern of the sentences. Vary the beginnings of some sentences. Join two sentences in any way you wish, adding appropriate connecting words or dropping unnecessary words. Punctuate correctly.

LEADING LADY

As a child, Michelle Robinson lived with her doting parents and brother. They lived in a one-bedroom apartment on Chicago's South Side. Her father believed in his children's potential. He disciplined them with only a look of severe disappointment. Michelle's brother Craig was a basketball star. He earned As almost effortlessly. She studied hard. She struggled to overcome her discomfort with test-taking. Craig won a scholarship to Princeton University. Michelle decided to apply there as well.

It was the 1980s. The Princeton campus was largely white. Some students assumed things. They assumed that Michelle and her two close friends came to Princeton through affirmative action, not achievement. The three young women had probing discussions. They discussed social barriers and success. Michelle majored in sociology, the study of human social behavior. Her thesis explored race, success, and the black community. Michelle had high grades and a maturing point of view. She attended Harvard Law School. She graduated. She joined a Chicago law firm.

First Lady Michelle Obama on a school visit

Her future husband was a dynamic young man. He was named Barack Obama. He interned at her firm. They soon married. They waited several years before having two girls. Barack's star climbed higher. Michelle successfully balanced the demands of motherhood, work, and intense campaigning. Suddenly, she was traveling the country and the world. She was meeting everyday people and royalty. To many, she represented the stylish, multitasking modern woman. The lessons of a lifetime served her well.

On November 4, 2008, Barack and Michelle Obama stepped into history, as President and First Lady of the United States.

LEADING LADY

_____

_____

_____

_____

_____

_____

_____

_____

_____

_____

_____

_____

_____

_____

_____

_____

CHAPTER 23

Revising for Language Awareness

A: Exact Language: Avoiding Vagueness

B: Concise Language: Avoiding Wordiness

C: Fresh Language: Avoiding Triteness

D: Figurative Language: Similes and Metaphors

A. Exact Language: Avoiding Vagueness

PRACTICE 1

Lively verbs are a great asset to any writer. The following sentences contain four overused general verbs—*to walk, to see, to eat,* and *to be*. In each case, replace the general verb in parentheses with a more exact verb *chosen to fit the context of the sentence*. Use a different verb in every sentence. Consult a dictionary or thesaurus* if you wish.

EXAMPLES In no particular hurry, we _____*strolled*_____ (walked) through the botanical gardens.

Jane _____*fidgets*_____ (is) at her desk and watches the clock.

———

* A thesaurus is a book of *synonyms*—words that have the same or similar meanings.

1. With guns drawn, three police officers _____ (walked) toward the door of the warehouse.

2 As we stared in fascination, an orange lizard _____ (walked) up the wall.

3. The four-year-old _____ (walked) onto the patio in her mother's high-heeled shoes.

4. A furious customer _____ (walked) into the manager's office.

5. Two people who _____ (saw) the accident must testify in court.

6. We crouched for hours in the underbrush just to _____ (see) a rare white fox.

7. Three makeshift wooden rafts were _____ (seen) off the coast this morning.

8. For two years, the zoologist _____ (saw) the behavior of bears in the wild.

9. There was the cat, delicately _____ (eating) my fern!

10. Senator Gorman astounded the guests by loudly _____ (eating) his soup.

11. All through the movie, she _____ (ate) hard candies in the back row.

12. Within seconds, Dan had bought two tacos from a street vendor and _____ (eaten) them both.

13. During rush hour, the temperature hit 98 degrees, and dozens of cars _____ (were) on the highway.

14. A young man _____ (is) on a stretcher in the emergency room.

15. Workers who _____ (are) at desks all day should make special efforts to exercise.

16. Professor Nuzzo _____ (was) in front of the blackboard, excited about this new solution to the math problem.

PRACTICE 2

The following sentences contain dull, vague language. Revise them using vivid verbs, specific nouns, and colorful adjectives. As the examples show, you may add and delete words.

EXAMPLES   A dog lies down in the shade.

A mangy collie flops down in the shade of a parked car

My head hurts

My head throbs

I have shooting pains in the left side of my head.

1. Everything about the man looked mean.

   _____

   _____

2. I feel good today for several reasons.

   _____

   _____

3. A woman in unusual clothes went down the street.

   _____

   _____

4. The sunlight made the yard look pretty.

   _____

   _____

5. What the company did bothered the townspeople.

   _____

   _____

6. The pediatrician's waiting room was crowded.

   _____

   _____

7. As soon as he gets home from work, he hears the voice of his pet asking for dinner.

_____

_____

8. The noises of construction filled the street.

_____

_____

9. When I was sick, you were helpful.

_____

_____

10. This college does things that make the students feel bad.

_____

_____

PRACTICE 3

A word that works effectively in one sentence might not work in another sentence. In searching for the right word, always consider the **context** of the sentence into which the word must fit. Read each of the following sentences for meaning. Then circle the word in parentheses that *most exactly fits* the context of the sentence.

EXAMPLE   Machu Picchu, which means "old peak" in the Quechua (words, language, lingo), is known as the "Lost City of the Incas."

1. Ever since the ruins of Machu Picchu were (buried, invented, discovered) in 1911 by Yale archaeologist Hiram Bingham, people all over the world have been fascinated by this mysterious site.

2. The ancient city (perches, hangs, wobbles) high atop a peak in the rugged Andes Mountains of Peru.

3. In the 1400s, using gray Andes granite, the Inca people (arranged, constructed, piled) the palace, temples, baths, and houses of Machu Picchu.

4. The carved stone blocks are so (strong, massive, humongous) that thousands of men would have been needed to move just one of them into place.

5. The city served not only as a (hideout, getaway, retreat) and fortress for the nobility but also as an observatory.

6. Many ceremonies took place around the Intihuatana stone, a kind of sundial that (casts, manufactures, emits) no shadow at noon on the two equinoxes, in March and in September.

7. According to legend, when spiritually sensitive people touch their foreheads to the Intihuatana stone, it (magically, accidentally, weirdly) opens their vision to the spirit world.

View of Machu Picchu, Peru

© Wes Walker/Lonely Planet Images

8. In 1533, Spanish conquistadors (ruthlessly, destructively, properly) destroyed the Inca civilization, but the invaders never found Machu Picchu.

9. Nevertheless, the cloud-capped city was (abandoned, missed, set aside) for 400 years.

10. Today, however, many tourists (enjoy, battle, are awed by) altitude sickness just to trek up the mountain and gaze upon this beautiful, well-preserved sanctuary.

PRACTICE 4

The following paragraph begins a mystery story. Using specific and vivid language, revise the paragraph to make it as exciting as possible. Then finish the story; be careful to avoid vague language.

The weather was bad. I was in the house alone, with a funny feeling that something was going to happen. Someone knocked at the door. I got up to answer it and found someone outside. She looked familiar, but I didn't know from where or when. Then I recognized her as a person from my past. I let her in although I was not sure I had done the right thing.

_____

_____

_____

_____

_____

_____

_____

_____

_____

_____

B. Concise Language: Avoiding Wordiness

The following sentences are *wordy*. Make them more *concise* by crossing out or replacing unnecessary words or by combining two sentences into one concise sentence. Rewrite each new sentence on the lines beneath, capitalizing and punctuating correctly.

EXAMPLES   The U.S. Census uncovers many interesting facts that have a lot of truth to them.

The U.S. Census uncovers many interesting facts.

In the year 1810, Philadelphia was called the cigar capital of the United States. The reason why was because the census reported that the city produced 16 million cigars each year.

In 1810, Philadelphia was called the cigar capital of the United States

because the census reported that the city produced 16 million each year.

1. The Constitution requires and says that the federal government of the United States must take a national census every ten years.

   _____

   _____

2. At first, the original function of the census was to ensure fair taxation and representation.

   _____

   _____

3. Since the first count in 1790, however, the census has been controversial. There are several reasons why the census has been controversial.

   _____

   _____

4. One reason why is because there are always some people who aren't included.

   _____

   _____

5. The 1990 census, for example, missed almost 5 million people, many of whom were homeless with no place to live.

   _____

   _____

6. For the 2000 census, the Census Bureau considered using statistical methods. The statistical methods would have been used instead of the traditional direct head count.

   _____

   _____

7. The Bureau would have directly counted about 90 percent of U.S. residents who live in the United States and then estimated the number and characteristics of the remainder of the rest of the people.

   _____

   _____

8. Those who opposed the idea believed that in their opinion statistical methods would have introduced new errors that were mistaken into the count.

   _____

   _____

9. The distribution of $100 billion in money, as well as the balance of power in the House of Representatives, depended on how and in which manner the census was conducted.

   _____

   _____

10. Despite controversy, the U.S. census still continues to serve a beneficial purpose that is for the good of the United States.

   _____

   _____

PRACTICE 6

Rewrite this essay *concisely*, cutting out all unnecessary words. Reword or combine sentences if you wish, but do not alter the meaning.

DR. ALICE HAMILTON, MEDICAL PIONEER

At the age of forty years old, Dr. Alice Hamilton became a pioneer in the field of industrial medicine. In 1910, the governor of Illinois appointed her to investigate rumors that people who were doing the work in Chicago's paint factories were dying from lead poisoning. The result of her investigation was the first state law that was passed to protect workers.

The following year, the U.S. Department of Labor hired this woman, Dr. Hamilton to study industrial illness throughout the country of the United States. In the next decade, she researched and studied many occupational diseases, including tuberculosis among quarry workers and silicosis—clogged lungs—among sandblasters. To gather information, Dr. Hamilton went to the workplace—deep in mines, quarries, and underwater tunnels. She also spoke to the workers in their homes where they lived.

With great zeal, Dr. Hamilton spread her message about poor health conditions on the job. What happened with her reports is that they led to new safety regulations, workers' compensation insurance, and improved working conditions in many industries. She wrote many popular articles and spoke to groups of interested citizens. In the year of 1919, she became the first woman to hold courses and teach at Harvard University. Her textbook which she wrote, *Industrial Poisons in the U.S.,* became the standard book on the subject. By the time she died in 1970—she was 101—she had done much to improve the plight of many working people. The reason why she is remembered today is because she cared at a time when many others seemed not to care at all.

C. Fresh Language: Avoiding Triteness

PRACTICE 7

Cross out clichés and trite expressions in the following sentences and replace them with fresh and exact language of your own.

1. Getting a good job in this cold cruel economy can be easier said than done.

2. Many Americans are living hand to mouth, and even college graduates may be hitting a brick wall in the job market.

3. The keys are to keep your chin up and think outside the box, says career coach Bob Martinez.

4. He offers three useful tips for job seekers who are between a rock and a hard place.

5. First, don't cling like there's no tomorrow to one limited career goal.

6. If your dream is to become assistant marketing director for the Portland Trailblazers, consider starting at any sports organization as low man on the totem pole by getting coffee and helping out.

7. Don't throw out the baby with the bathwater by ruling out an internship.

8. Next, don't rely only on tried and true websites like *monster.com*.

9. Reach out and touch someone by networking in person because having a contact inside the company is often the best way to get hired.

10. Last but not least, at job fairs or interviews, set yourself apart by bringing a writing sample or demonstrating your people skills.

D. Figurative Language: Similes and Metaphors

PRACTICE 8

The author of the following paragraph describes a lake as winter turns to spring. She uses at least two similes and two metaphors. Underline the similes and circle the metaphors.

Mornings, a transparent pane of ice lies over the meltwater. I peer through and see some kind of water bug—perhaps a leech—paddling like a sea turtle between green ladders of lakeweed. Cattails and sweetgrass from the previous summer are bone dry, marked with black mold spots, and bend like elbows into the ice.

—Gretel Erlich, "Spring," *Antaeus*

PRACTICE 9

Think of several similes to complete each sentence that follows. Be creative! Then underline your favorite simile, the one that best completes each sentence.

EXAMPLE   My English class is like   *an orchestra.*
the Everglades.
an action movie.
a vegetable garden.

1. Job hunting is like _____   2. Writing well is like _____

_____   _____

_____   _____

_____   _____

3. My room looks like _____

4. Marriage is like _____

_____

_____

_____

_____

_____

_____

PRACTICE 10

Think of several metaphors to complete each sentence that follows. Jot down three or four ideas, and then underline the metaphor that best completes each sentence.

EXAMPLE   Love is

a blood transfusion.

a sunrise.

a magic mirror.

a roller coaster ride.

1. The Internet is_____

3. My car is_____

_____

_____

_____

_____

_____

_____

2. Registration is_____

4. Courage is_____

_____

_____

_____

_____

_____

_____

CHAPTER 24

Putting Your Revision Skills to Work

Because revising, like writing, is a personal process, the best practice is to revise your own paragraphs and essays. Nevertheless, here is a first draft that needs revising.

Revise it *as if you had written it.* Mark your revisions on the first draft, using and building on the good parts, crossing out unnecessary words, rewriting unclear or awkward sentences, adding details, and perhaps reordering parts. Then, recopy your final draft on the lines. Especially, ask yourself these questions:

Are my verb tenses and pronouns consistent?
Have I used parallel structure to highlight parallel ideas?
Have I varied the length and type of my sentences?
Is my language exact, concise, and fresh?

First Draft

BREAKING THE YO-YO SYNDROME

For years, I was a yo-yo dieter. I bounced from fad diets to eating binges when I ate a lot. This leaves you tired and with depression. Along the way, though, I learned a few things. As a result, I personally will never go on a diet again for the rest of my life.

First of all, diets are unhealthy. Some of the low carbohydrate diets are high in fat. Accumulating fat through meat, eggs, and the eating of cheese can raise blood levels of cholesterol and led to artery and heart disease. Other diets are too high in protein and can cause kidney ailments, and other things can go wrong with your body, too. Most diets also leave you deficient in essential vitamins and minerals that are necessary to health, such as calcium and iron.

In addition, diets are short-term. I lose about ten pounds. I wind up gaining more weight than I originally lost. I also get sick and tired of the restricted diet. On one diet, I ate cabbage soup for breakfast, lunch, and dinner. You are allowed to eat some fruit on day one, some vegetables on day two, and so on, but mostly you are supposed to eat cabbage soup. After a week, I never want to see a bowl of cabbage soup again. Because the diet was nutritionally unbalanced, I ended up craving bread, meat, and all the other foods I am not supposed to eat. Moreover, in the short-term, all one loses is water. You cannot lose body fat unless you reduce regularly and at a steady rate over a long period of time.

The last diet I try was a fat-free diet. On this diet I actually gained weight while dieting. I am surprised to discover that you can gain weight on a fat-free diet snacking on fat-free cookies, ice cream, and cheese and crackers. I also learn that the body needs fat—in particular, the unsaturated fat in foods like olive oil, nuts, avocados, and salad dressings. If a dieter takes in too little fat, you are constantly hungry. Furthermore, the body thinks it is starving, so it makes every effort to try to conserve fat, which makes it much harder for one to lose weight.

In place of fad diets, I now follow a long-range plan. It is sensible and improved my health. I eat three well-balanced meals, exercise daily, and am meeting regularly with my support group for weight control. I am much happier and don't weigh as much than I used to be.

Revised Draft

BREAKING THE YO-YO SYNDROME

_____

_____

_____

_____

_____

_____

_____

"I'm going to order a broiled, skinless chicken breast, but I want you to bring me lasagna and garlic bread by mistake."

Unit 6 Reviewing the Basics

222

CHAPTER 25

The Simple Sentence

A: Defining and Spotting Subjects

B: Spotting Prepositional Phrases

C: Defining and Spotting Verbs

A. Defining and Spotting Subjects

PRACTICE 1

Circle the subjects in these sentences.

1. Do you know the origin and customs of Kwanzaa?

2. This African-American holiday celebrates black heritage and lasts for seven days—from December 26 through January 1.

3. Maulana Karenga introduced Kwanzaa to America in 1966.

4. In Swahili, Kwanzaa means "first fruits of the harvest."

5. During the holiday, families share simple meals of foods from the Caribbean, Africa, South America, and the American South.

6. Specific foods have special meanings.

7. For instance, certain fruits and vegetables represent the products of group effort.

8. Another important symbol is corn, which stands for children.

Lighting the candles at Kwanza

9. At each dinner, celebrants light a black, red, or green candle and discuss one of the seven principles of Kwanzaa.

10. These seven principles are unity, self-determination, collective work and responsibility, cooperative economics, purpose, creativity, and faith.

B. Spotting Prepositional Phrases

PRACTICE 2

Cross out the prepositional phrases in each sentence. Then circle the subject of the sentence.

1. From 6 A.M. until 10 A.M., Angel works out.

2. Local buses for Newark leave every hour.

3. Three of my friends take singing lessons.

4. That man between Ralph and Cynthia is the famous actor Hank the Hunk.

5. Near the door, a pile of laundry sits in a basket.

6. Toward evening, the houses across the river disappear in the thick fog.

7. Before class, Helena and I meet for coffee.

8. In one corner of the lab, beakers of colored liquid bubbled and boiled.

C. Defining and Spotting Verbs

PRACTICE 3

Underline the verbs in these sentences.

1. She exposes insurance cheats and lying spouses.

2. She spies on suspected nannies with a tiny camera.

3. Chardee Anderson might have become a police officer.

4. However, wearing a uniform every day did not appeal to her.

5. Instead, she became a private investigator.

6. Only one of every ten private investigators is a woman.

7. Women in this business might face criticism or even sexual harassment.

8. On the other hand, many clients prefer a female P.I. and can talk more freely with her.

9. Chardee enjoys her lack of routine and even the spy equipment.

10. Thanks to technology, cameras and tape recorders have gotten small enough to fit

into a Beanie Baby, a pair of sunglasses, or even a ballpoint pen.

PRACTICE 4　　**REVIEW**

Circle the subjects and underline the verbs in the following sentences. First, cross out any prepositional phrases.

1. Do you watch videos on YouTube?

2. This hugely popular website grew quickly out of an invention by three friends.

3. One night, Steve Chen shot a video of his pals Chad Hurley and Jawed Karim.

4. Surprisingly, the three buddies could find no easy way of sharing this video online.

5. Their solution was a video-sharing website.

6. Their friends loved it and inspired the young men to launch YouTube in 2005.

7. Within two years, YouTube had attracted millions of visitors and millions of dollars from investors.

8. Very easily, users can view or post videos on the site.

9. Today, YouTube's millions of videos inspire creativity, news reporting by everyday people, and some engaging craziness.

CHAPTER 26

Coordination and Subordination

A: Coordination

B: Subordination

C: Semicolons

D: Conjunctive Adverbs

E: Review

A. Coordination

PRACTICE 1

Read the following sentences for meaning. Then fill in the coordinating conjunction that *best* expresses the relationship between the two clauses. Don't forget to add the comma.

1. In 1853, a customer at Moon Lake Lodge in Saratoga, New York, thought his fried

   potatoes were too thick and soggy _____ he sent them back to the kitchen.

2. The Native-American/African-American chef, George Crum, took offense at this

   criticism of his cooking _____ he was a confident and cranky fellow.

3. Crum wanted to annoy his fussy customer_____ he angrily sliced some potatoes very thin, poured salt all over them, and fried them hard.

4. The chef expected the complaining patron to leave in a huff _____ he didn't.

5. Instead, the crispy potato thins pleased the customer immensely _____ he ordered more.

6. Crum, who soon opened his own restaurant, called his lucky invention "potato crunches" _____ he later renamed them "Saratoga Chips."

7. In the 1920s, traveling salesman Herman Lay began selling potato chips out of the trunk of his car _____ other companies began manufacturing them, too.

8. Now customers could order the tasty treat in restaurants _____ they could munch them at home.

9. However, chips at the bottom of the barrel or tin packaging would not stay fresh _____ would they stay crispy.

10. Entrepreneur Laura Scudder solved this problem by putting the chips between sheets of wax paper that she ironed together _____ the potato chip quickly became America's favorite snack.

PRACTICE 2

Combine these simple sentences with a coordinating conjunction. Punctuate correctly.

1. My daughter wants to be a mechanic. She spends every spare minute at the garage.

   _____

   _____

2. Ron dared not look over the edge. Heights made him dizzy.

_____

_____

3. Tasha's living room is cozy. Her guests always gather in the kitchen.

_____

_____

4. Meet me by the bicycle rack. Meet me at Lulu's Nut Shop.

_____

_____

5. In 1969, the first astronauts landed on the moon. Most Americans felt proud.

_____

_____

B. Subordination

PRACTICE 3

Read the following sentences for meaning. Then fill in the subordinating conjunction that _best_ expresses the relationship between the two clauses.

1. We could see very clearly last night _____ the moon was so bright.

2. Violet read _Sports Illustrated_ _____ Daisy walked in the woods.

3. _____ it is cold outside, our new wood-burning Franklin stove keeps us

   warm.

4. The students buzzed with excitement _____ Professor Hargrave

   announced that classes would be held at the zoo.

5. _____ his shoulder loosens up a bit, Ron will stay on the bench.

PRACTICE 4

Punctuate the following sentences by adding a comma where necessary. Put a *C* after any correct sentences.

1. Thousands of low-income children in Venezuela have been given a new life because Jose Antonio Abreu taught them to play classical music.

2. While some people only talked about the poverty and drugs destroying many young Venezuelans Abreu took action.

3. After he convinced government leaders that musical training builds self-worth, Abreu got funding to start children's orchestras.

4. The results have been amazing as communities proudly support their young musicians.

5. When the children practice their violins or oboes they are also learning discipline, valuable skills, and the joys of musical teamwork.

6. The program ignores pop and tropical musicians like Christina Aguilera and Oscar de Leon because Abreu wants his students to master classical artists like Mozart and Beethoven.

Brothers Wilfredo and Onil Galarraga received instruments and new opportunities, thanks to the Venezuelan Children's Orchestra.

7. Since the program was launched a generation of talented Venezuelan musicians is already performing, composing, and teaching classical music.

8. Because the program has been so successful it is the model for new youth orchestras now being formed throughout the world.

PRACTICE 5

Combine each pair of the following ideas by using a subordinating conjunction. Write each combination twice, once with the subordinating conjunction at the beginning of the sentence and once with the subordinating conjunction in the middle of the sentence. Punctuate correctly.

EXAMPLE

We stayed on the beach.
The sun went down.

We stayed on the beach until the sun went down.

Until the sun went down, we stayed on the beach.

_____

_____

1. This cactus has flourished.

2. I talk to it every day.

_____

_____

_____

_____

3. Ralph takes the train to Philadelphia.

4. He likes to sit by the window.

_____

_____

_____

_____

5. I had known you were coming.

6. I would have vacuumed the guest room.

_____

_____

_____

_____

7. He was the first person to eat a slice of meat between two pieces of bread.

8. The sandwich was named after the Earl of Sandwich.

_____

_____

_____

_____

9. Akila was about to answer the final question.

10. The buzzer sounded.

_____

_____

_____

_____

11. Few soap operas remain on the radio.

12. Daytime television is filled with them.

_____

_____

_____

_____

13. She connected the speakers.

14. The room filled with glorious sound.

_____

_____

_____

_____

15. The chimney spewed black smoke and soot.

16. Nobody complained to the local environmental agency.

_____

_____

_____

_____

C. Semicolons

PRACTICE 6

Combine each pair of independent clauses by placing a semicolon between them.

1. The senator appeared ill at ease at the news conference he seemed afraid of saying the wrong thing.

2. The new seed catalogue, a fifteen-hundred-page volume, was misplaced the volume weighed ten pounds.

3. On Thursday evening, Hector decided to go camping on Friday morning, he packed his bags and left.

4. This stream is full of trout every spring men and women with waders and fly rods arrive on its banks.

5. Not a single store was open at that hour not a soul walked the streets.

PRACTICE 7

Each independent clause that follows is the first half of a sentence. Add a semicolon and a second independent clause. Make sure your second thought is also independent and can stand alone.

1. At 2 A.M. I stumbled toward the ringing telephone _____

   _____

2. *People* magazine published my letter to the editor _____

   _____

3. The officer pulled over the speeding pickup truck _____

   _____

4. Cameras are not permitted in the museum _____

_____

5. Computer skills are increasingly important in many careers _____

_____

D. Conjunctive Adverbs

PRACTICE 8

Punctuate each sentence correctly by adding a semicolon, a comma, or both, where necessary. Put a C after any correct sentences.

1. I hate to wash my car windows nevertheless it's a job that must be done.

2. Sonia doesn't know how to play chess however she would like to learn.

3. Dean Fader is very funny in fact he could be a professional comedian.

4. Deep water makes Maurice nervous therefore he does not want to join the scuba dive team.

5. I like this painting; the soft colors remind me of tropical sunsets.

6. The faculty approved of the new trimester system; furthermore, the students liked it too.

7. Bill has an iPod plugged into his ear all day consequently he misses a lot of good conversations.

8. We toured the darkroom then we watched an actual photo shoot.

PRACTICE 9

Proofread this paragraph for coordination errors, missing punctuation, and one conjunctive adverb that does not express the right relationship between ideas. Add the correct punctuation or write your corrections above the lines, using a mix of semicolons and semicolons plus conjunctive adverbs.

(1) Successful college students learn how to take good notes in class. (2) One

excellent note-taking method is the Cornell method experts say that it actually

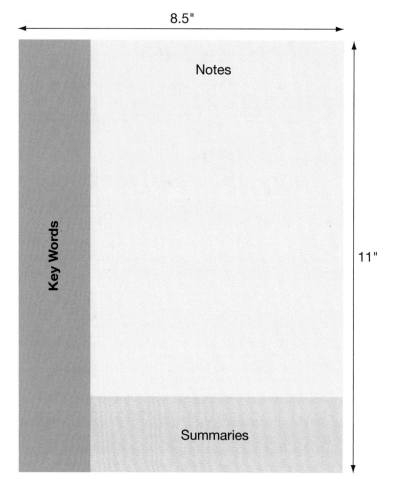

8.5"

Notes

Key Words

11"

Summaries

A sample page showing the Cornell note-taking method. Do you think this method would work better than the one you now use? Why or why not?

helps the brain learn. (3) A student using the Cornell method performs several steps. (4) Before class, he or she draws a line dividing notebook paper into two columns. (5) The narrower left-hand column will contain key words, and the wider right-hand column, notes. (6) During the lesson, the student records the professor's main ideas in the notes column, jotting important phrases, symbols, and abbreviations, but not complete sentences. (7) At the bottom of the page, the student leaves five or six lines blank. (8) As soon as possible after class, he or she rereads the notes and reduces them further by writing a few key words or questions in the left-hand column furthermore at the bottom of the page, the student writes a brief summary of the notes. (9) These "reducing" steps help the brain understand and remember the material, nevertheless, studying later for a test is easier. (10) To study, the student simply covers up the notes and recites the information aloud from memory, glancing at the key words and questions for hints. (11) Periodically reviewing like this helps the brain move course concepts gradually into long-term memory and improves recall on exams. (12) Finally, students should reflect on what they are learning, for example; they might ask how the ideas in their notes apply to real-life situations. Some people call the Cornell system the Five R's, for *record, reduce, recite, review*, and *reflect*.

E. Review

PRACTICE 10

Read each pair of simple sentences to determine the relationship between them. Then join each pair in three different ways, using the conjunctions or conjunctive adverbs in parentheses at the left. Punctuate correctly.

EXAMPLE

The company picnic was canceled.
Rain started to fall in torrents.

(for) *The company picnic was canceled, for the rain started to fall in torrents.*

_____

(because) *Because the rain started to fall in torrents, the company picnic was canceled.*

_____

(therefore) *The rain started to fall in torrents; therefore, the company picnic was canceled.*

1. My grandmother is in great shape.

   She eats right and exercises regularly.

   (for) _____

   _____

   (because) _____

   _____

   (therefore) _____

   _____

2. We just put in four hours paving the driveway.
   We need a long break and a cold drink.

   (since) _____

   _____

   (because) _____

   _____

   (consequently) _____

   _____

3. The bus schedule was difficult to read.
   Penny found the right bus.

   (but) _____

   _____

   (although) _____

   _____

   (however) _____

   _____

4. Don is an expert mechanic.

   He intends to open a service center.

   (and) _____

   _____

   (because) _____

   _____

   (furthermore) _____

   _____

5. We haven't heard from her.

   We haven't given up hope.

   (but) _____

   _____

   (although) _____

   _____

   (nevertheless) _____

   _____

PRACTICE 11

In your writing, aim for variety by mixing coordination, subordination, and simple sentences. Revise the following paragraphs to eliminate monotonous simple sentences. First, read the paragraph to determine the relationships between ideas; then choose the conjunctions that best express these relationships, making your corrections above the lines. Punctuate correctly.

Paragraph 1

Dating has always been a risky business. Television shows like *Blind Date* succeed. They let viewers leer at other people's embarrassing dates. Now the Internet is opening a whole new social frontier. It also is creating new dangers. Online, it is harder to spot nuts, flakes, and predators. We meet someone through e-mail. We lose our usual ways of judging people. According to Internet safety expert Parry Aftab, it is hard to gauge the truth of someone's statements. We cannot see, hear, and experience that person's eye contact, body language, dress, personal hygiene, and voice. Furthermore, most people lie. They begin to date online. Aftab says that men often fib about their income, fitness level, or amount of hair. Women shave pounds off their weight or years off their age. Cyber daters must remain skeptical, ask questions, and watch for red-flag comments. Your online love keeps calling herself Gilda, Bat Goddess of the Red Planet. It's probably time to log off.

"On the Internet, nobody knows you're a dog."

Paragraph 2

Businessman Robert Johnson has blazed new trails throughout his career. No existing television network targeted African Americans. Johnson created the Black Entertainment Television network. The company started with a tiny budget and just two hours of daily programming. It became a huge success. BET grew to be the largest black-owned and -operated company in the country. Johnson created new jobs for hundreds of people. He himself became America's first African-American billionaire. In 2005, he achieved yet another first. He became the first African American to gain controlling interest in an NBA team, the Charlotte Bobcats. One of his lifelong dreams had come true. He says that he is even prouder of another accomplishment. He wanted to create more economic opportunities for minorities. He has succeeded.

Paragraph 3

Cleopatra became Queen of Egypt at seventeen. She displayed a flair for ruling and was soon worshipped by her subjects. Julius Caesar, ruler of Rome, was sent to calm civil wars in Egypt in 51 B.C. Cleopatra was in hiding. She directed her servants to roll her up inside a large rug and smuggle her into the palace. Caesar was fifty-two and the most powerful man in the world. He was amazed to receive a gift-wrapped queen. Their relationship became one of history's greatest love stories. It lasted until Caesar's enemies murdered him. Later, Marc Antony came to Egypt to add African lands to the Roman Empire. He, too, fell in love with the spirited queen. He moved into her palace on the island of Antirhodos. This betrayal was too much for the Romans. Their navy attacked Cleopatra's fleet. Both Antony and Cleopatra killed themselves. They would not bow in defeat. The Romans smashed all statues of the queen. An earthquake sank her palace into the Mediterranean Sea. Fifteen hundred years passed. Undersea explorer Franck Goddio discovered Cleopatra's lost palace in 1996. Neither the Roman Empire nor the forces of nature could erase one of the most powerful and intriguing women who ever lived.

CHAPTER 27

Avoiding Sentence Errors

A: Avoiding Run-Ons and Comma Splices

B: Avoiding Fragments

A. Avoiding Run-Ons and Comma Splices

PRACTICE 1

Some of these sentences contain run-ons or comma splices; others are correct. Put a C next to the correct sentences. Revise the run-ons and comma splices in any way you choose. Be careful of the punctuation.

1. Identity theft is the fastest-growing crime in the United States it costs society $4 to $5 billion a year.

   Revised: _____

   _____

2. The identity thief doesn't just steal someone's cash or jewelry, he or she poses as that person to open new accounts, take out loans, or even buy houses.

   Revised: _____

   _____

3. For the victim, identity theft can mean the shock of violation, large financial losses, and ruined credit.

   Revised: _____

   _____

4. Individuals today must protect themselves against identity theft the U.S. Department of Justice recommends the SCAM approach.

   Revised: _____

   _____

5. S is for *stingy* people should be stingy about giving their valuable social security, bank account, and credit-card numbers to others.

   Revised: _____

   _____

6. C stands for *check* all financial statements carefully for unauthorized withdrawals or purchases.

   Revised: _____

   _____

7. The A in SCAM reminds everyone to *ask* periodically for a copy of his or her credit report fraudulent accounts and activity will show up there.

   Revised: _____

   _____

8. The final step is M, *maintaining* careful records of bank and financial accounts, these records can help dispute any problems.

   Revised: _____

   _____

9. Trash cans and dumpsters still provide identity thieves with most of their valuable information, a final S might stand for *shred*.

   Revised: _____

   _____

10. Old checks, bank records, and credit-card offers from today's mail should never be tossed out they should be shredded or burned.

Revised: _____

_____

PRACTICE 2

Proofread the following paragraph for run-ons and comma splices. Correct them in any way you choose.

(1) College costs have risen dramatically in recent years, many students now have to tap multiple resources to cover their expenses. (2) These students are using their own savings and getting monetary help from parents and other relatives. (3) In addition, 75 percent of all college students now work at least part-time earning a paycheck helps them make ends meet. (4) Before they consider working even longer hours, these students should learn to apply early and often for different kinds of financial aid. (5) Every year, they should fill out the Free Application for Federal Student Aid (FAFSA) form, ensuring consideration for grants that do not have to be repaid. (6) They should regularly check college newsletters or bulletin boards for scholarship announcements yet another option is applying for loans with reasonable repayment terms. (7) Financial survival is possible for college students experts say the secret is planning ahead, applying early, and combining different resources.

PRACTICE 3

Proofread the following essay for run-ons and comma splices. Correct them in any way you choose, writing your revised essay on a separate sheet of paper. Be careful of the punctuation.

HOW TO READ AN AD

(1) Most people insist that advertising does not affect them and that they tune out ads and commercials. (2) If these claims are true, however, why do companies spend billions a year on advertising? (3) For the Super Bowl alone, corporations rush to buy

30-second commercial spots at $3 million each, in fact, ads work very well, declares former advertising executive Stephen Garey, they bombard people with attractive pictures and the hidden message, "buy, buy, buy." (4) The best defense against this ad blitz is learning to read ads critically.

(5) Advertisers are master persuaders, their techniques are very different from those used in college and at work. (6) A student or worker often must take a stand, arguing for or against something he or she uses logical reasons and arguments to try and persuade others. (7) Advertisers, on the other hand, use illogical but powerful visual methods to

Study this ad for a famous cologne. Reread Practice 3, especially the list at the end of the second paragraph of this reading (on page 246). How many advertisers' "techniques of persuasion" can you spot in the ad?

Image courtesy of The Advertising Archives

persuade people to buy their products. (8) The Center for Media Literacy lists ten such "techniques of persuasion" in ads:

Humor	Friends	Fun	Sex appeal	Celebrity
Macho	Family	Nature	Cartoons	Wealth

(9) These techniques are emotional and indirect, often pictures are used to suggest pleasant associations with a product. (10) For instance, one ad might show happy people smoking, it links "friends" and "fun" with cigarettes. (11) Another ad shows a well-dressed man helping a beautiful woman into a car, associating "wealth," "macho," and perhaps "sex appeal" with that brand of automobile. (12) Flip through any popular magazine and see which techniques each ad uses look closely and ask yourself what *audience* is targeted by each ad. (13) What *methods* attract your attention and call to your dollars? (14) Are there *hidden messages*? (15) Looking critically at ads not only creates smarter consumers, it also trains the critical thinking skills that many professors and employers value.

B. Avoiding Fragments

PRACTICE 4

Some of these examples are fragments; others are complete sentences. Put a C next to the complete sentences. Revise the fragments any way you choose.

1. When Sandra completes her commercial jet training.

   Revised: _____

   _____

2. Loudly talking on his cell phone, Ivan strolled through the mall.

   Revised: _____

   _____

3. A city that I have always wanted to visit.

   Revised: _____

   _____

4. If she speaks Portuguese fluently, she will probably get the job.

   Revised: _____

   _____

5. The comic strip *Peanuts*, which was created by Charles Schultz.

   Revised: _____

   _____

6. Interviewing divorced people for her research project.

   Revised: _____

   _____

7. Although some students bring laptop computers to class.

   Revised: _____

   _____

8. Frantically, the disc jockey flipping through stacks of CDs.

   Revised: _____

   _____

PRACTICE 5

Now, proofread for fragments. Some of these examples are fragments; others are complete sentences. Put a C next to the complete sentences. Revise the fragments any way you choose.

1. To earn money for college.

   Revised: _____

   _____

2. Terrence, a graphic designer at *Sports Illustrated*.

   Revised: _____

   _____

3. Across the railroad tracks and down the riverbank.

   Revised: _____

   _____

4. A born comedian.

   Revised: _____

   _____

5. To answer phones for the AIDS Education Network.

   Revised: _____

   _____

6. On a coffee plantation in Jamaica.

   Revised: _____

   _____

7. That silver razor scooter.

   Revised: _____

   _____

8. To find a job that you love.

   Revised: _____

   _____

PRACTICE 6

Fragments are most likely to occur in paragraphs or longer pieces of writing. Proofread the paragraph below for fragments. Correct them in any way you choose, either adding the fragments to other sentences or making them into complete sentences.

(1) The sinking of the *Titanic* in 1912 has inspired fifteen motion pictures over the years. (2) All of them requiring special effects. (3) What set James Cameron's *Titanic* apart, however, was his attention to detail. (4) Following the blueprints and plans for the original ship. (5) Cameron's team created scaled sets and models accurate down to the rivets. (6) Scenes of the ship in the water were made possible through the brilliant use of computer technology and a small model. (7) A larger model of the liner's huge cargo hold was needed. (8) To show the ocean rushing into the ship. (9) Although the model was only a quarter as large as the original. (10) It still had enough room for period luggage and a brand-new Renault. (11) The largest model was a 775-foot replica of the luxury ship. (12) Which reproduced every detail, from the ship's name lettered on the façade to the chairs on the deck. (13) That set took almost a year to build. (14) And a good chunk of the $287 million that Cameron spent on the most expensive movie ever made.

PRACTICE 7

Proofread this essay for fragments. Correct them in any way you choose, either adding the fragments to other sentences or making them into complete sentences. Be careful of the punctuation.

HER FOCUS IS SUCCESS

(1) If the way we react to adversity reveals our true character. (2) Maria Elena Ibanez is extraordinary. (3) This successful computer engineer and businesswoman is a master at refusing to let obstacles keep her from a goal.

(4) In 1973, nineteen-year-old Maria Elena left Colombia and arrived alone in Miami. (5) Speaking just a few words of English. (6) Her goal was to learn fifty new words a day. (7) By talking to people and reading children's books. (8) Soon she spoke well

enough to enroll at Florida International University, earn a computer science degree, and so impressed college officials that they hired her as a programmer.

(9) In 1982, Maria Elena started her first company. (10) Because computers cost much more in South America than they did in the United States. (11) She decided to sell reasonably priced computers to South American dealers. (12) When some dealers hesitated to do business with such a young woman, she won their respect with her expertise and willingness to teach them about the new technology. (13) Soon she sold International Micro Systems. (14) The nation's fifty-fifth fastest growing private company, at a huge profit.

(15) In spite of this success, people laughed out loud when Maria Elena announced her new goal. (16) To sell computers throughout Africa. (17) She paid no attention and returned from her first selling trip with handfuls of orders. (18) Then in 1992, disaster struck.

(19) Hurricane Andrew plowed into Miami, exploding Maria Elena's house. (20) As she and her two small children hid in a closet. (21) In the morning, dazed, she walked to the offices and warehouse of her new company. (22) The building was a mangled mess of fallen walls, trees, wet paper, and smoking wires. (23) Sitting down on a curb, she cried, but as her employees began arriving. (24) She sprang into action.

(25) One worker said the company could set up in his home. (26) Which had electricity. (27) Working twenty-four hours a day and using cell phones, the employees called all their African customers. (28) To say everything was fine and their orders would be shipped on time. (29) International High Tech grew 700 percent that year. (30) Despite the most damaging hurricane in U.S. history.

(31) Maria Elena moved her company into its rebuilt offices. (32) Today she and the children live in an apartment. (33) Not a house. (34) Asked about losing every piece of clothing, every picture, every possession in her former home. (35) She laughs, says that most problems hide opportunities, and adds that now she has no lawn to mow.

PRACTICE 8 REVIEW

Proofread these paragraphs for run-ons, comma splices, and fragments. Correct the errors in any way you choose.

Paragraph 1

(1) In 1970, duct tape helped save the lives of the three astronauts aboard the damaged *Apollo 13* spacecraft, this strong, fabric-based adhesive tape is not just for fixing broken things any more. (2) Now rolls of duct tape, creativity, and more than a dash of humor can bloom into a college scholarship. (3) In 2001, the Duck Tape Company sponsored the first national "Stuck at Prom" contest. (4) After managers learned that some high school students were sculpting colored rolls of duct tape into dresses and tuxedos for their

Dressed head to toe in duct tape, the winners of the 2008 Stuck at Prom contest also scored college scholarships.

Courtesy Duck Tape® brand duct tape

senior proms. (5) The couple who designed the most imaginative and stylish formal wear from duct tape received a $5,000 scholarship to college. (6) The contest tapped into some goofy national yearning to design clothes with duct tape—or to laugh. (7) By 2008, 160 couples in forty-four states and four Canadian provinces competed the 2008 winners, for example, created her five-foot-wide pink hoop skirt with accents of black, white, and aqua his zebra-striped tuxedo jacket was accented with pink and aqua to match. (8) This jacket took 30 hours to make the 50-pound dress required 140 hours of labor and 134 rolls of duct tape. (9) Although the clothes were extremely heavy. (10) The college-bound couple says everyone loved their fashion statement. (11) In addition, the duct tape's insulating qualities made them the hottest couple on the dance floor.

Paragraph 2

(1) Some teenagers seem to start the day tired, they are worn out even before they leave for school. (2) Once in class, they might doze off, even in the middle of an exciting lesson. (3) Are these students lazy, have they stayed out too late partying? (4) Medical research provides a different explanation for the exhaustion of these teens. (5) As children become adolescents, they develop an increased need for sleep, especially in the morning. (6) Unfortunately, most American high schools start around 7:30 A.M. many students have to get up as early as 5:00 A.M. (7) Scientists suggest that if students could start school later in the day. (8) They might get the extra sleep they need. (9) To test this theory, many schools have begun to experiment with later hours. (10) Congress is even paying the extra operating costs for schools that start after 9:00 A.M. (11) The hope is that teens will be less tired, furthermore, because schools that start later will end later, students will be off the streets and out of trouble during the late afternoon. (12) Which is prime mischief time.

PRACTICE 9 REVIEW

Proofread this essay for run-ons, comma splices, and fragments. Correct the errors in any way you choose, writing your revisions above the lines.

WORDS FOR THE WISE

(1) Scrabble has been called America's favorite word game. (2) It was invented by Alfred Butts. (3) An architect who wanted to create a word game that required both luck and skill. (4) In 1938, Butts produced a board with 225 squares and 100 tiles with letters on them. (5) Each letter was worth a certain number of points, depending on how easy it was to use that letter in a word.

(6) Butts made fifty Scrabble sets by hand he gave them to his friends. (7) Who loved playing Scrabble. (8) Strangely, Butts could not interest a manufacturer in the game. (9) A friend of his, James Brunot, asked Butts for permission to manufacture and sell the game. (10) At first, Brunot too had little success. (11) Selling only a few sets a year. (12) Then the president of Macy's discovered the game on a vacation. (13) And stocked some sets for his store. (14) Overnight, Scrabble caught on a million sets sold in 1953.

(15) Butts and Brunot couldn't keep up with the demand they sold the rights to a game company. (16) The rest is history today 100 million Scrabble sets have been sold worldwide. (17) The game is also a successful learning tool. (18) for teaching spelling and vocabulary. (19) Half a million schoolchildren play it in school many adults play in local, national, and international Scrabble tournaments.

PRACTICE 10 REVIEW

Proofread this essay for run-ons, comma splices, and fragments. Correct the errors in any way you choose, writing your revisions above the lines.

ENGINEERING THE FUTURE

(1) Sometimes a childhood passion can lead to a rewarding career, James McLurkin's journey from Lego bricks to robots is a perfect example. (2) This engineer and teacher is now famous for his work in robotics. (3) He is the creator of SwarmBots, large numbers of small robots. (4) That are programmed to work together on a group task. (5) All his life, however, McLurkin has enjoyed building things.

As a child, he played for hours with Legos and cardboard boxes, like many future engineers, he wanted to understand how things worked. (7) Then a television program on PBS changed his life, the seventh grader watched in amazement as students in a well-equipped machine shop built their own robots. (8) It was "the coolest thing I had ever seen," he now says. (9) Impressed that the students were fiercely competitive and working on a high level. (10) He knew at that moment what he wanted to do.

(11) Education and drive turned his childhood passion into mastery, as a college student, McLurkin began to enter computer and robotics contests. (12) Which led to honors as a young inventor. (13) He earned a bachelor's degree in electrical engineering. (14) And then went on to receive a master's in that field and a second master's in computer science.

(15) Keeping an open mind and a spirit of play. (16) Have given him some of his best ideas. (17) The idea for SwarmBots, for instance, came from watching ants, bees, and other insects. (18) As they worked together in nature. (19) Today McLurkin champions technical education. (20) He loves to meet with students. (21) And inspire them to pursue engineering, computer science, and invention.

Robotics engineer McLurkin with some of his *SwarmBots*

CHAPTER 28

Present Tense (Agreement)

A. Defining Subject-Verb Agreement

PRACTICE 1

Underline the subject and circle the correct present tense verb.

1. Many people (thinks, think) of scientific research as unrelated to everyday life.

2. Professor John Trinkaus (challenges, challenge) this idea.

3. He and his business students (investigates, investigate) such issues as supermarket manners, driving violations, and people's real feelings about Brussels sprouts.

4. They (observes, observe) and (records, record) data to shed light on human behavior.

5. For example, most shoppers (grabs, grab) pastries and rolls with their hands instead of tongs or tissues.

6. Of 100 supermarket shoppers, eighty-five (exceeds, exceed) the express line limit.

7. Thanks to Trinkaus, we (knows, know) more about rude and dangerous drivers.

8. Many drivers (parks, park) in fire zones or illegally (snatches, snatch) handicapped parking spots.

9. Only six people in ten (stops, stop) fully at stop signs.

10. In all these studies, observers (notes, note) the vehicle type and driver's sex.

11. Over and over again, women in vans (ranks, rank) as the worst offenders.

12. With a straight face, Trinkaus (investigates, investigate) baseball cap style and pedestrian shoe color.

13. His writings often (stimulates, stimulate) laughter first, then thinking.

14. The eccentric professor proudly (displays, display) his 2003 IgNobel Prize, a joke award for goofy research.

15. According to admirers, his work (sheds, shed) serious light on modern American culture.

B. Three Troublesome Verbs in the Present Tense: *To Be, To Have, To Do*

PRACTICE 2

Write the correct present tense form of the verb in the space at the right of the pronoun.

To be	To have	To do
I _____	we _____	it _____
we _____	she _____	they _____
he _____	he _____	she _____
you _____	they _____	you _____
it _____	I _____	he _____
they _____	it _____	we _____
she _____	you _____	I _____

PRACTICE 3

Fill in the correct present tense form of the verb in parentheses.

1. Surfing _____ (to be) an extreme sport, and it _____ (to have) become very popular.

2. Most beginners _____ (to do) basic moves on dry land—lying on the board, kneeling, and then rising to a hunched standing position.

3. An ocean beach with gentle, regular waves _____ (to be) the ideal place to start surfing.

4. Expert surfers _____ (to have) exceptional skills and _____ (to be) at home in the monster waves off Hawaii or Australia.

5. An expert _____ (to do) a "roller coaster" by soaring from the bottom to the top of a giant wave and down again.

6. "Riding a tube" _____ (to be) a thrilling trip through the transparent green tunnel of a giant wave.

7. Hawaiian coastlines _____ (to have) some of the world's best surfing.

8. Banzai Pipeline in Oahu _____ (to be) a famous surfing break; it

   _____ excellent tubes and waves three stories high.

9. Oahu's Sunset Rip, a notorious break, _____ (to have) several international surfing competitions.

10. For the surfer, wipeouts, flying boards, and sharks _____ (to be) constant dangers.

11. Yet the sport _____ (to have) new converts every year.

12. Many say that it _____ (to be) a spiritual experience.

C. Special Singular Constructions

Underline the subject and circle the correct verb in each sentence.

1. Each of these ferns (needs, need) special care.

2. One of the customers always (forget, forgets) his or her umbrella.

3. Which one of the flights (goes, go) nonstop to Dallas?

4. Every one of those cameras (costs, cost) more than I can afford.

5. Either you or Doris (is, are) correct.

6. Either of these flash drives (contain, contains) the information you need.

7. Do you really believe that one of these oysters (holds, hold) a pearl?

8. Neither of the twins (resembles, resemble) his parents.

9. One of the scientists (believes, believe) he can cure baldness.

10. Each of these inventions (has, have) an effect on how we spend our leisure time.

D. Separation of Subject and Verb

PRACTICE 5

Read each sentence carefully for meaning. Cross out any phrase or clause that separates the subject from the verb. Underline the subject and circle the correct verb.

1. The plums in that bowl (tastes, taste) sweet.

2. The instructions on the package (is, are) in French and Japanese.

3. Our new community center, which has a swimming pool and tennis courts, (keeps, keep) everyone happy.

4. The lampshades that are made of stained glass (looks, look) beautiful at night.

5. All the CD players on that shelf (comes, come) with a remote control.

6. A movie that lasts more than three hours usually (puts, put) me to sleep.

7. The man with the dark sunglasses (looks, look) like a typical movie villain.

8. The two nurses who check blood pressure (enjoys, enjoy) chatting with the patients.

9. The function of these metal racks (remains, remain) a mystery to me.

10. The lizard on the wall (has, have) only three legs.

E. Sentences Beginning with *There* and *Here*

PRACTICE 6

Underline the subject and circle the correct verb in each sentence.

1. There (goes, go) Tom Hanks.

2. There (is, are) only a few seconds left in the game.

3. Here (is, are) a terrific way to save money—make a budget and stick to it!

4. There (has, have) been robberies in the neighborhood lately.

5. Here (is, are) the plantains you ordered.

6. Here (comes, come) Jay, the television talk-show host.

7. There (is, are) no direct route to Black Creek from here.

8. There (seems, seem) to be something wrong with the doorbell.

9. Here (is, are) the teapot and sugar bowl I've been looking for.

10. There (is, are) six reporters in the hall waiting for an interview.

F. Agreement in Questions

PRACTICE 7

Underline the subject and circle the correct verb in each sentence.

1. How (does, do) the combustion engine actually work?

2. Why (is, are) Robert and Charity so suspicious?

3. Where (is, are) the new suitcases?

4. Which tour guide (have, has) a pair of binoculars?

5. (Are, Is) Dianne and Ramone starting a mail-order business?

6. What (seems, seem) to be the problem here?

7. Why (is, are) those boxes stacked in the corner?

8. (Is, Are) the mattress factory really going to close in June?

9. How (does, do) you explain that strange footprint?

10. Who (is, are) those people on the fire escape?

G. Agreement in Relative Clauses

PRACTICE 8

Underline the antecedent of the *who, which,* or *that*. Then circle the correct verb.

1. Most patients prefer doctors who (spends, spend) time talking with them.

2. The gnarled oak that (shades, shade) the garden is my favorite tree.

3. Laptop computers, which (has, have) become very popular recently, are still fairly expensive.

4. My neighbor, who (swims, swim) at least one hour a day, is seventy years old.

5. Planning ahead, which (saves, save) hours of wasted time, is a good way to manage time effectively.

6. Employers often appreciate employees who (asks, ask) intelligent questions.

7. This air conditioner, which now (costs, cost) $800, rarely breaks down.

8. Everyone admires her because she is someone who always (sees, see) the bright side of a bad situation.

9. He is the man who (creates, create) furniture from scraps of walnut, cherry, and birch.

10. Foods that (contains, contain) artificial sweeteners may be hazardous to your health.

PRACTICE 9   REVIEW

Proofread the following essay for verb agreement errors. Correct any errors by writing above the lines.

JOB HUNTING? THINK GREEN.

(1) These days, many job fairs and sites features green jobs, or green-collar jobs. (2) Just what is a green job? (3) A green job provide solid wages yet preserves rather than drains the earth's resources. (4) Workers who build hybrid cars have green jobs. (5) So do people who install "green roofs" on buildings—garden areas that purifies the air and prevent

diseases like asthma. (6) Green-collar employees often take pride in their work because they contribute to the health of the community. (7) Many colleges now offer courses that prepares students for a greener workforce. (8) Robert, Cheree, and Han illustrates this trend.

(9) Robert Gomez of Oakland, California, remembers his shock at losing a good job in commercial construction two years ago. (10) Today, at 52, thanks to a poster in the unemployment office, Robert have a certificate in solar panel installation from Merritt College and a new lease on life. (11) He installs solar energy panels on homes and buildings, a job he enjoys. (12) According to career counselors, people like Robert does well even during hard times because they stay flexible and get new training.

(13) Cheree Williams wants a green career. (14) She attends Evergreen State College in Eugene, Oregon, a school that wins awards for its environmental efforts. (15) Cheree study in the Food, Health, and Sustainability program; she learns earth-friendly farming methods in the school's organic garden. (16) With her degree, she hope to work in the public schools, building children's health and achievement through wise food choices.

Solar panel installation is a green job in demand.

(17) A third example is Han Bae, who loves chemistry and cars. (18) A career in the growing biofuels industry make sense for him, he believes. (19) At Central Carolina Community College, Han gets hands-on experience making and testing new fuels because a factory right on campus makes ethanol from different plant sources. (20) College vehicles actually runs on these fuels.

(21) Nationwide, enrollment in green courses increase every year, touching fields as diverse as prison administration and small business entrepreneurship.

CHAPTER 29

Past Tense

A: Regular Verbs in the Past Tense

B: Irregular Verbs in the Past Tense

C: A Troublesome Verb in the Past Tense: *To Be*

D: Troublesome Pairs in the Past Tense: *Can/Could, Will/Would*

A. Regular Verbs in the Past Tense

PRACTICE 1

Fill in the past tense of the regular verbs in parentheses.*

1. On July 8, 1947, the headline of the *Daily Record* in Roswell, New Mexico,

   _____ (announce) the U.S. military's capture of a "flying saucer."

2. Events surrounding this incident _____ (produce) one of the most famous

   and controversial UFO stories of all time.

3. A local sheep rancher first _____ (stumble) upon a large field of wreckage

   that _____ (resemble) sheets of tough, wafer-thin metal.

-----

* If you have questions about spelling, see Chapter 39, "Spelling," Parts D, E, and F, in the companion text.

4. Several people who _____ (stop) at the crash site _____ (report) seeing bodies of space aliens.

5. Army officials _____ (gather) the fragments, _____ (transport) them to the Roswell Army Air Field, and _____ (issue) a press release about a mysterious disc.

6. Soon afterward, however, the military _____ (change) its story and _____ (identify) the object as a fallen weather balloon.

7. Reporters and the public _____ (ignore) the incident for 30 years, but in 1978, an Army major who _____ (search) the wreckage _____ (accuse) the military of lying.

8. Other eyewitnesses to the crash _____ (admit) seeing strange bodies, which they _____ (portray) as short, hairless beings with large heads.

9. Over sixty years later, scientists are debating whether the military actually _____ (seize) and _____ (study) the remains of beings from outer space.

10. In 2008, astronaut and scientist Edgar Mitchell _____ (drop) a bombshell, stating that an alien craft indeed _____ (crash) at Roswell and the government _____ (cover) it up.

B. Irregular Verbs in the Past Tense

PRACTICE 2

Fill in the past tense of the regular and irregular verbs in parentheses. If you are not sure of the past tense, use the reference chart "Irregular Verbs in the Past Tense" in Chapter 29, Part B, of the companion text. Do not guess.

HISPANIC HEROES: SHAKING UP HOLLYWOOD

(1) For much of the last century, Hispanics in Hollywood _____ (remain) a small minority. (2) Many Latin actors either _____ (accept) such stereotyped roles as the gardener or _____ (change) their names, hoping to snag better roles. (3) Jo Raquel Tejada _____ (choose) the last name Welch, and Ramon Estevez _____ (become) Martin Sheen. (4) But a new century _____ (bring) deeper change—in the form of determined individuals who _____ (dream) of making or starring in movies and then _____ (fight) to open doors.

(5) Director Robert Rodriguez, for instance, _____ (succeed) after a rocky beginning. (6) As a young Texan, Rodriguez was rejected by the film school to which he _____ (apply). (7) Instead of getting discouraged, the twenty-three-year-old _____ (take) off for Mexico with a movie camera, some friends, and $7,000. (8) The result was the film *El Mariachi*, a Spanish-language action comedy that Rodriguez later _____ (sell) to Columbia Pictures for worldwide distribution. (9) After that, he _____ (keep) entertaining moviegoers with low-budget, action-packed English-language films like *Desperado, Spy Kids*, and *From Dusk Till Dawn*. (10) He _____ (rake) in millions with his violent shoot-'em-up scenes and special effects. (11) Perhaps more important, Rodriguez _____ (put) Hispanics in top roles—for instance, casting Antonio Banderas as a dad, not a Hispanic dad, in *Spy Kids*. (12) "I find that the best way through a closed door," Rodriguez once _____ (announce), "is to kick it open." (13) Another Hispanic who _____ (help) make her own opportunities is Mexican-born actress and producer Salma Hayek. (14) Ironically, it was Rodriguez who _____ (battle) Hollywood for approval to cast this unknown

actress in one of *Desperado*'s leading roles. (15) She _____ (do) not disappoint

him, and her performance _____ (catapult) her to fame. (16) From the time she

was thirteen, Hayek _____ (admire) Frida Kahlo and _____ (long) to play

the spirited Mexican painter in a film about her life. (17) Behind the scenes, Salma

_____ (strategize) brilliantly to get the movie made, secure rights, and beat out

Madonna for the part. (18) In the end, Hayek _____ (produce) and

_____ (star) in *Frida*, which _____ (open) in 2002. (19) Her

performance in that lead role _____ (earn) her an Academy Award nomination.

(20) This movie and Salma's depiction of the brainy scientist in *Spy Kids* _____

(expand) Hollywood's ideas about "suitable" Hispanic roles.

Salma Hayek as Mexican painter Frida Kahlo, the dream role for which she fought

© Miramax/Courtesy Everett Collection

(21) Rodriguez and Hayek are just two examples of the new infusion of talent in American movies. (22) In 2005, the mentor and his leading lady _____ (find) themselves together again—on a magazine cover. (23) Both _____ (win) spots on *Time* magazine's list of the 25 Most Influential Hispanics in the United States.

C. A Troublesome Verb in the Past Tense: *To Be*

PRACTICE 3

Circle the correct form of the verb *to be* in the past tense. Do not guess. If you are not sure of the correct form, use the reference chart "Irregular Verbs in the Past Tense" in Chapter 29, Part B, of the companion text.

1. Oprah Winfrey (was, were) always an avid reader.

2. In fact, books (was, were) sometimes her only comfort during her difficult childhood and painful adolescence.

3. When her producers (was, were) considering a TV book club, the world's most popular talk-show host (was, were) sure she could get the whole country reading.

4. Her first book club selection (was, were) *The Deep End of the Ocean* by Jacquelyn Mitchard, the story of a kidnaped child; the public's rush to buy books (wasn't, weren't) anticipated.

5. Mitchard's publishers (was, were) astonished to have to reprint the book nearly twenty times; all in all, 900,000 hardcovers and over 2 million paperbacks (was, were) sold.

6. Every book club pick (was, were) a huge success, and even people who didn't read found they (was, were) eagerly awaiting Winfrey's next selection.

7. When Oprah closed the club in 2002, her e-mail and phone lines (was, were) flooded with protests.

8. So readers (was, were) happy when Oprah revived the club in 2003, focusing on only classic authors like William Faulkner, John Steinbeck, and Carson McCullers.

9. In 2008, a bold online version of the book club (was, were) launched when Oprah and author Eckhart Tolle led online discussions of Tolle's spiritual self-help book, *A New Earth.*

10. For ten weeks, their interactive Web Seminars (was, were) attended by over 700,000 people from around the world.

D. Troublesome Pairs in the Past Tense: *Can/Could, Will/Would*

PRACTICE 4

Fill in either the present tense *can* or the past tense *could*.

1. Tom is so talented that he ⸺⸺⸺ play most music on the piano by ear.

2. He ⸺⸺⸺ leave the hospital as soon as he feels stronger.

3. Last week we ⸺⸺⸺ not find fresh strawberries.

4. When we were in Spain last summer, we ⸺⸺⸺ see all of Madrid from our hotel balcony.

5. As a child, I ⸺⸺⸺ perform easily in public, but I ⸺⸺⸺ no longer do it.

6. Anything you ⸺⸺⸺ do, he ⸺⸺⸺ do better.

7. Nobody ——————— find the guard after the robbery yesterday.

8. These days, Fred ——————— usually predict the weather from the condition of his bunions.

PRACTICE 5

Fill in either the present tense *will* or the past tense *would*.

1. Sean expected that he ——————— arrive at midnight.

2. Sean expects that he ——————— arrive at midnight.

3. I hope the sale at the used car lot ——————— continue for another week.

4. I hoped the sale at the used car lot ——————— continue for another week.

5. When Benny had time, he ——————— color-code his computer disks.

6. When Benny has time, he ——————— color-code his computer disks.

7. The chefs assure us that the wedding cake ——————— be spectacular.

8. The chefs assured us that the wedding cake ——————— be spectacular.

PRACTICE 6   REVIEW

Proofread the following essay for past tense errors. Then write the correct past tense form above the line.

VIDEO GAME NATION

(1) In 1972, when Nolan Bushnell introduced the first video game to the mass market, few people imagined what the future hold. (2) Bushnell call his new company Atari; the game was Pong. (3) To play, two people simply bounced a digital ball back and forth on a black-and-white console, turning knobs to control their paddles. (4) Primitive by today's standards, Pong were a sensation in arcades and bars across the United States. (5) In 1975, Atari's home version of Pong outsolded all other items in the Sears Christmas catalog. (6) But that was just the beginning. (7) Over the next thirty-five years, electronic games

becomed one of America's most popular pastimes, spawning a booming industry and new jobs.

(8) During the 1980s, the first generation of gamers flock to arcades to play Pac-Man, Donkey Kong, and Centipede. (9) Far-sighted tech companies like Sony, Nintendo, and Microsoft seen this growing market and gone to work. (10) They create home consoles, handheld systems, and of course, more and better games. (11) With the evolution of eye-popping 3-D graphics, realistic sound and action, and imaginative characters, video games begin to look more like television and movies than the electronic paddle-and-ball game that started it all. (12) The public kept buying. (13) In 2004 alone, sales of game consoles and software total $6.2 billion.

(14) As the industry grew, so do controversy. (15) Critics warned that gamers just set on the couch instead of playing outside. (16) Many worryied about the violent content of some games. (17) Others argued that the puzzle-based adventure games of the 1990s and early 2000s teached useful skills. (18) Gamers has to reason, invent strategies, and foresee the consequences of their actions. (19) Despite the controversy, video games are now part of life for most American children, teens, and even adults. (20) In recent years, the average age of the video game player rise to thirty.

(21) Some gamers longed to work in the field, but they needed training. (22) They knowed that companies, hoping to create the latest, greatest game, formed development teams composed of graphic designers, artists, musicians, computer programmers, and other technicians. (23) So it were students themselves who clamor for degree programs to teach them the necessary skills. (24) Some colleges—like New York's Rensselaer Polytechnic Institute and Pittsburgh's Carnegie Mellon University—responded quickly. (25) They establish interdisciplinary programs to prepare students for the fast-moving video game industry of the future.

CHAPTER 30

The Past Participle

A. Past Participles of Regular Verbs

PRACTICE 1

The first sentence of each pair that follows contains a regular verb in the past tense. Fill in *have* or *has* plus the past participle of the same verb to complete the second sentence.

1. Arlen Ness earned his title, King of the Choppers.

   Arlen Ness _____ _____ his title, King of the Choppers.

2. Since 1967, Ness designed and manufactured one-of-a-kind motorcycles.

   Since 1967, Ness _____ _____ and _____ one-of-a-kind motorcycles.

3. The craftsmanship, performance, and eye-popping style of Ness bikes attracted worldwide attention.

   The craftsmanship, performance, and eye-popping style of Ness bikes

   _____ _____ worldwide attention.

4. Shaquille O'Neal and Aerosmith's Steven Tyler ordered custom Ness creations.

   Shaquille O'Neal and Aerosmith's Steven Tyler _____ _____

   custom Ness creations.

5. A master builder and bike painter, Arlen Ness received many first-place trophies.

   A master builder and bike painter, Arlen Ness _____ _____

   many first-place trophies.

6. Crowds lined up just to glimpse his elongated yellow chopper, "Top Banana."

   Crowds _____ _____ up just to glimpse his elongated

   yellow chopper, "Top Banana."

7. Ness picked witty names like "Jelly Belly" for many bikes.

   Ness _____ _____ witty names like "Jelly Belly" for many bikes.

Arlen Ness rides "Top Banana," one of his eye-popping choppers.

From the book, *Arlen Ness, The King of Choppers,* by Michael Lichter.
© Michael Lichter

8. The curvy, green beauty, "Smooth-Ness," and the silver monster, "Mach Ness," both played on his famous name.

The curvy, green beauty, "Smooth-Ness," and the silver monster, "Mach Ness," both _____ _____ on his famous name.

9. Corey Ness joined his father's multimillion dollar company.

Corey Ness _____ _____ his father's multimillion dollar company.

10. Custom motorcycles turned into big business.

Custom motorcycles _____ _____ into big business.

B. Past Participles of Irregular Verbs

PRACTICE 2

The first sentence of each pair that follows contains an irregular verb in the past tense. Fill in *have* or *has* plus the past participle of the same verb to complete the second sentence.

1. Sean took plenty of time buying the groceries.

Sean _____ _____ plenty of time buying the groceries.

2. We sent our latest budget to the mayor.

We _____ _____ our latest budget to the mayor.

3. My daughter hid her diary.

My daughter _____ _____ her diary.

4. The jockey rode all day in the hot sun.

The jockey _____ _____ all day in the hot sun.

5. Hershey, Pennsylvania, became a great tourist attraction.

   Hershey, Pennsylvania, _____ _____ a great tourist attraction.

6. The company's managers knew about these hazards for two years.

   The company's managers _____ _____ about these hazards for two years.

7. Carrie floated down the river on an inner tube.

   Carrie _____ _____ down the river on an inner tube.

8. At last, our team won the bowling tournament.

   At last, our team _____ _____ the bowling tournament.

9. Larry and Marsha broke their long silence.

   Larry and Marsha _____ _____ their long silence.

10. Science fiction films were very popular this past year.

    Science fiction films _____ _____ very popular this past year.

PRACTICE 3

Complete each sentence by filling in *have* or *has* plus the past participle of the verb in parentheses. Some verbs are regular, some are irregular.

1. Soccer _____ _____ (gain) popularity in the United States ever since the 1994 World Cup was held in Pasadena, California.

2. Sports fans _____ _____ (see) the enthusiasm and passion that soccer arouses in such countries as Argentina, Brazil, Italy, and Portugal.

3. The United States also _____ _____ (demonstrate) that it can win games in the biggest soccer competition in the world.

4. The U.S. women's soccer team _____ _____ (win) worldwide respect, earning Olympic gold medals in 2004 and again in 2008.

Kozue Ando of Japan and Shannon Boxx of the U.S. vie for the ball during the 2008 Olympics.

5. The names of female stars like Mia Hamm _____ _____ (become) household words, along with great male players like David Beckham.

6. Consequently, television coverage of matches _____ _____ (increase).

7. Now Major League Soccer officials _____ _____ (announce) plans to add new soccer franchises in Portland, Oregon, Vancouver, British Columbia, and other cities.

8. Significantly, the game _____ _____ (grow) in popularity with suburban boys and girls.

9. The parents of these children _____ _____ (encourage) them to play a relatively safe but exciting sport.

10. Experts say that this generation, which _____ _____ (fall) in love with soccer, will likely change the future of American athletics.

C. Using the Present Perfect Tense

PRACTICE 4

Read these sentences carefully for meaning. Then circle the correct verb—either the **past tense** or the **present perfect tense**.

1. He (directed, has directed) the theater group for many years now.

2. Emilio lifted the rug and (has swept, swept) the dust under it.

3. She (went, has gone) to a poetry slam last night.

4. For the past four years, I (took, have taken) art classes in the summer.

5. We (talked, have talked) about the problem of your lateness for three days; it's time for you to do something about it.

6. While he was in Japan, he (took, have taken) many photographs of shrines.

7. She (won, has won) that contest ten years ago.

8. The boxers (fought, have fought) for an hour, and they look very tired.

9. He (applied, has applied) to three colleges and attended the one with the best sociology department.

10. The auto mechanics (had, have had) a radio show together for five years and are now extremely popular.

D. Using the Past Perfect Tense

PRACTICE 5

Read these sentences carefully for meaning. Then circle the correct verb—either the *past tense* or the *past perfect tense*.

1. Tony came to the office with a cane last week because he (sprained, had sprained) his ankle a month ago.

2. As Janice (piled, had piled) the apples into a pyramid, she thought, "I should become an architect."

3. Juan (finished, had finished) his gardening by the time I (drove, had driven) up in my new convertible.

4. The man nervously (looked, had looked) at his watch and then walked a bit faster.

5. Roberto told us that he (decided, had decided) to enlist in the Marines.

6. The caller asked whether we (received, had received) our free toaster yet.

7. Last week he told me that he (forgot, had forgotten) to mail the rent check.

8. As the curtain came down, everyone (rose, had risen) and applauded the Brazilian dance troupe.

9. Scott (closed, had closed) his books and went to the movies.

10. The prosecutor proved that the defendant was lying; until then I (believed, had believed) he was innocent.

E. Using the Passive Voice (*To Be* and the Past Participle)

PRACTICE 6

Fill in the correct *past participle* form of the verb in parentheses to form the passive voice. If you are not sure, check the reference chart "Irregular Verbs, Past and Past Participle" in Chapter 30, Part B, of the companion text.

1. The barn was ——————— (build) by friends of the family.

2. These ruby slippers were ——————— (give) to me by my grandmother.

3. A faint inscription is ——————— (etch) on the back of the old gold watch.

4. At the garden party, Sheila and Una were ——————— (bite) by mosquitoes and gnats.

5. The getaway car is always ——————— (drive) by a man in a gray fedora.

6. Her articles have been ——————— (publish) in the *Texas Monthly*.

PRACTICE 7

Whenever possible, write in the *active* not the *passive* voice. Rewrite these sentences in the active voice, making all necessary verb and subject changes. Be sure to keep the sentence in the original tense.

EXAMPLE

Too many personal questions were asked by the interviewer.

The interviewer asked too many personal questions.

1. The shot was blocked by the goalie.

   _____

2. Her reputation was hurt by her rudeness.

   _____

3. The law boards were passed by Eduardo and Noah.

   _____

4. The noisy group was warned by the usher.

   _____

5. We were shown how to create PowerPoint slides by the instructor.

   _____

F. Using the Past Participle as an Adjective

PRACTICE 8

Use the past participle form of the verb in parentheses as an adjective in each sentence.

1. My ———————— (use) laptop was a great bargain at only $200.

2. Bob is highly ———————— (qualify) to install a water heater.

3. The ———————— (air-condition) room was making everyone shiver.

4. The newly ———————— (rise) cinnamon bread smelled wonderful.

5. Were you ———————— (surprise) to hear about my raise?

6. He feels ———————— (depress) on rainy days.

7. She knows the power of the ———————— (write) word.

8. My gym teacher seems ———————— (prejudice) against short people.

9. The ———————— (embarrass) child pulled her jacket over her head.

10. We ordered ———————— (toss) salad, ———————— (broil) salmon,

   ———————— (mash) potatoes, and ———————— (bake) apple rings.

PRACTICE 9

Proofread the following paragraph for errors in past participles used as adjectives. Correct the errors by writing above the lines.

(1) To experience the food of another culture is to appreciate that culture in new ways. (2) A fine example is the traditional Chinese wedding banquet, where each beautiful dish is chosen, prepare, and presented to carry a promise for the couple's future. (3) Carefully

season shark's fin soup opens the feast; this rare and expensive treat signifies health and long life to both family lines. (4) Each table receives its own glazed Peking Duck to indicate the couple's fidelity. (5) In Chinese tradition, chicken represents the phoenix, a magic bird that rises from the ashes, and lobster represents the dragon. (6) Often combine and bake in a single dish, these two foods mark the peaceful union of two families. (7) Because the Chinese word for fish sounds like "abundance," a whole steamed fish is offered to the newly marry couple—a wish for prosperity. (8) At the end of the meal, satisfy guests enjoy dessert buns filled with lotus seeds, promising fertility and future children. (9) It should come as no surprise that an old-fashion Chinese banquet can last an entire day.

PRACTICE 10   REVIEW

Proofread the following essay for past participle errors. Correct the errors by writing above the lines.

LAUGHING AT THE NEWS

Comedian and fake news anchor Stephen Colbert

(1) In recent years, many people have stop reading newspapers and watching the nightly news. (2) Meanwhile, "fake news" comedy shows like *The Daily Show with Jon Stewart* and *The Colbert Report* have growed more popular. (3) Watch by many people, they are the only source of news for 40 percent of those 18 to 29.

(4) Since the mid-1970s, generations of television viewers have seen NBC's *Saturday Night Live* mock the news with its "Weekend Update," where comic actors posing as news anchors offer a few sentences about a current issue, follow by a punch line. (5) SNL's writers have took aim at everything from global warming and the budget crisis to world leaders. (6) Actress and writer Tiny Fey outdid herself in 2008 with her impressions of vice presidential candidate Sarah Palin, complete with winks, "beauty pageant walkin'," and a phony moose shoot dead on stage. (7) View millions of times on YouTube, Fey's skits are classics.

(8) Mixing a little news with a lot of laughs has rose to new heights on *The Daily Show* and *The Colbert Report* (pronounced "repore" with a silent *t* like the host's name). (9) These news parodies feature anchormen delivering updates, complete with video clips, reports from correspondents on location, and interviews with real politicians, authors, and celebrities.

(10) The topics are all lift from current headlines, but the wise-cracking hosts, with their over-spray hair and intense facial expressions, have became masters at mining humor from their guests. (11) In one interview, Colbert revealed that a congressman who wanted the Ten Commandments display in every American courtroom could name only three commandments. (12) Adore by their fans, both hosts have won Emmys.

(13) As the line between news and comedy has blur, questions are being raise about the effects of "infotainment." (14) Worry about the trend, CNN reporter Christiane Amanpour fears viewers are becoming less educate. (15) Others insist that those who watch comedy news think more critically and that humor comes closer to the truth than wooden seriousness.

CHAPTER 31

Nouns

A: Defining Singular and Plural

B: Signal Words: Singular and Plural

C: Signal Words with *of*

A. Defining Singular and Plural

PRACTICE 1

Make these singular nouns plural.

1. man _____	11. maid-of-honor _____
2. half _____	12. criterion _____
3. foot _____	13. shelf _____
4. son-in-law _____	14. mouse _____
5. moose _____	15. child _____
6. life _____	16. father-in-law _____
7. tooth _____	17. knife _____
8. medium _____	18. deer _____
9. woman _____	19. secretary _____
10. crisis _____	20. goose _____

B. Signal Words: Singular and Plural

Some of the following sentences contain incorrect singulars and plurals. Correct the errors. Put a C after correct sentences.

1. By three years old, most children have firm ideas about how men and woman should behave.

2. Children develop their concepts about gender differences through *conditioning*, a process of learning that reinforces certain behaviors while discouraging other.

3. Conditioning occurs through the messages delivered by parents, peer, and the media.

4. Research shows that parents begin to treat their childrens differently as early as twenty-four hour after birth.

5. Fathers hold their infant girls gently and speak softly to them, but they bounce baby boys, playing "airplane" and tickling their feets.

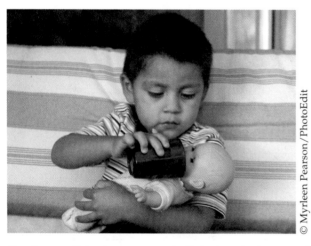

Gender conditioning starts early. Is it okay for boys to play with dolls and girls with trucks?

6. Mothers, too, condition gender roles; they reward little girls who play quietly and help with chores, while excusing the loud play of boys as natural.

7. Once in school, children quickly learn that certain kinds of make-believe—such as playing house or having tea parties—are girls' games; boys are encouraged by their friend to crash cars and shoot toy guns.

8. While the boundaries are less rigid for girls at this stage, most boys who show any interest in feminine clothes or activity will be mocked by their peers.

9. Many TV ad play a key conditioning role by showing boys involved in sports or jobs and girls playing indoors with toy ovens or dolls.

10. By limiting choices for most child, perhaps we ignore many talents and interest that might greatly enhance their lifes and society as a whole.

C. Signal Words with *of*

PRACTICE 3

Fill in your own nouns in the following sentences. Use a different noun in each sentence.

1. Since Jacob wrote each of his _____ with care, the As came as no surprise.

2. You are one of the few _____ I know who can listen to the radio and play video games at the same time.

3. Naomi liked several of the new _____ but remained faithful to her long-time favorites.

4. Many of the _____ carried laptops.

5. Determined to win the Salesperson of the Year award, Clyde called on all of his _____ two or three times a month.

6. One of the _____ makes no sense.

PRACTICE 4 REVIEW

Proofread the following essay for errors in singular and plural nouns. Correct the errors above the lines.

HAPPINESS 101

(1) At Harvard University, up to 900 student per semester pack a lecture hall for Professor Tal Ben-Shahar's course on happiness. (2) Called "Positive Psychology," the class explores current research on what makes peoples truly happy. (3) It is one of the most popular course on campus. (4) Students learn that they are more likely to experience joy if they participate in activitys that they find meaningful as well as pleasurable. (5) For example, a person who enjoys playing the piano might perform once a month for the residents of a nursing homes, thus adding meaning to pleasure. (6) Students also discover that more happiness comes to people who accept every one of their feeling—even fear, sadness, and anger—without self-judgment.

(7) Professor Ben-Shahar's students learn a few more criterion for a cheerful life. (8) They find out that rushing to do too much in a short time increases anxiety and depression, while simplifying life increases enjoyment. (9) Furthermore, several study prove that expressing gratitudes can lift a person's spirits, so it seems the many woman and man who keep a daily gratitude journals are on to something.

(10) One of the most important lesson, though, is that contentment depends on a person's state of mind, not his or her status or bank account. (11) Happy people see the glasses as half full rather than half empty. (12) They also view all of their failure not as disasters or crisis but learning opportunities. (13) Fortunately, research indicates that this kind of optimisms can be learned. (14) Those who are able to shift their thoughts to focus on the positive can change their lifes for the better.

PRACTICE 5 — THINKING AND WRITING TOGETHER

In a group with classmates, reach agreement about which one of Professor Ben-Shahar's principles for happiness in Practice 4 is the most important. What three reasons best explain why your group reached this conclusion? Pick one person to jot down the group's ideas. Be prepared to share your reasoning with the class.

Reasons _____

_____

_____

_____

_____

_____

_____

_____

CHAPTER **32**

Pronouns

A: Defining Pronouns and Antecedents

B: Making Pronouns and Antecedents Agree

C: Referring to Antecedents Clearly

D: Special Problems of Case

E: Using Pronouns with *-self* and *-selves*

A. Defining Pronouns and Antecedents

PRACTICE 1

In each sentence, a pronoun is circled. Write the pronoun first and then its antecedent, as shown in the example.

EXAMPLE

Have you ever wondered why we exchange rings in (our) wedding ceremonies?

our   we

1. Today when people buy wedding rings, (they) follow an age-old tradition.

_____

2. Rich Egyptian grooms gave (their) brides gold rings five thousand years ago.

_____

3. To Egyptian couples, the ring represented eternal love; (it) was a circle without beginning or end.   _____

4. By Roman times, gold rings had become more affordable, so ordinary people could also buy (them).   _____

5. Still, many a Roman youth had to scrimp to buy (his) beloved a ring.   _____

6. The first bride to slip a diamond ring on (her) finger lived in Venice about five hundred years ago.   _____

7. The Venetians knew that setting a diamond in a ring was an excellent way of displaying (its) beauty.   _____

8. Nowadays, two partners exchange rings to symbolize the equality of (their) relationship.   _____

B. Making Pronouns and Antecedents Agree

PRACTICE 2

Fill in the correct pronoun and circle its antecedent. Make sure each pronoun agrees in number and person with its antecedent.

1. Anyone can become a good cook if _____ tries.

2. Someone dropped _____ lipstick behind the bookcase.

3. No one in the mixed doubles let _____ guard down for a minute.

4. Everybody wants _____ career to be rewarding.

5. Everyone is entitled to _____ full pension.

6. Mr. Hernow will soon be here, so please get _____ contract ready.

7. One should wear a necktie that doesn't clash with _____ suit.

8. The movie theater was so cold that nobody took off _____ coat.

PRACTICE 3

Fill in the correct pronoun and circle its antecedent. Make sure each pronoun agrees in number and person with its antecedent.

1. Each of the men wanted to be _____ own boss.

2. One of the saleswomen left _____ sample case on the counter.

3. Every one of the colts has a white star on _____ forehead.

4. Neither of the actors knew _____ lines by heart.

5. Neither of the dentists had _____ office remodeled.

6. Each of these arguments has _____ flaws and _____ strengths.

7. Every one of the jazz bands had _____ own distinctive style.

8. Either of these telephone answering machines will work very well if _____ is properly cared for.

PRACTICE 4

Read each sentence carefully for meaning. Circle the antecedent and then fill in the correct pronoun.

1. My family gave me all _____ support when I went back to school.

2. The government should reexamine _____ domestic policy.

3. The college honored _____ oldest graduate with a reception.

4. Eco-Wise has just begun to market a new pollution-free detergent that _____ is proud of.

5. The panel will soon announce _____ recommendations to the hospital.

6. The two teams gave _____ fans a real show.

7. The jury deliberated for six days before _____ reached a verdict.

8. After touring the Great Pyramid, the class headed back to Cairo in _____ air-conditioned bus.

C. Referring to Antecedents Clearly

Revise the following sentences, removing vague, repetitious, or ambiguous pronoun references. Make the pronoun references clear and specific.

1. In this book it says that hundreds of boys are injured each year copying wrestling stunts they see on TV.

    Revised: _____

    _____

2. On the radio they warned drivers that the Interstate Bridge was closed.

    Revised: _____

    _____

3. Sandra told her friend that she shouldn't have turned down the promotion.

    Revised: _____

    _____

4. In North Carolina they raise tobacco.

    Revised: _____

    _____

5. The moving van struck a lamppost; luckily, no one was injured, but it was badly damaged.

    Revised: _____

    _____

6. Professor Grazel told his parrot that he had to stop chewing telephone cords.

   Revised: ——————————————————————————

   ——————————————————————————————————

7. On the news, it said that more Americans than ever are turning to non-traditional medicine.

   Revised: ——————————————————————————

   ——————————————————————————————————

8. Keiko is an excellent singer, yet she has never taken a lesson in it.

   Revised: ——————————————————————————

   ——————————————————————————————————

9. Vandalism was once so out of control at the local high school that they stole sinks and lighting fixtures.

   Revised: ——————————————————————————

   ——————————————————————————————————

10. Rosalie's mother said she was glad she had decided to become a paralegal.

    Revised: ——————————————————————————

    ——————————————————————————————————

D. Special Problems of Case

PRACTICE 6

Determine the case required by each sentence, and circle the correct pronoun.

1. Harriet and (he, him) plan to enroll in the police academy.

2. A snowdrift stood between the subway entrance and (I, me).

3. Tony used the software and then returned it to Barbara and (I, me, myself).

4. The reporter's questions caught June and (we, us) off guard.

5. By noon, Julio and (he, him) had already cleaned the garage and mowed the lawn.

6. These charts helped (she, her) and (I, me) with our statistics homework.

7. Professor Woo gave Diane and (she, her) extra time to finish the geology final.

8. Between you and (I, me), I have always preferred country music.

PRACTICE 7

Circle the correct pronoun.

1. Your hair is much shorter than (she, her, hers).

2. We tend to assume that others are more self-confident than (we, us).

3. She is just as funny as (he, him).

4. Is Hanna as trustworthy as (he, him)?

5. Although they were both research scientists, he received a higher salary than (she, her).

6. I am not as involved in this project as (they, them).

7. Sometimes we become impatient with people who are not as quick to learn as (we, us).

8. Michael's route involved more overnight stops than (us, our, ours).

PRACTICE 8

Circle the correct pronoun.

1. (Who, Whom) will deliver the layouts to the ad agency?

2. To (who, whom) are you speaking?

3. (Who, Whom) prefers hiking to skiing?

4. For (who, whom) are those boxes piled in the corner?

5. The committee will award the scholarship to (whoever, whomever) it chooses.

6. (Who, Whom) do you wish to invite to the open house?

7. At (who, whom) did the governor fling the cream pie?

8. I will hire (whoever, whomever) can use a computer and speak Korean.

E. Using Pronouns with -self and -selves

Fill in the correct reflexive or intensive pronoun. Be careful to make pronouns and antecedents agree.

1. Though he hates to cook, André _____ sautéed the mushrooms.

2. Rhoda found _____ in a strange city with only the phone number of a cousin whom she had not seen for years.

3. Her coffee machine automatically turns _____ on in the morning and off in the evening.

4. The librarian and I rearranged the children's section _____.

5. When it comes to horror films, I know that you consider _____ an expert.

6. They _____ didn't care if they arrived on time or not.

7. After completing a term paper, I always buy _____ a little gift to celebrate.

8. Larry _____ was surprised at how quickly he grew to like ancient history.

REVIEW

Proofread the following essay for pronoun errors. Then correct the pronoun error above the line, in any way you choose.

THE MANY LIVES OF JACKIE CHAN

(1) Few movie stars can claim a career as unusual as him. (2) For one thing, Jackie Chan performs his death-defying stunts hisself. (3) Although he was a huge star in Asia for more than twenty years, fame eluded him in the United States until recently.

(4) Chan was born in Hong Kong in 1954. (5) Because him and his parents were so poor, he was sent to live and study at the Peking Opera School. (6) There, they trained him in

acting, dancing, singing, sword fighting, and kung fu. (7) When the school closed in 1971, their lessons paid off for Chan in an unexpected way.

(8) Chan worked as a stuntman and fight choreographer and landed acting roles in several films, including Bruce Lee's *Enter the Dragon*. (9) Lee, he died in 1973, and Chan was the natural choice to fill Lee's shoes. (10) In several films, Chan tried to imitate Lee, but the films were unsuccessful. (11) In 1978, however, Chan came up with the idea of turning Lee's tough style into comedy. (12) *Snake in the Eagle's Shadow* and *Drunken Master* were hilarious hits; it established "kung fu comedy." (13) Jackie Chan became one of Hong Kong's most popular stars.

(14) However, Hollywood directors did not appreciate Chan as a stuntman, actor, comedian, director, and scriptwriter all in one, and its early American films flopped. (15) Chan understood his own strengths better than them. (16) He returned to Hong Kong, but him and his fans always believed he could make a U.S. comeback. (17) This happened when *Rumble in the Bronx*, China's most popular film ever, was dubbed in English. (18) Finally, they began to appreciate this manic, bruised, and battered action hero who films were refreshingly nonviolent. (19) Since then, Chan's U.S. films, like *Rush Hour, Rush Hour 2*, and *The Medallion*, are being received almost as well as its Hong Kong counterparts.

CHAPTER 33

Prepositions

A: Working with Prepositional Phrases

B: Prepositions in Common Expressions

A. Working with Prepositional Phrases

PRACTICE 1

Fill in the correct prepositions in the following sentences. Be especially careful of *in* and *on*.

1. _____ a little town _____ the coast of the Dominican Republic, baseball is a way of life.

2. Once known for cattle and sugar, San Pedro de Macoris has been exporting world-class baseball players _____ the major leagues _____ fifty years.

3. Hall-of-Famer Juan Marichal and slugger Manny Ramirez are just two Dominicans who have made names _____ themselves _____ the majors.

4. Other stars born in or _____ San Pedro de Macoris are Pedro Martinez, Alfonso Soriano, and David Ortiz.

5. Baseball was first introduced _____ the island _____ American mill and plantation owners, who encouraged their workers to learn the game.

6. Because equipment was expensive, boys from poor families often batted _____ a tree branch, using a rolled-up sock _____ place _____ a ball.

7. Each young man dreamed that he would be discovered _____ the baseball scouts and sent to play _____ *las ligas mayores*.

8. Amazing numbers _____ these players succeeded, and many Dominican athletes later returned to invest _____ the local economy.

9. For example, Robinson Cano bought 6000 baseball uniforms _____ youngsters and donated two ambulances _____ the town.

10. Major league teams, including the Dodgers, Giants, and Expos, now operate year-round training camps _____ the island, hoping to cultivate the athletes _____ tomorrow.

B. Prepositions in Common Expressions

PRACTICE 2

Fill in the preposition that correctly completes each of the following expressions.

1. In 2008, political involvement among college freshmen reached a 40-year high, according _____ the annual American Freshman survey.

2. Every year since 1966, the Higher Education Research Institute has been responsible _____ this survey of hundreds of thousands of college students.

3. The fascinating results show what students each year hope _____, worry

_____, complain _____, depend _____, and hold dear.

4. In sharp contrast _____ freshmen in 2000, who did not care about politics,

those surveyed in 2008 were very interested _____ the presidential election.

5. Experts say that the September 11, 2001 terrorist attacks on the United States

contributed _____ this new sense of responsibility.

6. College students are more concerned _____ environmental issues, with over 45

percent approving _____ programs to preserve the planet.

7. Almost 75 percent say that responding _____ climate change must be a priority.

8. American students are very comfortable with diversity; in fact, a majority believe that

they are capable _____ working well with people whose beliefs are different

_____ their own.

9. A record half of college freshmen are dealing _____ financial pressures and say

they must work while attending college to help pay expenses.

10. To succeed _____ balancing work and school, many students are relying even

more _____ sources of strength like friends, family, and spiritual beliefs.

PRACTICE 3 REVIEW

Proofread this essay for preposition errors. Cross out the errors and write corrections
above the lines.

DR. BEN CARSON, PIONEER BRAIN SURGEON

(1) Today, Dr. Benjamin Carson of Johns Hopkins Hospital is internationally known as the
man to call from tricky brain surgeries in children. (2) He routinely takes out challenging
cases such as removing parts of the brain to stop seizures or repairing deformities of the

skull and face. (3) On 1987, he made medical history over successfully separating a pair of conjoined (or Siamese) twins in a twenty-two-hour operation.

(4) This gifted physician was not always a high achiever, however. (5) As a child, he grew up fatherless on Detroit. (6) He now says that, like many off the people he knew, he had a low opinion at himself. (7) Consequently, his grades were poor, and he was prone with violent outbursts and disruptive behavior. (8) Nevertheless, his mother, a high-school dropout who worked two or three jobs at a time to support her two sons, believed he was capable to doing better and refused to give out on him. (9) Convinced that education provides the only escape against poverty, she insisted that Ben and his brother read and complete their homework. (10) Thanks on her encouragement, Ben experienced a turning point one day when a teacher brought rock samples at school. (11) Because of a book he had read, Ben was able to identify all off them. (12) Suddenly, he knew that he wasn't the slow learner he had always thought himself to be. (13) Today Dr. Carson declares, "When I thought I was stupid, I acted like a stupid person. (14) When I thought I was smart, I acted

Dr. Ben Carson holds a press conference about a difficult brain surgery.

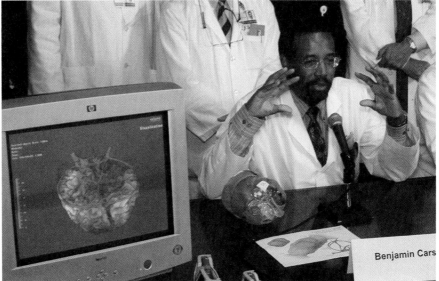

like a smart person and achieved like a smart person." (15) His hunger of knowledge grew, and he rose on the top of his class, going on to attend Yale University.

(16) Nonetheless, Carson would have to overcome another obstacle. (17) Even as late as his first year of medical school, a faculty adviser counseled him to drop off because he wasn't "medical school material." (18) Fortunately, he ignored this advice, by then having discovered his strengths. (19) He knew that he was a careful person with excellent hand-eye coordination. (20) He enjoyed dissecting things, and he could think three dimensionally. (21) With these skills, he decided, he could specialize on brain surgery.

(22) Today Dr. Carson performs three to five life-saving operations a day. (23) On addition, he and his wife have founded the Carson Scholars, a scholarship program for students who succeed on academic subjects. (24) He said he got the idea when he visited schools to speak and saw huge trophies honoring athletic achievements but none for academic achievers. (25) He invested $500,000 of his own money to start rewarding children like he once was about trophies, publicity, and money for college. (26) These scholars are the ones, Carson believes, "who will keep us number 1, not the guy with the 25-foot jump shot."

CHAPTER **34**

Adjectives and Adverbs

A: Defining and Using Adjectives and Adverbs

B: The Comparative and the Superlative

C: A Troublesome Pair: *Good/Well*

A. Defining and Using Adjectives and Adverbs

PRACTICE 1

Circle the correct adjective or adverb in parentheses. Remember that adjectives modify nouns or pronouns; adverbs modify verbs, adjectives, or adverbs.

1. Have you ever seen (real, really) emeralds?

2. Try to do your work in the library (quiet, quietly).

3. We will (glad, gladly) take you on a tour of the Crunchier Cracker factory.

4. Lee, a (high, highly) skilled electrician, rewired his entire house last year.

5. She made a (quick, quickly) stop at the scanner.

6. It was (awful, awfully) wet today; the sleet filled our shoes.

7. The fans from Cleveland (enthusiastic, enthusiastically) clapped for the Browns.

8. Are you (sure, surely) this bus stops in Dusty Gulch?

9. He (hasty, hastily) wrote the essay, leaving out several important ideas.

10. It was a funny joke, but the comedian told it (bad, badly).

11. Tina walked (careful, carefully) down the icy road.

12. Sam swims (poor, poorly) even though he spends hours posing on the beach.

13. Sasha the crow is an (unusual, unusually) pet and a (humorous, humorously) companion.

14. The painting is not (actual, actually) a Picasso; in fact, it is a (real, really) bad imitation.

15. It is an (extreme, extremely) hot day, and I (sure, surely) could go for some (real, really) orange juice.

B. The Comparative and the Superlative

PRACTICE 2

Write the comparative or the superlative of the words in parentheses. Remember: Use the comparative to compare two items; use the superlative to compare more than two. Use *-er* or *-est* for one-syllable words; use *more* or *most* for words of more than one syllable.*

1. The ocean is _____ (cold) than we thought it would be.

2. Please read your lines again, _____ (slowly) this time.

3. Which of these two roads is the _____ (short) route?

4. Which of these three highways is the _____ (short) route?

5. Belkys is the _____ (busy) person I know.

6. That red felt hat with feathers is the _____ (outlandish) one I've

    seen.

_____

* If you have questions about spelling, see Chapter 39, "Spelling," Part G, in the companion text.

7. Today is _____ (warm) than yesterday, but Thursday was the

   _____ (warm) day of the month.

8. The down coat you have selected is the _____ (expensive) one in

   the store.

9. Each one of Woody's stories is _____ (funny) than the last.

10. As a rule, mornings in Los Angeles are _____ (hazy) than

    afternoons.

11. Is Paolo _____ (tall) than Louie? Is Paolo the _____

    (tall) player on the team?

12. If you don't do these experiments _____ (carefully), you will blow

    up the chemistry lab.

13. This farmland is much _____ (rocky) than the farmland in Iowa.

14. Therese says that Physics 201 is the _____ (challenging) course she

    has ever taken.

15. Mr. Wells is the _____ (wise) and _____

    (experienced) leader in the community.

PRACTICE 3

Proofread the following paragraph for comparative and superlative errors. Cross out
unnecessary words and write your corrections above the lines.

(1) Wikipedia is a free online encyclopedia that offers information about thousands
of topics. (2) Created in 2001, it has become one of the most popularest sites on
the Internet—and one of the most controversial. (3) Unlike *Britannica* and other
encyclopedias of a more early time, Wikipedia is not an expensive set of books; it exists

only online at **www.wikipedia.org.** (4) Its most great innovation is also its most biggest problem: readers can also help write content. (5) The "wiki" software allows anyone who visits the site to add or edit an entry. (6) Supporters believe that thousands of minds produce entries that are often completer and accurater than those in traditional encyclopedias. (7) Yet mistakes and sabotage have occurred. (8) A U.S. Congressperson changed his Wikipedia profile to make it positiver. (9) The entry on Harriet Tubman, rescuer of southern slaves, gave the wrong birthplace and stated as fact several disproved stories. (10) Jokers, vandals, and even racists have planted lies in some entries. (11) Wikipedia's 800 volunteer administrators labor to approve each change, making sure that a revised entry is more effectiver than the previous one. (12) While correcting such errors is more easier and fast than in print encyclopedias, some teachers and professors caution students not to cite Wikipedia as an information source.

EXPLORING ONLINE

http://www.wikipedia.org

Choose a subject that interests you and evaluate the Wikipedia entry. First, read the Wikipedia article; take notes or print it. Now visit the library and check the facts. Ask the librarian if you need help. Did you find any false information, or is the entry reliable? How would you rate Wikipedia, based on this one entry?

C. A Troublesome Pair: *Good/Well*

PRACTICE 4

Fill in either the adjective *good* or the adverb *well* in each blank.

1. Corned beef definitely goes _____ with cabbage.

2. How _____ do you understand Spanish?

3. He may not take phone messages very —————, but he is ————— at handling

computer problems.

4. Exercise is a ————— way to stay in shape; eating ————— will help you

maintain ————— health.

5. Tony looks ————— in his new goatee.

6. This is a ————— arrangement: I wash, you dry.

7. On rainy nights, Sheila loves to curl up with a ————— book.

8. The old Persian carpet and oak desk are a ————— match; they go —————

together.

9. Both teams played —————; it was a ————— game.

10. They are ————— neighbors and are ————— liked in the community.

PRACTICE 5

Fill in the correct comparative or superlative of the word in parentheses.

1. Lucinda is a ————— (good) chemist than she is a mathematician.

2. Bascomb was the ————— (bad) governor this state has ever had.

3. When it comes to staying in shape, you are ————— (bad) than I.

4. Of the two sisters, Leah is the ————— (good) markswoman.

5. You can carry cash when you travel, but using a credit card is —————

(good).

6. Our goalie is the ————— (good) in the league; yours is the —————

(bad).

7. When it comes to bad taste, movies are ——————— (bad) than television.

8. Your sore throat seems ——————— (bad) than it was yesterday.

9. Gina likes snorkeling ——————— (good) than fishing; she loves scuba diving

——————— (good) of all.

10. A parka is the ——————— (good) protection against a cold wind; it is certainly

——————— (good) than a scarf.

PRACTICE 6   REVIEW

Proofread the following essay for adjective and adverb errors. Correct errors by writing above the lines or crossing out unnecessary words.

JULIA MORGAN, ARCHITECT

(1) Julia Morgan was one of San Francisco's most finest architects, as well as the first woman licensed as an architect in California. (2) In 1902, Morgan became the first woman to finish successful the program in architecture at the School of Fine Arts in Paris. (3) Returning to San Francisco, she opened her own office and hired and trained a very talented staff that eventual grew to thirty-five full-time architects. (4) Her first major commission was to reconstruct the Fairmont Hotel, one of the city's bestest-known sites, which had been damaged bad in the 1906 earthquake. (5) Morgan earned her reputation by designing elegant homes and public buildings out of inexpensively and available materials and by treating her clients real good. (6) She went on to design more than 800 residences, stores, churches, offices, and educational buildings, most of them in California.

(7) Her bestest customer was William Randolph Hearst, one of the country's most rich newspaper publishers. (8) Morgan designed newspaper buildings and more than twenty pleasure palaces for Hearst in California and Mexico. (9) She maintained a private plane and pilot to keep her moving from project to project. (10) The most big and famousest of her undertakings was sure San Simeon. (11) Morgan worked

on it steady for twenty years. (12) She converted a large ranch overlooking the Pacific into a hilltop Mediterranean village composed of three of the beautifullest guest houses in the world. (13) The larger of the three was designed to look like a cathedral and incorporated Hearst's fabulous art treasures from around the world. (14) The finished masterpiece had 144 rooms and was larger than a football field. (15) San Simeon is now one of the most visited tourist attractions in California and seems to grow popularer each year.

CHAPTER 35

The Apostrophe

A: The Apostrophe for Contractions

B: The Apostrophe for Ownership

C: Special Uses of the Apostrophe

A. The Apostrophe for Contractions

PRACTICE 1

Proofread these sentences and, above the lines, supply any apostrophes missing from the contractions.

1. When Edvard Munch painted *The Scream* in his native Norway in 1893, he couldnt have

    known that it would become world-famous—and the center of an unsolved mystery.

2. The painting shows an anguished person whos either screaming or covering his ears to

    muffle a scream.

3. Its become such a powerful symbol of modern stress and anxiety that its sometimes

    printed on office mugs as a joke.

4. But art lovers and stressed-out jokers arent the only ones whove admired *The Scream*.

5. Incredibly, the pictures been stolen twice, and the second time, it wasnt recovered.

The Scream by Edvard Munch

6. In 1994, thieves snatched one of four versions of the painting from a gallery in Oslo, Norway, yet theyve since been convicted, and the painting was found unharmed.

7. But in August 2004, shocked visitors at Norways Munch Museum couldnt believe it when two armed bandits ripped another version of the painting out of the wall and escaped.

8. Experts dont agree on an exact figure, but theyve guessed that *The Scream* is worth between $50 and $70 million.

9. Thieves usually demand a ransom for such a famous artwork because they cant sell it openly.

10. However, those whove stolen *The Scream* didnt ask for money, and the crime remains one of the great unsolved art heists of all time.

B. The Apostrophe for Ownership

Proofread the following sentences and add apostrophes where necessary to show ownership. In each case, ask yourself if the word already ends in -s. Put a C after any correct sentences.

1. Bills bed is a four-poster.

2. Martha and Davids house is a log cabin made entirely by hand.

3. Somebodys cell phone was left on the sink.

4. During the eighteenth century, ladies dresses were heavy and uncomfortable.

5. Have you seen the childrens watercolor set?

6. Mr. James fried chicken and rice dish was crispy and delicious.

7. The class loved reading about Ulysses travels.

8. The Surgeon Generals latest report was just released.

9. Our citys water supply must be protected.

10. He found his ticket, but she cannot find hers.

11. Every spring, my grandmothers porch is completely covered with old furniture for sale.

12. Jacks car is the same color as ours.

13. Celias final, a brilliant study of pest control on tobacco farms, received a high grade.

14. The mens locker room is on the right; the womens is on the left.

15. The program is entering its final year.

C. Special Uses of the Apostrophe

PRACTICE 3

Proofread these sentences and add an apostrophe wherever necessary.

1. Cross your *t*s and dot your *i*s.

2. I would love a months vacation on a dude ranch.

3. Too many *and*s make this paragraph dull.

4. Those *9*s look crooked.

5. You certainly put in a hard days work!

PRACTICE 4   REVIEW

Proofread the following essay for apostrophe errors. Correct the errors by adding apostrophes above the lines where needed and crossing out those that do not belong.

THE TRUE STORY OF SUPERMAN

(1) Sometimes, things just dont work out right. (2) That's how the creators of Superman felt for a long time.

(3) Supermans first home wasnt the planet Krypton, but Cleveland. (4) There, in 1933, Superman was born. (5) Jerry Siegels story, "Reign of Superman," accompanied by Joe Shuster's illustrations, appeared in the boys own magazine, *Science Fiction*. (6) Later, the teenagers continued to develop their idea. (7) Superman would come to Earth from a distant planet to defend freedom and justice for ordinary people. (8) He would conceal his identity by living as an ordinary person himself. (9) Siegel and Shuster hoped their characters strength and morality would boost peoples spirits' during the Great Depression.

(10) At first, the creators werent able to sell their concept; then, Action Comics' Henry Donnenfield bought it. (11) In June of 1938, the first *Superman* comic hit the stands. (12) Superman's success was immediate and overwhelming. (13) Finally, Americans had a hero who wouldnt let them down! (14) Radio and TV shows, movie serials, feature films, and generations of superheroes' followed.

(15) While others made millions from their idea, Siegel and Shuster didnt profit from its' success. (16) They produced Superman for Action Comics for a mere fifteen dollars a page until they were fired a few years later when Joe Shusters eyes began to fail. (17) They sued, but they lost the case. (18) For a long time, both lived in poverty, but they continued to fight. (19) In 1975, Siegel and Shuster finally took their story to the press; the publicity won them lifelong pensions. (20) The two mens long struggle had ended with success.

CHAPTER 36

The Comma

A. Commas for Items in a Series

PRACTICE 1

Punctuate the following sentences:

1. At the banquet, Ed served a salad of juicy red tomatoes crunchy green lettuce and stringless snap beans.

2. As a nursing assistant, Reva dispensed medication disinfected wounds and took blood samples.

3. Ali visited Santa Barbara Concord and Berkeley.

4. Hiking rafting, and snowboarding are her favorite sports.

5. The police found TV sets blenders and blow dryers stacked to the ceiling in the abandoned house.

6. I forgot to pack some important items for the trip to the tropics: insect repellent sunscreen and antihistamine tablets.

7. Don't eat strange mushrooms walk near the water or feed the squirrels.

8. Everyone in class had to present an oral report write a term paper and take a final.

9. We brought a Ouija board a Scrabble set and a Boggle game to the party.

10. To earn a decent wage make a comfortable home and educate my children—those are my hopes.

B. Commas with Introductory Phrases, Transitional Expressions, and Parentheticals

PRACTICE 2

Punctuate the following sentences:

1. Frankly I always suspected that you were a born saleswoman.

2. All twelve jurors by the way felt that the defendant was innocent.

3. On every April Fools' Day he tries out a new, dumb practical joke.

4. In fact Lucinda should never have written that poison-pen letter.

5. Close to the top of Mount Washington the climbers paused for a tea break.

6. To tell the truth that usher needs a lesson in courtesy.

7. Near the end of the driveway a large lilac bush bloomed and brightened the yard.

8. He prefers as a rule serious news programs to the lighter sitcoms.

9. To sum up Mr. Choi will handle all the details.

10. During my three years in Minnesota I learned how to deal with snow.

C. Commas for Appositives

PRACTICE 3

Punctuate the following sentences.

1. The Rock the popular wrestler and actor starred in movies and made a video with musician Wyclef Jean.

2. Long novels especially ones with complicated plots force me to read slowly.

3. Rolando a resident nurse hopes to become a pediatrician.

4. I don't trust that tire the one with the yellow patch on the side.

5. Tanzania a small African nation exports cashew nuts.

6. Watch out for Phil a man whose ambition rules him.

7. Ms. Liu a well-known nutritionist lectures at public schools.

8. A real flying ace Helen will teach a course in sky diving.

9. We support the Center for Science in the Public Interest a consumer education and protection group.

10. My husband Bill owns two stereos.

D. Commas with Nonrestrictive and Restrictive Clauses

PRACTICE 4

Set off the nonrestrictive relative clauses in the following sentences with commas. Note that *which* usually begins a nonrestrictive relative clause and *that* usually begins a restrictive clause. Remember: Restrictive relative clauses are *not* set off by commas. Write a *C* after each correct sentence.

1. Olive who always wanted to go into law enforcement is a detective in the Eighth Precinct.

2. Employees who learn to use the new computers may soon qualify for a merit raise.

3. Polo which is not played much in the United States is very popular in England.

4. A person who always insists upon telling you the truth is sometimes a pain in the neck.

5. Statistics 101 which is required for the business curriculum demands concentration and perseverance.

6. Robin who is usually shy at large parties spent the evening dancing with Arsenio who is everybody's favorite dance partner.

7. This small shop sells furniture that is locally handcrafted.

8. His uncle who rarely eats meat consumes enormous quantities of vegetables, fruits, and grains.

9. Pens that slowly leak ink can be very messy.

10. Valley Forge which was the site of Washington's winter quarters draws many tourists every spring and summer.

E. Commas for Dates and Addresses

PRACTICE 5

Punctuate the following sentences. Write a C after each correct sentence.

1. The unusual names of many American towns reflect our history and sense of humor.

2. In February 1878, Ed Schieffelin told friends that he was joining the California Gold Rush, and they warned, "The only thing you'll find out there will be your own tombstone."

3. But Schieffelin found silver in Arizona and named his settlement Tombstone, now famous for the shootout at the O.K. Corral on October 26 1881.

4. The residents of another mining town wanted to honor the chicken-like ptarmigan bird, but an argument about the word's spelling led them to select Chicken Alaska instead.

5. It was Christmas Eve, December 24 1849 when residents of a small rural community chose to name their town Santa Claus.

6. Every Christmas since the 1920s, volunteers have replied to the thousands of children's letters that pour into the town's post office, located at 45 N. Kringle Place Santa Claus Indiana 47579.

7. Hell, Michigan, got its name when crusty resident George Reeves was asked his opinion and replied, "I don't care. You can name it Hell if you want to."

8. At a 10K race there on August 13 2005 runners went home with T-shirts announcing, "I Ran Thru Hell."

9. On January 20 2000 the town of Halfway Oregon became the "World's First Dot Com City" when it officially changed its name to Half.com.

10. Choosing the right name can be difficult, as the folks who founded Nameless Tennessee can attest.

F. Minor Uses of the Comma

Punctuate the following sentences.

1. Yes I do think you will be famous one day.

2. Well did you call a taxi?

3. The defendant ladies and gentlemen of the jury does not even own a red plaid jacket.

4. Cynthia have you ever camped in the Pacific Northwest?

5. No I most certainly will not marry you.

6. Oh I love the way they play everything to a salsa beat.

7. The class feels Professor Molinor that your grades are unrealistically high.

8. He said march not swagger.

9. Perhaps but I still don't think that the carburetor fits there.

10. We all agree Ms. Crawford that you are the best jazz bassist around.

REVIEW

Proofread the following essay for comma errors—either missing commas or commas used incorrectly. Correct the errors above the lines.

PIXAR PERFECT

(1) A company called Pixar has transformed animated films. (2) It was started in 1986 by Steven Jobs the head of Apple Computer and creator of the iPod and iPhone. (3) Applying technical imagination to story-telling Pixar has produced some of the most successful and beloved movies ever made. (4) *Toy Story, A Bug's Life Monsters, Inc. Finding Nemo* and *Wall-E* appealed to both children and adults by combining engaging stories memorable characters, and cutting-edge computer animation.

Wall-E and Eve dance in space in Pixar's *Wall-E*.

(5) Pixar's action-packed plots carry emotional punch. (6) In *Finding Nemo* for instance, Nemo's father searches for his missing son in the vast ocean and learns about the bonds of family love. (7) *Monsters, Inc.* explores the theme of facing fears as it follows two monsters attempting to return a wayward toddler to her room. (8) In *Wall-E*, an outdated robot on the abandoned planet Earth meets a sleek robot from space falls in love and helps save the planet.

(9) Pixar populates these plots with lovable heroes and diabolical villains. (10) Although none of them is technically a human characters like Woody, Buzz Lightyear, Sully, Nemo, and Wall-E win moviegoers' hearts with their "humanity." (11) Woody is upset when a new toy replaces him as the favorite. (12) Lonely Wall-E longs to win the the heart of shiny Eve. (13) The characters seem even more real because stars like Ellen Degeneres, Tom Hanks, Tim Allen, John Goodman, and Billy Crystal bring their voices to life.

(14) Finally Pixar animators use the latest computer-animation technology and meticulous detail to create realistic 3-D images. (15) Monster Sully's shaggy blue coat

ripples in the wind for example because animators created a separate computer model for each of its 2.3 million individual hairs. (16) To convey strong emotion with almost no words *Wall-E*'s animators studied the movements of machines like NASA's Mars Rover and watched silent films and those with little dialogue such as *2001: A Space Odyssey*.

(17) Pixar's films have impressed critics as well as audiences. (18) In fact its movies have won 205 Academy Awards Golden Globes and other top film prizes.

EXPLORING ONLINE

http://www.pixar.com/howwedoit/#

The site, "How We Make a Movie," offers a quick tour through a Pixar process. Notice the clear, step-by-step presentation that helps make a complicated series of steps understandable—just as good process writing does.

CHAPTER 37

Mechanics

A: Capitalization

B: Titles

C: Direct Quotations

D: Minor Marks of Punctuation

A. Capitalization

PRACTICE 1

Capitalize wherever necessary in the following sentences. Put a C after each correct sentence.

1. Barbara Kingsolver, a well-known novelist, nonfiction writer, and poet, was born on april 8, 1955, in annapolis, maryland.

2. She grew up in rural kentucky and then went to college in indiana; after graduating, she worked in europe and since then has lived in and around tucson, arizona.

3. In college, Kingsolver majored first in music and then in biology; she later withdrew from a graduate program in biology and ecology at the university of arizona to work in its office of arid land studies.

4. Kingsolver's first novel, *The Bean Trees*, has become a classic; it is taught in english classes and has been translated into more than sixty-five languages.

5. The main character, named taylor greer, is considered one of the most memorable women in modern american literature.

6. In a later novel, *The Poisonwood Bible*, Kingsolver follows the family of a baptist minister in its move to the congo.

7. The fanaticism of reverend price brings misery to his family and destruction to the villagers he tries to convert to christianity.

8. Kingsolver's writing always deals with powerful political and social issues, but her novels don't sound preachy because she is a wonderful storyteller.

9. She has won awards and prizes from the american library association and many other organizations; she also has earned special recognition from the united nations national council of women.

10. This gifted writer, who plays drums and piano, performs with a band called rock bottom remainders; other band members are also notable writers—stephen king, amy tan, and dave barry.

B. Titles

PRACTICE 2

Capitalize these titles correctly. Do not underline or use quotation marks in this practice.

1. inside women's college basketball

2. the genius of frank lloyd wright

3. breath, eyes, memory

4. an insider's guide to the music industry

5. the orchid thief

6. dave barry's guide to marriage and/or sex

7. how to build a website

8. a history of violence in american movies

9. harry potter and the goblet of fire

10. currents from the dancing river

PRACTICE 3

Wherever necessary, underline or place quotation marks around each title in the sentences below so that the reader will know at a glance what type of work the title refers to. Put a *C* after any correct sentence.

EXAMPLE   Two of the best short stories in that volume are "Rope" and "The New Dress."

1. African American writer Langston Hughes produced his first novel, Not Without Laughter, when he was a student at Lincoln University in Pennsylvania.

2. By that time, he had already been a farmer, a cook, a waiter, and a doorman at a Paris nightclub; he had also won a prize for his poem The Weary Blues, which was published in 1925 in the magazine Opportunity.

3. In 1926 Hughes wrote his famous essay The Negro Artist and the Racial Mountain, which appeared in the Nation magazine; he wanted young black writers to write without shame or fear about the subject of race.

4. Because he spoke Spanish, Hughes was asked in 1937 by the newspaper the Baltimore Afro-American to cover the activities of blacks in the International Brigades in Spain during the Spanish Civil War.

5. For the rest of his life, he wrote articles in newspapers such as the San Francisco Chronicle, the New York Times, and the Chicago Defender.

6. In fact, for more than twenty years he wrote a weekly column for the Chicago Defender in which he introduced a character named Simple, who became popular because of his witty observations on life.

7. The stories about Simple were eventually collected and published in five books; two of those books are Simple Speaks His Mind and Simple Takes a Wife.

8. In 1938, Hughes established the Harlem Suitcase Theater in Manhattan, where his play Don't You Want to Be Free? was performed.

9. Because Hughes's poetry was based on the rhythms of African American speech and music, many of his poems have been set to music, including Love Can Hurt You, Dorothy's Name Is Mud, and Five O'Clock Blues.

10. Few modern writers can rival Hughes's enormous output of fine poems, newspaper articles, columns, and novels.

C. Direct Quotations

PRACTICE 4

Insert quotation marks where necessary in each sentence. Capitalize and punctuate correctly.

1. The sign reads don't even think about parking here.

2. Alexander Pope wrote to err is human, to forgive divine.

3. Well, it takes all kinds she sighed.

4. He exclaimed you look terrific in those jeweled sandals

5. The article said Most American children do poorly in geography.

6. These books on ancient Egypt look interesting he replied but I don't have time to read them now.

7. Although the rain is heavy she said we will continue harvesting the corn.

8. Give up caffeine and get lots of rest the doctor advised.

9. The label warns this product should not be taken by those allergic to aspirin.

10. Red, white, and blue Hillary said are my favorite colors.

D. Minor Marks of Punctuation

PRACTICE 5

Punctuate these sentences with colons, dashes, or parentheses.

1. Calvin asked for the following two light bulbs, a pack of matches, a lead pencil, and a pound of grapes.

2. They should leave by 11 30 P.M.

3. The designer's newest fashions magnificent leather creations were generally too expensive for the small chain of clothing stores.

4. Harvey the only Missourian in the group remains unconvinced.

5. She replied, "This rock group The Woogies sounds like all the others I've heard this year."

6. If you eat a heavy lunch as you always do remember not to go swimming immediately afterward.

7. By 9:30 P.M., the zoo veterinarian a Dr. Smittens had operated on the elephant.

8. Note these three tips for hammering in a nail hold the hammer at the end of the handle, position the nail carefully, and watch your thumb.

9. Whenever Harold Garvey does his birdcalls at parties as he is sure to do everyone begins to yawn.

10. Please purchase these things at the hardware store masking tape, thumbtacks, apple-green paint, and some sandpaper.

PRACTICE 6 REVIEW

Proofread the following essay for errors in capitalization, quotation marks, colons, parentheses, and dashes. Correct the errors by writing above the lines.

THE PASSION OF THOMAS GILCREASE

(1) Thomas Gilcrease, a descendant of creek indians, became an instant Millionaire when oil was discovered on his homestead in 1907. (2) He spent most of his fortune collecting objects that tell the story of the american frontier, particularly of the Native American experience. (3) The Thomas Gilcrease institute of american history and arts in Tulsa, oklahoma, is the result of his lifelong passion.

(4) This huge collection more than 10,000 works of art, 90,000 historical documents, and 250,000 native american artifacts, spans the centuries from 10,000 B.C. to the 1950s. (5) Awed visitors can view nearly 200 George Catlin paintings of Native American life. (6) They can walk among paintings and bronze sculptures by Frederic Remington with names like *The Coming And Going Of The Pony Express* that call up images of the West. (7) Museumgoers can admire Thomas Moran's watercolors that helped persuade Congress to create yellowstone, the first national park. (8) In addition, visitors are treated to works by modern Native Americans, such as the display of wood sculptures by the cherokee Willard Stone.

Mourning Her Brave by George de Forest Brush, a painting in the Gilcrease Collection. Name five details in the painting that create its somber mood.

(9) The museum also houses many priceless documents an original copy of the declaration of independence, the oldest known letter written from the new world, and the papers of Hernando Cortés. (10) A new glass storage area even allows visitors to view the 80 percent of the holdings that are not on display. (11) Thousands of beaded moccasins and buckskin dresses line the shelves, and a collection of magnificent war bonnets hangs from brackets.

(12) When the Gilcrease Institute opened its doors on May 2, 1949, *Life* magazine declared it is the best collection of art and literature ever assembled on the American frontier and the Indian. (13) Thousands of visitors agree.

CHAPTER 38

Putting Your Proofreading Skills to Work

This chapter gives you the opportunity to put your proofreading skills to work in real-world situations. As you proofread the paragraphs and essays that follow, you must look for any—and every—kind of error, just as you would in the real world of college or work. The first three practices tell you what kinds of errors to look for; if you have trouble, go back to those chapters in the companion text and review. The other practices, however, contain a random mix of errors and give you no clues at all.

PRACTICE 1   **PROOFREADING**

Proofread this paragraph, correcting any errors above the lines. To review, see these chapters in the companion text and the exercises in this workbook.

> Chapter 27   run-ons, comma splices, fragments
> Chapter 28   present tense problems, subject-verb agreement
> Chapter 29   past tense problems
> Chapter 30   past participle problems

(1) Mount Everest is the tallest mountain in the world. (2) The highest point on Earth, and the dangerous dream of every mountain climber. (3) Everest set in the Himalaya Mountains of central Asia and rise 29,028 feet. (4) The deadliest threat to climbers are not the steep, icy slopes or even the bitter cold and ferocious winds it is the lack of

air. (5) Air at the top of Everest has only one-third the oxygen of air below, so without preparation, the average person would live less than an hour at the summit. (6) In fact, altitude sickness begin at 8,000 feet, with headache, nausea, and confusion. (7) At 12,000 feet, the brain and lungs starts filling with fluid, which can lead to death. (8) How, then, has anyone ever climbed Everest, the answer is acclimatization. (9) Mountaineers climb slowly, about 2,000 feet a day, and they drink huge amounts of water. (10) They also carry oxygen. (11) Amazingly, in 1980, the first person to climb Everest solo was also the first to climb it without oxygen. (12) That was Reinhold Messner from Italy. (13) Who later wrote in *Climbing* magazine that the lack of air "saps your judgment and strength, even your ability to feel anything at all. I don't know how I made it." (14) Over 210 climbers have died scaling Mount Everest, nonetheless, this danger keeps tempting others to try their skills and their luck.

PRACTICE 2   PROOFREADING

Proofread this paragraph, correcting any errors above the lines. To review, see these chapters in the companion text and the exercises in this workbook.

Chapter 21   inconsistency of number or person, parallelism problems
Chapter 27   run-ons, comma splices, fragments
Chapter 28   present tense problems, subject-verb agreement
Chapter 30   past participle problems
Chapter 35   apostrophe errors

(1) American culture emphasizes quick results we pick up fast food and do our banking in drive-through lanes. (2) We buy gadgets that promise to save you time. (3) We even call ahead for restaurant seating, so we wont have to wait for a table. (4) Now a new trend know as *speed dating* becoming popular in big cities like Los Angeles, Chicago, and

Boston. (5) Also called pre-dating or "McDating". (6) This activity is suppose to reduce the time that busy single people spend getting to know each other. (7) Speed dating events are arranged by companies like HurryDate and 8MinuteDating. (8) At these events, even numbers of men and women are paired off, each couple chats for eight to ten minutes while trying to determine potential compatibility. (9) Then a bell rings, and everyone switch partners. (10) At the end of the session, participants who are interest in each other are provide with each other's phone and e-mail contacts. (11) Some say that speed dating is ideal for people who are busy, who dislike the bar scene, or who hope to lessen the pain of rejection. (12) Others calls it drive-through dating, just another crazy American fad.

PRACTICE 3   PROOFREADING

Proofread this paragraph, correcting any errors above the lines. To review, see these chapters in the companion text and the exercises in this workbook.

Chapter 27   run-ons, comma splices, and fragments
Chapter 29   past tense errors
Chapter 30   past participle problems
Chapter 34   adjective and adverb errors

(1) Lea Salonga, a talented Broadway performer, has became a role model for aspiring young actors, both in the United States and her native Philippines. (2) Born in Manila, Salonga began performing at age seven. (3) After she won a small part in a local production of *The King and I*. (4) Her popularity grew quickly. (5) She acted in many theater productions, recorded a number of albums. (6) And even star in her own children's television show, called *Love, Lea*. (7) Through it all, Salonga's parents focused on her education and good manners rather than her fame. (8) When British talent scouts arrived in Manila, they were charm by the gracious young woman with the beautiful soprano

voice and cast her immediate as the lead in their new musical *Miss Saigon*. (9) Salonga was only twenty when she won a Tony award for her sensitive portrayal of a Vietnamese woman who sacrifices her own life to give her child a more better one. (10) Since then, Salonga has starred in some of the popularest Broadway musicals, landed a role in *As the World Turns*, and singing the soundtrack for the female leads in the Disney films *Aladdin* and *Mulan*. (11) Despite her success, Salonga remains close to her family and her traditional upbringing. (12) Her first kiss occurred on the set of *Miss Saigon* she was chaperoned on dates until she turned twenty-one. (13) Salonga's parents have encouraged her to complete her college education. (14) With her balanced lifestyle and much achievements, Lea Salonga encourages other young people to follow their dreams without loosing sight of their roots.

PRACTICE 4   PROOFREADING

This passage contains many of the errors you have learned to avoid. Proofread each sentence carefully, and then correct each error above the line.

(1) Do you know your learning style? (2) Finding out might help you succeed in college. (3) A learning style is a preferred way of taking in new information. (4) The four major learning styles is *visual, auditory, reading/writing*, and *hands-on*. (5) Most people use all of these method, however, one method might work more better than others. (6) For example, Lupe discovered in college that she has a dominant *visual* learning style. (7) New facts or concepts are most clearest to her if they are presented in diagrams, charts, photographs, or videos. (8) Lupe realized that she can deepen her understanding by drawing pictures to depict the information she hears and reads. (9) Nathan, on the other hand, has a dominant *auditory* style he needs to hear spoken explanations and

also talk about what he is learning. (10) He absorbs course work best by reading aloud, participation in class discussions, and tape-recording and then listening to his notes. (11) Terrell has a *reading/writing* style. (12) Because his mind soaks up information best in the form of written words. (13) Terrell enjoys learning through books, handouts, PowerPoint presentations, and notes, he benefits from writing summaries and journal entries to process what he sees and hears. (14) The fourth learning style—*hands-on*—describe the preference of Emilio, who learns most efficient by moving, doing, and using all his sense. (15) Whenever possible, he tries to handle objects, participate in performances, conduct hands-on experiments, and use trial-and-error. (16) An understanding of learning styles give each of these students new skills to help master any academic subject.

PRACTICE 5   **PROOFREADING**

This passage contains many of the errors you have learned to avoid in Unit 6. Proofread each sentence carefully, and then correct each error above the line.

(1) If you want to eat well and do our planet a favor become a Vegetarian. (2) Most vegetarian's eat eggs, milk, dairy products and fish. (3) All youre giving up are leathery steak's and overcooked chicken. (4) A vegetarian dinner might begin with a greek salad of, crisp cucumbers, sweet red onion black olives, and a sprinkling of feta cheese. (5) Youll think you're sitting in a little café overlooking the mediterranean sea. (6) For the main course, head to mexico for tamale pie. (7) A rich, flavorful dish made of pinto beans's, brown rice, green peppers and tomatoes. (8) On the table of course is a loaf of warm bread.

(9) Do you have room for dessert? how about some ben and jerrys ice cream, made in vermont? (10) As you linger over a cup of french espresso coffee think how your vegetarian meal was delicious, nutritious, and a help to our planet. (11) If more people ate vegetarian the land given to raising cattle and crops to feed cattle could be used for raising grain, many of the worlds hungry people could be fed. (12) To read about vegetarianism, get the best-known guide *laurels kitchen: a handbook for vegetarian cookery and nutrition.*

PRACTICE 6   PROOFREADING

This essay contains many of the errors you have learned to avoid. Proofread each sentence carefully, and then correct each error above the line.

(1) Some of the most popularest programs on television today are the *CSI* dramas, which depict crime scene investigators using state-of-the-art equipment and old-fashioned detective work to solve crimes. (2) These shows not only entertain 60 million

TV shows like *CSI: NY* have prompted many people to train for CSI careers.

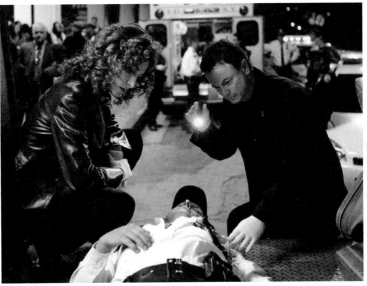

© CBS/Courtesy Everett Collection

viewers a week but have also stimulate great interest in forensics as a career, in fact, demand for training has reached record levels. (3) According to the American academy of forensic sciences, the many jobs in forensics allows people to apply their love of science to the pursuit of justice and public safety.

(4) Forensic scientists are curious, detail-oriented people whom like to think and puts puzzles together. (5) They also need to work good in groups. (6) Unlike *CSI* characters on TV, who perform many varied tasks, real forensic scientists usually specialize on one area and then pool their expertise to help police nab criminals. (7) For example, crime scene examiners go to the places where crimes have occurred to locate, photograph, collect, and transportation of physical evidence like fingerprints and blood samples. (8) On the other hand, crime laboratory analysts stay in the lab. (9) Using microscopes, DNA tests, firearms tests, and other techniques and equipments to make sense of crime scene evidence.

(10) Each of these jobs require a bachelor's degree. (11) Two specialtys requiring a master's degree are forensic anthropology; which involves identifying people from skeletal remains. And psychological profiling. (12) Using behavioral clues to "read" the mind of a killer or other criminal. (13) One specialty, medical examiner, requires a medical degree. (14) Although this is the highest-paid forensics career. (15) It requires a tough personality able to perform autopsies on crime victims to determine exact cause of death. (16) Real-world forensic scientists admit that their jobs are not quite as glamorous as those of their television counterparts however, they describe their work as challenging, interesting, and with rewards.

PRACTICE 7   PROOFREADING

This essay contains many of the errors you have learned to avoid. Proofread each sentence carefully, and then correct each error above the line.

IN THE MARKET FOR A USED CAR?

(1) For several year's now, used car sales have exceeded new car sales. (2) Good used cars can be founded at dealers, (3) And through newspaper ads. (4) You might also let your friends know your in the market for a used car, they might know of someone who wants to sell their car. (5) Wherever you look for a used car keep the following tips in mind.

(6) First shop before you need the car. (7) This way you can decide exactly what type of car suit you most best. (8) Do you want a compact. (9) Or a midsize car? (10) What features are important to you? (11) Should you get an american-made car or a japanese, german, or other import? (12) If you shop when you are'nt desperate, you are more likely to make a good choice and negotiate good.

(13) Second narrow your choices to three or four cars, and do some research. (14) Start with the *kelley blue book used car price manual*, online at **http://www.kbb.com.** (15) The blue book as its called for short gives the current value by model year and features. (16) Its also a good idea to check *consumer reports* magazine. (17) Every april issue lists good used car buys and cars to avoid. (18) Based on what you learn go back and test-drive the cars that interest you the mostest. (19) Drive each for at least an hour, drive in stop-and-go traffic in the highway, in winding roads, and in hills.

(20) When you do decide on a car ask your mechanic to look at it. (21) Be sure to get a written report that include an estimate of what repair's will cost. (22) Money spent at

this point is money spent wise, if the seller wont allow an inspection, take your business elsewhere.

(23) When you buy a used car you want dependability and value. (24) Follow these tip's, youll be able to tell a good buy when you see it.

PRACTICE 8 PROOFREADING

This essay contains many of the errors you have learned to avoid. Proofread each sentence carefully, and then correct each error above the line.

GATORS AND CROCS

(1) With their scaly bodies slit eyes and long tails, alligators and crocodiles look a lot like dinosaurs. (2) In fact alligators and crocodiles descended from the same family as dinosaurs. (3) While its true that alligators and crocodiles look a lot alike, they differ in three ways.

(4) First alligators and crocodiles are found in different parts of the world. (5) Alligators be found in china, central america, and south america. (6) On the other hand, crocodiles are found in africa (especially around the nile river), australia, southeast asia, india, cuba, and the west indies. (7) Only in the southern united states is both alligators and crocodiles found. (8) In all cases however alligator's and crocodile's live in hot, tropical regions. (9) Reptiles are cold-blooded, so at temperatures below 65 degrees, alligators and crocodiles gets sluggish and cannot hunt.

(10) Alligators and crocodiles also differ in appearance. (11) Alligators has broader flatter snouts that are rounded at the end. (12) Crocodiles has narrower almost triangular snouts.

(13) The best way to tell the difference is to view both from the side when they have their mouths closed, you can see only upper teeth on an alligator, but you can also see four lower teeth on a croc. (14) If you get really close you can see that alligators have a space between they're nostrils whereas the nostrils of crocs are very close together.

(15) Finally alligators and crocodiles are temperamentally different. (16) Alligators are not aggressive they are even a bit shy. (17) They will lie in wait along a river bank for prey when on land, they move slow and uneven. (18) Crocodiles, however, are much more aggressive. (19) They are fast and mean, they often stalk they're prey. (20) The australian freshwater crocodile and the nile crocodile can even run on land, with their front and back legs working together like a dog. (21) Nile crocodiles kill hundred's of people every year.

(22) Alligators and crocodiles have outlived the dinosaurs, but they might not survive hunters who want to turn them into shoes wallets briefcases and belts. (23) In 1967, the u.s. government declared alligators an endangered species. (24) Fortunately american alligators have repopulated and are now reclassified as threatened. (25) Importing crocodile and alligator skins are banned worldwide, but some species is still threatened. (26) These frightening and fascinating ancient creatures need help worldwide if they are to survive.

Unit 7 Strengthening Your Spelling

CHAPTER 39

Spelling

A. Suggestions for Improving Your Spelling

Use the suggestions found in the companion text to improve your spelling, and then use the exercises here to practice what you have learned.

B. Computer Spell Checkers

With a group of four or five classmates, read this poem, which "passed" spell check. Can your group find and correct all the errors that the spell checker missed?

Eye halve a spelling check her,

It came with my pea see.

It clearly marques four my revue,

Miss steaks eye can knot sea.

I've run this poem threw it.

Your Shirley please too no

Its letter perfect in it's weigh.

My checker tolled me sew.

C. Spotting Vowels and Consonants

Write *v* for vowel and *c* for consonant in the space on top of each word. Be careful of the *y*.

EXAMPLE

$\frac{c}{h}\ \frac{v}{o}\ \frac{c}{p}\ \frac{v}{e}\ \frac{c}{d}$

1. __ __ __ __
   r e l y

2. __ __ __ __
   y a w n

3. __ __ __ __ __ __ __
   p e r h a p s

5. __ __ __ __ __
   f o r g e

4. __ __ __ __ __ __ __
   i n s t e a d

6. __ __ __ __ __ __ __ __ __
   b y s t a n d e r

D. Doubling the Final Consonant (in Words of One Syllable)

PRACTICE 3

Which of the following words should double the final consonant? Check to see whether the word ends in *cvc*. Then add the suffixes *-ed* and *-ing*.

EXAMPLES

Word	Last Three Letters	-ed	-ing
drop	*cvc*	*dropped*	*dropping*
boil	*vvc*	*boiled*	*boiling*
1. tan			
2. brag			
3. mail			
4. peel			
5. wrap			

PRACTICE 4

Which of the following words should double the final consonant? Check for *cvc*. Then add the suffixes *-er* or *-est*.

EXAMPLES

Word	Last Three Letters	-*er*	-*est*
wet	cvc	wetter	wettest
cool	vvc	cooler	coolest
1. deep			
2. short			
3. red			
4. dim			
5. bright			

E. Doubling the Final Consonant (in Words of More Than One Syllable)

PRACTICE 5

Which of the following words should double the final consonant? First, check for *cvc*; then check final stress. Then add the suffixes *-ed* and *-ing*.

EXAMPLES

Word	Last Three Letters	-*ed*	-*ing*
repel	cvc	repelled	repelling
enlist	vcc	enlisted	enlisting
1. happen			
2. admit			

3. offer   _____   _____   _____

4. prefer   _____   _____   _____

5. compel   _____   _____   _____

F. Dropping or Keeping the Final *E*

PRACTICE 6

Add the suffix indicated for each word.

EXAMPLES

hope + ing = _____*hoping*_____

hope + ful = _____*hopeful*_____

1. love + able = _____   6. complete + ness = _____

2. love + ly = _____   7. enforce + ment = _____

3. pure + ly = _____   8. enforce + ed = _____

4. pure + er = _____   9. arrange + ing = _____

5. complete + ing = _____ 10. arrange + ment = _____

PRACTICE 7

Add the suffix indicated for each word.

EXAMPLES

come + ing = _____*coming*_____

rude + ness = _____*rudeness*_____

1. guide + ance = _____   3. sincere + ly = _____

2. manage + ment = _____   4. like + able = _____

5. dense + ity = _____   8. response + ible = _____

6. polite + ly = _____   9. judge + ment = _____

7. motive + ation = _____   10. fame + ous = _____

G. Changing or Keeping the Final *Y*

PRACTICE 8

Add the suffix indicated to each of the following words.

EXAMPLES

marry + ed = _____*married*_____

buy + er = _____*buyer*_____

1. try + ed = _____   6. wealthy + est = _____

2. vary + able = _____   7. day + ly = _____

3. worry + ing = _____   8. duty + ful = _____

4. pay + ed = _____   9. display + s = _____

5. enjoy + able = _____   10. occupy + ed = _____

PRACTICE 9

Add the suffix in parentheses to each word.

1. beauty (fy) _____   2. betray (ed) _____

   (ful) _____   (ing) _____

   (es) _____   (al) _____

3. lonely (er) _____

    (est) _____

    (ness) _____

4. study (es) _____

    (ous) _____

    (ing) _____

H. Adding -*S* or -*ES*

Add -*s* or -*es* to the following nouns and verbs, changing the final *y* to *i* when necessary.

EXAMPLES

sketch _____*sketches*_____

echo _____*echoes*_____

1. watch _____

2. tomato _____

3. reply _____

4. company _____

5. bicycle _____

6. piano _____

7. donkey _____

8. dictionary _____

9. boss _____

10. hero _____

I. Choosing *IE* or *EI*

Pronounce each word out loud. Then fill in either *ie* or *ei*.

1. bel __ __ ve

2. __ __ ght

3. ch __ __ f

4. soc __ __ ty

5. h __ __ ght

6. ach __ __ ve

7. effic __ __ nt   10. rec __ __ ve   13. v __ __ n

8. n __ __ ther   11. fr __ __ nd   14. for __ __ gn

9. cash __ __ r   12. consc __ __ nce   15. perc __ __ ve

PRACTICE 12 REVIEW

Test your knowledge of the spelling rules in this chapter by adding suffixes to the following words. If you have trouble, the part in which the rule appears is shown in parentheses.

	Part		**Part**
1. nerve + ous _____	(F)	6. occur + ed _____	(E)
2. drop + ed _____	(D)	7. carry + ing _____	(G)
3. hope + ing _____	(F)	8. tomato + s/es _____	(H)
4. busy + ness _____	(G)	9. believe + able _____	(F)
5. radio + s/es _____	(H)	10. day + ly _____	(G)

PRACTICE 13 REVIEW

Circle the correctly spelled word in each pair.

1. writting, writing   6. piece, peice

2. receive, recieve   7. resourceful, resourcful

3. begining, beginning   8. argument, arguement

4. greif, grief   9. marries, marrys

5. relaid, relayed   10. thier, their

J. Spelling Lists

PRACTICE 14   **REVIEW**

Proofread the following essay for spelling errors. (Be careful: There are misspelled words from both the exercises in this chapter and the spelling list.) Correct any errors by writing above the lines.

MAN'S BEST CLONE

(1) Ever since the sucessful cloning of Dolly the sheep in 1996, scientists have experimented with cloning other animals. (2) Now a Texas company is offerring cloning services to people who want to copy their favorite cat or dog. (3) Losing a beloved pet is dificult for anyone, so it should come as no suprise that some greiving pet owners are hurrying to resurrect their furry friends.

(4) Genetic Savings & Clone already has preserved the tissue of hundreds of pets whose owners hope one day to cuddle a clone. (5) Freezing a DNA sample from Fido or Fluffy costs over a thousand dollars, with yearly maintenance around $100. (6) Once the cloning process is perfected, creating the replacment animal will cost $10,000 more— making Fluffy II one expensive little cat!

(7) Ironically, experts tell owners of pricey purebred animals to forget about cloneing. (8) The bloodlines that produce the look and behavor of pure breeds work nearly as well as cloning. (9) On the other hand, if Fido has four or five breeds in his blood, he truly is a unique mutt and a good posibility for cloning.

(10) Critics say cloning pets is ridiclous. (11) Because both genes and enviroment determine animal behavior, puting a piece of Fido in the fridge will not guarentee good results. (12) Owners who beleive thier copycat will have the same adoreable personality as the original kitty are bound to be disapointed. (13) The Humane Society opposes cloning,

urging lonely pet owners to adopt an abandoned animal at their local shelter instead. (14) With thousands of strays needing homes, creating a copy cat or dog seems like a waste of money and scientific resources. (15) But people are so tyed to their pets that Genetic Savings & Clone might well remain a booming busyness.

CHAPTER 40

Look-Alikes/ Sound-Alikes

PRACTICE 1

Fill in *a, an,* or *and.*

1. The administration building is _____ old brick house on top of

   _____ hill.

2. _____ artist _____ two students share that studio.

3. The computer in my office has _____ flat screen _____

   _____ CD burner.

4. For lunch, Ben ate _____ tofu sandwich, _____ apple,

   _____ two bananas.

PRACTICE 2

Fill in *accept* or *except.*

1. Jan has read all of Shakespeare's comedies _____ one.

2. Please _____ my apologies.

3. Unable to _____ defeat, the boxer protested the decision.

4. Sam loves all his courses _____ chemistry.

PRACTICE 3

Fill in *affect* or *effect*.

1. You are mistaken if you think alcohol will not _____ your judgment.

2. Attractive, neat clothing will have a positive _____ on a job.

3. Hot, humid summers always have the _____ of making me lazy.

4. We will not be able to _____ these changes without the cooperation of the employees and the union.

PRACTICE 4

Fill in *been* or *being*.

1. Have you _____ to Rib Heaven yet?

2. Pete thinks his phone calls are _____ taped.

3. Are you _____ secretive, or have I _____ imagining it?

4. Yoko has never _____ to Omaha!

PRACTICE 5

Fill in *buy* or *by*.

1. You can't _____ happiness, but many people try.

2. Lee _____ sand _____ the ton for his masonry business.

3. Please drop _____ the bookstore and _____ some novels; I want to read all weekend.

4. _____ _____ out his partners, Joe became sole owner of the firm.

PRACTICE 6

Fill in *it's* or *its*.

1. Put the contact lens in _____ case, please.

2. _____ about time H.T. straightened up the rubble in his room.

3. The company offered some of _____ employees an early retirement option.

4. You know _____ cold when the pond has ice on _____ surface.

PRACTICE 7

Fill in *know, knew, no,* or *new*.

1. I _____ he's _____ in town, but this is ridiculous.

2. If I _____ then what I _____ now, I wouldn't have made so many mistakes when I was young.

3. Abe and Gabe _____ that they have _____ chance of winning the marathon.

4. _____, I don't _____ the way to Grandma's house, you hairy weirdo.

PRACTICE 8

Fill in *lose* or *loose*.

1. When Ari studies in bed, he _____ the _____ change from his pockets.

2. Several layers of _____ clothing can warm you in winter.

3. Don't _____ any sleep over tomorrow's exam.

4. If you _____ that _____ screw, the handle will fall off.

PRACTICE 9

Fill in *past* or *passed*.

1. As Jake _____ the barn, he noticed a man talking to the reindeer.

2. To children, even the recent _____ seems like ancient history.

3. Mia _____ up the opportunity to see a friend from her _____.

4. This Bible was _____ down to me by my mother; it contains records of our

   family's _____.

PRACTICE 10

Fill in *quiet, quit,* or *quite.*

1. The stone cottage is a _____ place in which to study.

2. Kali is _____ dedicated to her veterinary career.

3. Don't _____ your job, even though you aren't _____ happy
   with the working conditions.

4. Each day when he _____ work, Dan visits a _____ spot in the park.

PRACTICE 11

Fill in the correct form of *rise* or *raise.*

1. The loaves of bread have _____ perfectly.

2. The new mayor _____ his arms in a victory salute.

3. Once the sun has _____, Pete _____ the shades.

4. We all _____ as the bride walked down the aisle.

PRACTICE 12

Fill in *sit* or *set*.

1. Please _____ your briefcase here. Would you like to _____ down?

2. Have they _____ in on a rehearsal before?

3. Tomas _____ the chair by the window and _____ down.

4. Sorry, I wouldn't have _____ here if I had known you were returning.

PRACTICE 13

Fill in *suppose* or *supposed*.

1. Why do you _____ wolves howl at the moon?

2. I _____ you enjoy reggae.

3. Detective Nguyen is _____ to address the Citizens' Patrol tonight.

4. Wasn't Erik _____ to meet us at five?

PRACTICE 14

Fill in *their, there,* or *they're*.

1. If _____ not _____ on time, we will leave without them.

2. _____ two of the most amusing people I know.

3. _____ are two choices, and _____ both risky.

4. Two mail carriers left _____ mail bags _____ on the steps.

5. The motorcycles roared _____ way into town.

6. Don't worry about _____ performance in the race because

   _____ both tough.

PRACTICE 15

Fill in *then* or *than*.

1. First, Cassandra kicked off her shoes; _____ she began to dance.

2. Jupiter's diameter is eleven times larger _____ Earth's.

3. If you're more familiar with this trail _____ I, _____ you should lead the way.

4. Fran lived in Chicago _____; now she lives in Los Angeles.

PRACTICE 16

Fill in *through* or *though*.

1. _____ study and perseverance, Charelle earned her degree in three years.

2. Dee usually walks to work, _____ she sometimes rides the bus.

3. Julio strode _____ the bank as _____ he owned it.

4. Clayton is a Texan _____ and _____.

PRACTICE 17

Fill in *to, too,* or *two*.

1. Please take my daughter _____ the movies _____.

2. Dan, _____, took _____ hours _____ complete the exam.

3. Luis went _____ Iowa State for _____ semesters.

4. This curry is _____ hot _____ eat and _____ good _____ resist.

PRACTICE 18

Fill in *use* or *used*.

1. Marie _____ to drive a jalopy that she bought at a _____ car lot.

2. We will _____ about three gallons of paint on this shed.

3. Can you _____ a _____ laptop?

4. Pam _____ to _____ a pick to strum her guitar.

PRACTICE 19

Fill in *weather* or *whether*.

1. In fine _____, we take canoe rides on the lake.

2. _____ or not you like Brazilian food, you'll love this dish.

3. The _____ person never said _____ or not it would snow.

4. In 1870 a national _____ service was established.

PRACTICE 20

Fill in *where*, *were*, or *we're*.

1. _____ going to Hawaii _____ the sun always shines.

2. _____ you standing _____ we agreed to meet?

3. There _____ two high-rise apartment houses _____ the ballpark used to be.

4. _____ determined to attend college though we don't yet know

    _____.

PRACTICE 21

Fill in *whose* or *who's*.

1. _____ convertible is this?

2. Tanya, _____ in my history class, will join us for dinner.

3. We need someone in that position _____ dependable, someone

   _____ abilities have already been proven.

4. _____ biology textbook is this?

PRACTICE 22

Fill in *your* or *you're*.

1. _____ sitting on _____ hat.

2. When _____ ready to begin _____ piano lesson, we'll leave.

3. Let _____ adviser help you plan _____ course schedule.

4. When _____ with _____ friends, _____ a different
   person.

PRACTICE 23

Write a paragraph in your notebook using as many of the look-alikes and sound-alikes as
possible. Exchange paragraphs with a classmate and check each other's work.

PRACTICE 24   REVIEW

The following essay contains a number of look-alike/sound-alike errors. Proofread for
these errors, writing the correct word above the line.

ISABEL ALLENDE

(1) Possibly the best-known female writer of Latin-American literature, Isabel Allende has survived many political and personal tragedies. (2) Most of those events have found there way into her books. (3) Born in 1942, Allende was raise by her mother in Chile after her parents' divorce. (4) When her uncle, President Salvador Allende, was killed during a military coup in 1973, she fled. (5) For the next seventeen years, she lived in Venezuela, were she was unable to find work and felt trapped in a unhappy marriage.

(6) One day, learning that her grandfather was dying in Chile, Allende began to write him a long letter; that letter grew until it became her first novel. (7) Still her most famous book, *The House of the Spirits* established Allende's style of writing, which combines political realism and autobiography with dreams, spirits, an magic. (8) The novel, which was banned in Chile, was translated into more then twenty-five languages and in 1994 was made into a movie.

(9) Buy 1988, Allende had divorced, moved to northern California, remarried, and written her fourth novel, *The Infinite Plan*, which is her second husband's story. (10) Her next book traced the profound affect on Allende of the death of her daughter, Paula. (11) The book *Paula*, like *The House of the Spirits*, was suppose to be a letter, this time too her daughter, who lay in a coma in a Madrid hospital.

(12) After *Paula* was published, Allende stopped writing for several years. (13) She started again in 1996, on January 8, the same day of the year that she had begun every one of her books. (14) The result was *Aphrodite*, a nonfiction book about food and sensuality that was quiet different from Allende's passed work. (15) With renewed energy to right again, Allende spun the tale of an independent woman who leaves her home in Chile to

move to San Francisco during the Gold Rush. (16) Two novels, *Daughter of Fortune* and *Portrait in Sepia*, complete her story.

(17) Isabel Allende is famous for been a passionate storyteller who's writing captures both the Latin-American and the universal human experience. (18) As the first Latina to write a major novel in the mystical tradition, she not only created a sensation, but she paved the way for other female Hispanic writers, including Julia Alvarez and Sandra Cisneros.

Additional Help and Practice for ESL/ELL Students*

Count and Noncount Nouns

PRACTICE 1

Choose the correct word in each pair in the following sentences. Be prepared to explain your choice.

1. After moving to the condominium, they decided to buy new (furniture, furnitures).

2. An important key to learning a second language is memorizing (vocabulary, vocabularies).

3. The crew took a lot of video (equipment, equipments) to the film shoot.

4. This class was difficult because of all the (homework, homeworks) we had to complete.

5. This class was difficult because of all the (exercise, exercises) we had to complete.

6. The (scissor, scissors) lay on the color copier.

7. Waldo set up some computer (network, networks) for the company.

8. The patient's (respiration, respirations) seemed normal.

---

* For more help on these topics, see the Appendix in the companion text.

PRACTICE 2

Circle the correct word in each pair in the following sentences. Be prepared to explain your choice.

1. I always have (coffee, coffees) with dessert. Please give us two Persian (coffee, coffees) and two orders of baklava.

2. You have work (experience, experiences) in this field, I see. Tell me about your various (experience, experiences) at the ABC Company, where you held several positions.

3. Ship builders use a lot of (iron, irons) to build cruise and war ships.

4. Most modern (iron, irons) are made of plastic and steel, so they are light and easy to use.

5. To make Maria's wonderful salsa, you need to grill some fresh (corn, corns).

6. He had several (corn, corns) from years of wearing tight leather shoes.

7. If all cars had both front and side air bags, more (life, lives) would be saved.

8. How (time, times) passes! We have met several (time, times) by chance since we became engineers.

Articles with Count and Noncount Nouns

PRACTICE 3

Cross out *a* or *an* if it is used incorrectly in the sentences below. Be ready to explain your answers.

1. We need *a* special luggage for the camping trip.
2. She gave us *an* advice that helped our project succeed.
3. She gave us *a* piece of advice that helped our project succeed.
4. They are transferring to *a* university located somewhere in Los Angeles.
5. To drive on California freeways, one needs *a* patience.
6. I am in the mood for *a* fish, perhaps *a* piece of salmon and *a* green vegetable.
7. Mr. Lee will offer *a* help if you give him *a* call.
8. We heard *a* laughter coming from the other room.

PRACTICE 4

Write the article *the* where needed in each blank. Write X where no article is needed. Be prepared to explain your answers. (More than one answer is correct in some cases.)

Who said that _____ life never changes? Recent research has shown that _____ human body has changed significantly, especially during _____ past 200 years. Dr. Robert Fogel at _____ University of Chicago and other scientists around world have concluded that a significant change in _____ peoples' physical size has taken place. They note that _____ modern humans are much taller and heavier than _____ people were only a couple of centuries ago. _____ same scientists also found that humans today are much healthier than their ancestors. _____ Chronic diseases occur 10 to 25 years later than they used to, and older people today experience fewer disabilities. _____ same trend was also found for _____ mental health. _____ average IQ, for example, has increased for decades, and mental illnesses are diagnosed and treated much more effectively today. Because of these changes, we now enjoy _____ happier, healthier, longer, and more productive lives.

Verbs Followed by a Gerund or an Infinitive

PRACTICE 5

Circle the correct form (gerund or infinitive) to follow the verb in each sentence.

1. Many Americans enjoy (to watch, watching) television.

2. Because this is the store's busy season, we will postpone (to visit, visiting) our friends until spring.

3. Yuri asked Mia (to repair, repairing) the DVD player.

4. Mae Lee regretted (to miss, missing) the auto show.

5. Barring any unforeseen problems, the family expects me (to complete, completing) my degree by this summer.

6. Bae will persuade Edgar (to join, joining) us at the library.

7. Please keep (to sing, singing). We both want (to hear, hearing) another song.

8. Remember that Bruno's party is a surprise, so please do not mention our (to go, going) to the bakery and (to buy, buying) this huge cake.

PRACTICE 6

Circle the correct verb in each sentence. If you need help, review the verb lists.

1. I (prefer, want) listening to NPR during breakfast.

2. Ichiro (suggests, hopes) to finish his coursework this semester so that he can graduate in May.

3. Given the high cost of housing, he (plans, recommends) sharing an apartment with another serious student.

4. The mayor (hoped, advised) the city council not to pass legislation that would hurt local retailers.

5. Now that she has a good job, she can (afford, consider) to buy a new car.

6. I enjoyed the evening very much. I (appreciate, thank) your inviting me.

7. Several students (decided, kept) working after the chemistry lab closed.

8. He (loves, anticipates) to get up early and go running along the river.

For more practice in ESL-related issues in English, visit the CourseMate for *Evergreen Compact*.

Credits

This page constitutes an extension of the copyright page. We have made every effort to trace the ownership of all copyrighted material and to secure permission from copyright holders. In the event of any question arising as to the use of any material, we will be pleased to make the necessary corrections in future printings. Thanks are due to the following authors, publishers, and agents for permission to use the material indicated.

Pages 35–36: Reprinted courtesy of SPORTS ILLUSTRATED: "A New Dawn" by Sam Moses, April 23, 1990. Copyright © 1990 Time Inc. All rights reserved.

Page 129: From www.fin.ucar.edu/sass/hess/ergo/posture.html. Reprinted by permission of University Corporation of Atmospheric Research.

Pages 133–134: From VANDERMEY/MEYER/VAN RYS/SEBRANEK. STUDENT VOICES: A SAMPLING OF COLLEGE WRITING, 3E. © 2009 Heinle/Arts & Sciences, a part of Cengage Learning, Inc. Reproduced by permission. www .cengage.com/permissions

Revising and Proofreading Symbols

The following chart lists common writing errors and the symbols that instructors often use to mark them. For some errors, your instructor may wish to use symbols other than the ones shown. You may wish to write these alternate symbols in the blank column.

Standard Symbol	Instructor's Alternate Symbol	Error
adj		Incorrect adjective form
adv		Incorrect adverb form
agr		Incorrect subject-verb agreement
		Incorrect pronoun-antecedent agreement
apos		Missing or incorrect apostrophe
awk		Awkward expression
cap		Missing or incorrect capital letter
case		Incorrect pronoun case
⊙		Missing or incorrect comma
coh		Lack of coherence
⊙		Missing or incorrect colon
con d		Inconsistent discourse
con p		Inconsistent person
con t		Inconsistent verb tense
coord		Incorrect coordination
cs		Comma splice
⊝		Missing or incorrect dash
dev		Incomplete paragraph or essay development
dm		Dangling or confusing modifier
ed		Missing -ed, past tense or past participle
frag		Sentence fragment
¶		Missing indentation for new paragraph
⓪		Missing or incorrect parenthesis
‖		Faulty parallelism
pl		Missing or incorrect plural form
pp		Incorrect past participle form
⊙⓪⑦		Missing or incorrect end punctuation
quot		Missing or incorrect quotation marks
rep		Unnecessary repetition
ro		Run-on sentence
⊙		Missing or incorrect semicolon
sub		Incorrect subordination
sp		Spelling error
		Look-alike, sound-alike error
sup		Inadequate support
title		Title needed
trans		Transition needed
trite		Trite expression
ts		Poor or missing topic sentence or thesis statement
u		Lack of paragraph or essay unity
w		Unnecessary words
◠		Too much space
℘		Words or letters to be deleted
?		Unclear meaning
^		Omitted words
~		Words or letters in reverse order